D1292075

THE CATHEDRALS OF
ITALY

Uniform with this volume

THE CATHEDRALS OF SPAIN
  By John Harvey

THE CHATEAUX OF FRANCE
  By Ralph Dutton

In preparation

THE CATHEDRALS OF FRANCE
  By R. P. Howgrave-Graham

1   ORVIETO: façade, 1310–c. 1600

THE CATHEDRALS
OF ITALY

by

J. W. Franklin, M.A.

With photographs by
A. F. Kersting and others

London
B. T. BATSFORD LTD

First published, 1958

MADE AND PRINTED IN GREAT BRITAIN BY
WILLIAM CLOWES AND SONS, LTD, LONDON AND BECCLES
FOR THE PUBLISHERS
B. T. BATSFORD LTD
4 FITZHARDINGE STREET, PORTMAN SQUARE, LONDON, W.1

To
ANNA CARLA

PREFACE

Unlike in England, France or Spain, there is in Italy no style of architecture peculiar to the cathedral. The art of Italy, which is so patently, often exquisitely, decorative is as well looked for in the small church as in the large, domestic as well as ecclesiastical building. Some admirable cathedrals are small, like Torcello or Turin, but some of the most important and splendid churches such as St Mark's, Venice, S. Pietronio at Bologna and the Basilica of S. Francesco at Assisi, were never intended for the episcopal seat. Thus the cathedrals only incompletely represent the vast corpus of Italian art and architecture, but exhibit, nonetheless, the principal elements in its history. A selection has been made from the large number of cathedrals of all periods from the fourth to the nineteenth century; it is hoped that the way in which they are treated will be welcomed by those, in particular, who wish to spend more than five minutes in any one of them or who look for a general view of the factors contributing to the present state of the most notable examples. These long years of almost unremitting artistic activity are not to be described and assessed with impunity; may the undertaking be granted some leniency by those who feel that any particular monument or artist has been unreasonably neglected. It will be observed, for example, that scarcely any reference is made to Sardinia. The architecture of that island is not outstanding and close affinities are apparent with the styles prevalent in the homelands of its several possessors, whether Pisan, Genoese, French or Spanish. This principle has largely governed my selection.

To represent the principal architectural schools of these centuries, thirty-four cathedrals have been chosen for particular discussion. Others are referred to in an introductory survey of the significant developments in architecture and church decoration. The choice has been limited to provide the visitor to Italy with a fuller idea of outstanding individual monuments and, at the same time, it is hoped to give the general reader some conception of the stimulating quality, variety and interest of ecclesiastical architecture in Italy. Of the great number of cathedrals, most of which are listed in an appendix, not all are exceptional artistically or architecturally. Their hall-mark is variety; one inconspicuous building is a rare survival from the darkest centuries of European history; another is the masterpiece of an outstanding creative age. The most refined taste and the utmost vulgarity of gaudy decoration are found in close proximity. There is in fact, something for everyone; Italian churches symbolize the essence of the Catholic world.

The subject of this book, one of a series on the cathedral churches of Europe, was suggested to me by John Harvey and the publisher, to each of

9

whom I am deeply obliged. It is, in fact, the first new survey of Italian church architecture to be published in England for nearly half a century although there have, of course, been numerous monographs on particular aspects of the subject. It has not been possible, or felt suitable to burden these pages with footnotes to support the views and theories expressed in them; many of my sources are listed in the works included in the bibliography on page 269. Therefore, I would whole-heartedly acknowledge here my indebtedness to those many scholars on whose work I have based many of my conclusions. In so far as the views I have expressed differ from those most commonly accepted they are what I hold personally in the light of the evidence at my disposal at the time of writing.

I wish to express my most grateful thanks to the Dean and Chapter of Westminster Abbey for sabbatical leave during the summer of 1955 to enable me to visit almost all the cathedrals here described, and to those many English and Italian friends who have encouraged and assisted me in this undertaking. I would thank in particular John Parkin, without whose constant support and enlightened criticism little would have been accomplished; John O'Neilly, for many discussions on architectural problems, and for preparing the plan of Pavia cathedral; Nicoletta Bornoncini and Dr D. P. J. Wood for invaluable assistance in the arduous reading of proofs; Lucia Pallavicini, Librarian of the Italian Institute of Culture in London, and her staff; the staff of the London Library, but for the existence of which nothing could have been done at all; and A. F. Kersting, for his splendid photographs, specially taken to illustrate the book.

Kensington New Town, 1957   J. W. F.

CONTENTS

11

CONTENTS

ACKNOWLEDGMENT

THE Author and Publishers wish to thank the following for the illustrations appearing in this book:

Exclusive News Agency Ltd., for fig. 79; Fotocelere, Torino, for fig. 10; Foto-Stampa Angeli, Terni, for fig. 59; Gabinetto Fotografico Nazionale, for figs. 7, 14, 34, 43, 53, 55, 78, 103, 104, 106, 117, and 118; Ian Graham, for figs. 18, 35, 42 and 98; A. F. Kersting, F.R.P.S., for figs. 1, 3, 4, 6, 8, 9, 11–13, 15–17, 19–22, 25, 26, 30, 31, 38–40, 44–6, 48, 49, 54, 57, 63, 66, 68, 70, 71, 75, 76, 82–5, 87–97, 99, 105, 107–11, 113–16 and 119; Istituto di Studi Liguri, Albenga, for fig. 5; The Mansell Collection, for figs. 80 and 81; M. Moretti, Orvieto, for fig. 58; Museo del Duomo, for fig. 65; Museo del Duomo and Casa Editrice Gino Giusti, Firenze, for fig. 64; figs. 27, 28, 41, 47, 50–2, 56, 60–2, 69, 72–4, 77, 101, 102 and 112 are reproduced from G. Dehio and G. v. Bezold: *Die kirchliche Baukunst des Abendlandes*; fig. 100 from F. H. Jackson: *Shores of the Adriatic*; figs. 24, 32 and 36 from A. Santini: *San Pietro e le Basiliche Constantiniane*; fig. 37 from G. F. Buonamici: *Metropolitana di Ravenna*; fig. 29 from W. J. Anderson: *The Architecture of the Renaissance in Italy*; fig. 86 from F. Gianini: *Il Duomo di Pavia*. Thanks are due to the Society of Antiquaries for providing facilities for the photographing of figs. 2 and 23.

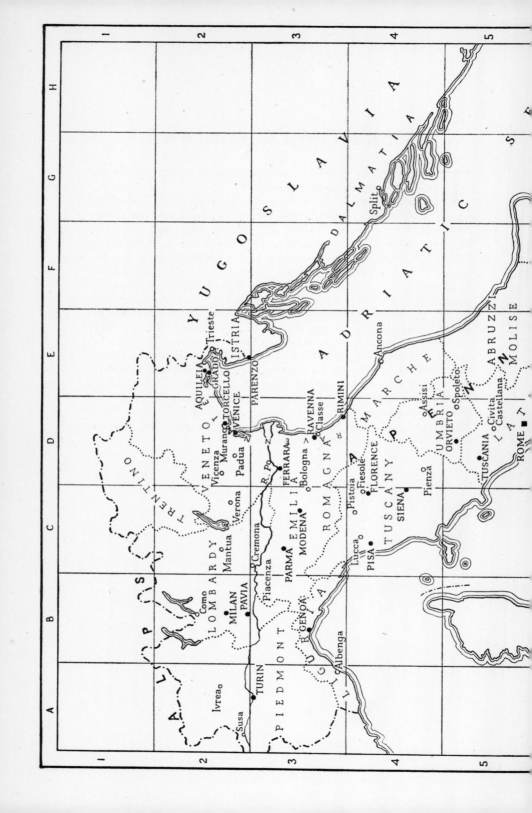

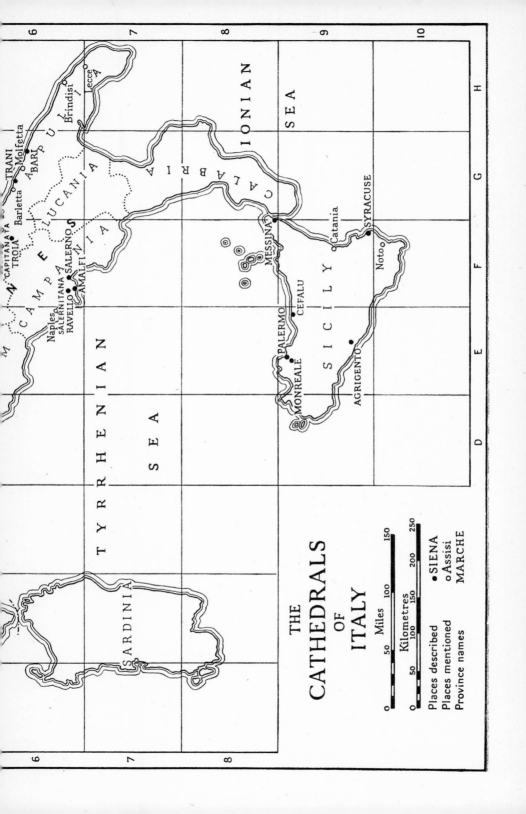

THE
CATHEDRALS
OF
ITALY

Miles
0   50   100   150

Kilometres
0   50   100   150   200   250

Places described   ●SIENA
Places mentioned   oAssisi
Province names   MARCHE

LIST OF ILLUSTRATIONS

The numerals in parentheses in the text refer to the *figure numbers* of the illustrations

17

LIST OF ILLUSTRATIONS

LIST OF ILLUSTRATIONS

LIST OF ILLUSTRATIONS

2 ROME: St Paul's outside the Walls. A section across the nave and aisles, begun 386.
An engraving from G. B. Piranesi's "Vedute di Roma", c. 1750

3 ROME: St Paul's outside the Walls. Rebuilt by L. Poletti after
the fire of 1823

4   RAVENNA: S. Apollinare in Classe. A Ravennate basilica, begun 535–8

5   ALBENGA: baptistery, built about 400. The amphorae were originally part of the vault. Window tracery is of ninth century

The History and Architecture of
Italian Cathedrals

THE CATHEDRAL IN ITALY

THAT there should be 275 bishoprics in Italy today demands some explanation to the English reader. It is to be sought in the development of ecclesiastical organization from the earliest days of Christianity. The social unit of Mediterranean countries is the town or city and in Italy most of the population, both agricultural workers and artisans, especially in the south, dwell together in cities large and small. Just as the cities were a basis for Roman administration so the early Christian Church adopted the main centres and provinces of the pagan Empire for its purposes. There were communities of Christians in Italy even in the lifetime of the Apostles and in each principal city there was one church served from an early date by a 'bishop', assisted by several presbyters. These mother churches became the cathedrals* of later centuries. It must be remembered that the organization and growth of the Church north of the Alps was dependent on factors not applicable to Italy. In France and Spain the Romans had imposed a city civilization on a largely pastoral community so that there were relatively few administrative centres. In England, the missionaries from Rome in the sixth and seventh centuries depended on the protection of the Anglo-Saxon kingdoms and the sees established by them were unusually large in area and few in number.

The earliest Christian centres in Italy included notably Rome, Syracuse, Naples and Milan. With the official establishment of Christianity in the fourth century, organization became more effective and widespread. The subdivision of the peninsula during the fifth and sixth centuries caused a considerable multiplication in the number of sees,

---

* The cathedral of an Italian city is often known as the *Duomo*, the House of God. The term "cathedral" has been used throughout the text to avoid confusion.

23

especially in the Byzantine provinces, the Ravennate in the north and Apulia in the south-east. With the thorough reorganization of the Church and a strengthening of the central authority of Rome during the eleventh and twelfth centuries, the establishment of dioceses in that period, especially in the Papal States and in the newly formed kingdom of the Normans, settled the ecclesiastical subdivisions of the peninsula. After that period few new dioceses were erected and these commonly for political convenience. The disturbance caused by Napoleon made possible a thorough reorganization and many dioceses were amalgamated in 1818 and in 1844. Of the total number of dioceses on the mainland and islands 38 have metropolitan archbishops and 154 have bishops or suffragans; 83 are archbishoprics and bishoprics immediately subject to the Holy See. Excluding seven suburbicaran sees, the cardinals' titular churches and the five patriarchal basilicas in Rome, the number of Italian towns with churches which have, or once certainly had, cathedral status is 341 (*see* Appendix).

The cathedrals of Italy have been for centuries objects of sincere devotion and deep veneration. Some of them have stood for as long as 1,500 years and represent the very roots of West European Church tradition. Over this space of time, the continuous and vigorous developments in architectural planning and design in new building and in the renovation of the old, have had an unparalleled influence on trends throughout Christendom, especially in Western Europe. For the transmission of ideas in liturgical practice and ecclesiastical organization the great pilgrimage and trade routes had particular importance. With Rome at its heart and the main arteries from all Europe crossing every part of Italy to the fount of Catholic institutions, the natural Italian genius has been discovered and sought by all. So it is scarcely surprising that we constantly find in Italy as a whole, hardly less than in Rome itself, the sources of many innovations in European art. This traffic has been reciprocated and the exchange fostered to general spiritual and artistic advantage.

On the mainland and the adjacent islands, innumerable monuments stand as an impressive record of the vigorous, passionate and devout nature of the people; Etruscan remains, Greek and Roman ruins, mediaeval and modern secular and ecclesiastical buildings. The roots of Italian architecture are firmly planted in classic soil and the remains of antique buildings and ornament in Italy have always been a direct source of inspiration to its artists. It is an assimilation of classical mass and line that distinguishes Italian architecture from that of northern countries. Even Gothic ideas, when they crossed the Alps, were interpreted according to a fundamentally different principle. No lack of imaginative development is responsible for the apparent continuation of the Romanesque pattern when "High Gothic" reigned elsewhere. Basically even the "unclassical" styles reflected the classical. Italian architects pursued a different course from northern masters and accomplished the glories of the Renaissance and Baroque through the structural principles of the Romanesque and the decorative use of Gothic. The Italian artist has always been a master of decoration and his greatest attainments are the fusion of decoration with harmonious architectural proportions; the forms are traditional and the native sense of proportion is combined with a firm control of sculptural texture and colour.

Italian church architecture grew up with the Church out of the tottering fabric of the Empire. Just as the architecture of pagan Rome had been disseminated wherever imperial authority was recognized so, at first, the forms of building used in Christian Rome were generally adopted in the West. During the "Dark Ages", however, each new kingdom developed a style determined by the nature of its people, their environment and the climate. While natural barriers were not absolute, the Alps were more hindrance than the sea to the interchange of knowledge. Italy was open to influences from the eastern shores of the Mediterranean which did not reach North Europe for several centuries and, notwithstanding the havoc wrought by war, some lights of civilization continued to burn in the peninsula. The principal provinces of Italy differed markedly in their traditions and their way of life. This is clearly reflected in the variety of their art and architecture. The strong local habits ingrained through the centuries, far more than the influences received in different ways from elsewhere, determined the course of stylistic development. It is convenient to group certain regions together to indicate the general trends and characteristics apparent in different parts of the country. The areas proposed have a general unity, but it must be borne in mind that political circumstances have frequently so confused the relationships between even one city and another that no boundaries can be clear-cut. The most important regions in the history of Italian architecture are Lombardy with Piedmont, Romagna and Emilia, the Veneto with the "Ravennate", Tuscany with Umbria and the Marches, Rome with Latium and Campania, Apulia and Sicily. Liguria, Sardinia, the Abruzzi, Trentino, Lucania and Calabria are of relatively slight interest for their ecclesiastical architecture. In each province the development of Romanesque, the effect of Gothic, the contribution to the Renaissance and indulgence in the Baroque have been marked by persistent local mannerisms.

The relation between Church and State is reflected in the history of architectural development as much in early centuries as later. The most notable schools of art and architecture in any period are located in centres which have enjoyed some more than transient political advantage.

The first important Christian churches to be built in western Europe are to be found in Rome. From them are ultimately derived the highly developed church plans of the Middle Ages with the exception of some features introduced from the Byzantine Empire. Not only were the accepted principles of construction and planning of the late Roman Empire employed in the earliest churches but, in Italy, the Church alone continued the tradition of large-scale building. The new Rome on the Bosphorus absorbed the architectural genius of the Empire, and the great Imperial Baths and the Basilica of Maxentius in Rome, and the Palace of Diocletian at Split on the Dalmatian coast were among the last significant examples of secular architecture to be erected before the founding of Constantinople.

The basilican form was adopted for the new Imperial foundations and other churches were commonly modelled on them. The basilica served throughout the Roman Empire in various rôles such as market halls and law-courts. It was suited to the accommodation of a large congregation and was not difficult to build. The basilican plan comprised a long nave between single or double aisles divided by arched or trabeated colonnades, a clerestory and a timber roof. At one end was the apse but there was no transept (*see* p. 32). In front of the church was an atrium or forecourt, or else only a single colonnaded portico or narthex, across the façade. Another important type of early building common to architectural practice in Rome was on a "centralized" plan and was adopted for use as a baptistery (5). The later developments of church planning depended as much on the materials available as on the requirements of the liturgy of the church. In Italy the great majority of churches are built of brick, even the vast St Peter's. While there remained a plentiful supply of classical Roman buildings, and it seemed inexhaustible, their columns and other materials were re-used in every part of Italy. Only in limited areas, notably the foothills of the Alps, Apulia and Sicily, are there supplies of good freestone which are suitable for more massive construction. Consequently the timber-roofed church continued to be erected and there was no need to alter the simple traditional techniques in construction. The development of Italian architecture has, therefore, been materially different from that north of the Alps. The vaulting of churches was limited to apses and low side-aisles until the twelfth century, when main vaults, almost invariably in brick, were introduced.

The marked height and accentuated vertical lines of North European churches were not acceptable in Italy and only gained a precarious footing in the very north-east of Lombardy and the Veneto during the fourteenth and fifteenth centuries. In the Italian church of every century the horizontal lines are dominant and recall the classical style of Rome. To this aspect of innate Italian taste may be attributed the manner in which Gothic forms were treated. They were rarely assimilated in their structural quality, but were very widely employed for decorative purposes. The Romanesque structural technique, as a consequence, persisted until it was suddenly transmuted by the significant technical accomplishment of Brunelleschi. His solution of the problem of covering a large space with a high cupola vindicated what may seem the backwardness of Italy in mediaeval structural methods. Without the persistence of the traditional Italian structure and the high development of decorative forms, the fifteenth-century Renaissance in architecture would not have been accomplished. Again, without the formulation of church design in the sixteenth century the freedom of Italian Baroque decoration would not have been possible.

The evolution of many aspects of church planning has depended on liturgical practice and, so far as the Western Church is concerned, this today springs from Rome. For a long time, however, the Roman rite was only one of several and was itself subject to uncertainty and variation. There were other rites like the Gallican in France, the Ambrosian in Lombardy and the Sarum in England which the Roman largely displaced only after some centuries. From the earliest Christian times, liturgical practice in Rome was predominantly Greek, but the ceremonial of Greek Christianity was probably not formulated until Justinian's reign in the sixth century. Not only did Greek practice persist in Italy during the period where large parts were subject to Byzantium but even today there are communities of Catholics in Italy using Byzantine liturgies. It is therefore not possible to indicate precise rules which may have been followed in the furnishing of ancient churches. However, in Italy there are several important instances of churches and cathedrals whose early planning and liturgical furniture survive remarkably intact, or may be reconstructed, from the sixth, eighth, eleventh and twelfth centuries (*see* Parenzo, Rome, Salerno and Monreale).

The orientation of the oldest basilicas varies but the entrance was usually at the west end; St Peter's faces the opposite way because of its special site. The celebrant of the Mass used to face the congregation over the altar. As in Rome today, this practice is occasionally continued at Parenzo and at S. Ambrogio in Milan. The altar itself has always been made of stone; sometimes a block but more commonly as a table or, from the sixteenth century, a sarcophagus. It is usually only placed against a wall, with a reredos, in side-chapels. The principal altar is normally free-standing but in Sicily, at Monreale and Cefalù for example, it occupies the apse. In early cases, like St Peter's and S. Apollinare in Classe, the single altar stood in the middle of the nave (4), but in the seventh century that at St Peter's was moved to a place over the shrine on the chord of the apse. The important result of this step was that the altar, covered by a baldacchino, henceforth stood above the shrine or tomb of the martyr or saint buried in the church (see Florence, Modena, St Mark's, Venice, Milan). Beneath the altar the shrine was made accessible from the rear by means of a crypt and was laid open to view from the nave by the excavation of a "confessio" in the floor. This feature was not reserved for the Apostolic basilicas and was widely adopted in Italy though rarely elsewhere. The confessio assumed grandiose proportions in the sixteenth century in Rome, but in general it was technically part of the crypt.

In the apse behind the altar was placed the episcopal chair. It was sometimes raised high up, as at Torcello (42), and surrounded by a hemicycle of stepped benches for the presbyters as in Byzantine churches. The presbytery, in those cases where this system was followed, occupied the area behind the altar and, in later times, was provided with elaborate choir stalls. This was no invariable rule, however, and the presbytery was frequently enclosed by a parapet wall between the nave and sanctuary as at Salerno, Monreale and St Mark's, Venice. An essential part of the liturgical furniture was the ambo, a form of pulpit usually fitted with a lectern. These are found often in pairs (92), one on each side of the nave, and were used for the readings of the Epistle and Gospel. A particular form of manuscript scroll, the exultet, was written to be read from the ambo, so that the illustrations could be seen by the congregation. Peculiar to the papal basilicas in Rome are the Porta Santa, or Holy Door, and the Loggia of the Benediction. The Holy Door is, in each case, the extreme right-hand one of the five great "west" doors, and is kept sealed except during the Holy Jubilee Years, which were initiated by Pope Boniface VIII in 1300. From the loggia over the narthex the Popes give their benediction to the world.

One of the most striking survivals of liturgical practice in Italy, rarely found north of the Alps, is the great baptistery. The baptistery was an essential adjunct of a community's principal church, either as a separate structure as at St John Lateran, Rome, and at Ravenna, or incorporated in the building as at St Paul's, Rome. The tradition thus established was in later centuries perpetuated in North Italy on a grandiose scale as at Pisa, Parma and Cremona. The baptizand was not, apparently, obliged to undergo total immersion; he is represented in pictures up to the tenth century as standing in the font while the priest pours water over his head. The baptistery was also used for the instruction of the catechumens before baptism. Since it was the custom for the bishop to administer baptism for the whole diocese only three times a year, at Easter, Pentecost and Epiphany, and then only at his cathedral, the reason for the erection of baptisteries on such a large scale during the twelfth century is more readily understandable. There seems to be no rule for the site of the baptistery. Though the earliest examples adjoined one side of the basilica, others stood at the west end as at Florence (*61*), Parenzo (*41*) and Torcello.

One other form of building employed at an early date which was to have a significant influence on church design was the martyrium; Old St Peter's, as originally built, was one. This great church was planned to honour the shrine of the Apostle and to provide a hall for the celebration of his Feast. It was the custom in pagan Rome to celebrate the anniversaries of the dead with a banquet, a practice continued by Christians in the Catacombs. The nave of St Peter's was apparently built for this purpose and screened off from the transept in which stood the shrine; the nave and the transept were in fact two separate, though conjoined, buildings. The banquets were soon stopped as they occasioned unseemly riots and the special distinction between the nave and transept was forgotten. The plan of so illustrious a model was, however, eagerly adopted and by the eleventh century it had become a commonplace in church design.

Ecclesiastical decoration is of the greatest significance in history; its importance is due, firstly, to its value as a record of ideas when Christianity was the primary medium for expression and, secondly, to the lack of secular art. It is not possible in this book to do more than indicate some of the more important aspects of the various arts, especially sculpture and mosaic decoration, in so far as they relate to the architecture and furnishing of the cathedrals.

The earliest Christian art was, like architecture, naturally enough, expressed in the same media as late Roman pagan art. Such decoration continued until the strength of Roman culture in the West dwindled away. Sculptures in stucco and marble with mosaic pictures and marble veneer were applied to walls and furniture. Evidence of this remains today principally in Rome and the Ravennate (39), and brilliant mosaics, especially in Venice, Sicily and Rome, are among the greatest splendours of mediaeval Italy. The new spirit of a strengthened Hellenistic art was introduced from Byzantium under the Emperor Justinian and continued to influence the iconography and manner of Italian art until the thirteenth century. But in every detail, whether it be the architectural line or the bronze doors, the classical tradition provided a firm base on which the individual artist developed his self-expression. The characteristic colourfulness of buildings and the expressive figure sculpture gave rich decorative values to church architecture from the thirteenth century onward, to which the use of fresco-painting and occasionally of coloured glass windows made a splendid contribution. The culmination of Italian personal expression was the Humanist Renaissance when patrons and artists combined to provide the finest and most beautiful work of which they were capable. After the panache of the Renaissance came the doldrums of sixteenth-century "mannerism", the sharp reaction to which, on the part of a few outstanding personalities like Bernini and Borromini, made the Baroque period one of the most exciting in the history of Italian art. The scene is dulled by the formal academism and imitation which afflicted Europe in the eighteenth and nineteenth centuries. That is still with us in the hands of the competent restorer but the new Italy shows that the spirit once so conspicuous an element in European art and life is by no means dead.

The patronage of art in Italy has not only been left in the hands of Emperors and the Papal Curia. Many of the most important mediaeval cathedrals were erected on the initiative and responsibility of individual communes like Florence and Milan. Among the phenomena of the Renaissance was the unremitting concern of the humanist for things of religion whether he were one of the great few like Lodovico Sforza, Il Moro, of Milan or one of the many petty despots like Sigismondo Malatesta of Rimini.

THE EARLY CENTURIES OF THE CHRISTIAN CHURCH

THE history of Christian architecture begins in Imperial Rome. Christianity was not declared the State religion of Rome until the year 380. Before that, however, encouraged by the conversion of the

Emperor Constantine in 312, and the new freedom from persecution, an underground movement was transformed into an imperial religion with all the consequences of official recognition. Meetings had no longer to be held in private houses and catacombs; worship could be conducted openly. For many years pagan cults and Christian worship were conducted side by side, but though Christians were again persecuted under Julian the Apostate, paganism could not prevail for long against the appeal of personal redemption, and the Church grew rapidly in numbers. The Church became necessary not only for Salvation but also for the security of life and property as well; a rôle which it maintained through the centuries. Out of this early period emerged the forms of ecclesiastical architecture.

During the fourth century the Church acquired an increasing self-confidence and power. Political disturbances and the weakening of Imperial government encouraged many leading officers of the Church to undertake local secular responsibilities whereby their authority was rapidly enhanced. Its organization was not yet centralized but depended on Oecumenical Councils, or general councils of bishops. The bishop of Rome was then but one of many, though certainly one of the most illustrious. It was in the second half of the century when absences of the Emperors from Rome increased in length and frequency that the authority of the bishop of Rome was first established in secular matters. The authority of a bishop was related to the political importance of his See as well as to the merits of its traditional foundation. Thus, for purely political reasons the bishop of Constantinople was declared in 381 to be second only to the bishop of Rome. This in itself presaged the importance Rome was to hold for the Church in the West.

The capital of the Western Empire was moved from one place to another in the fourth century. Of these, Milan was favoured by notable buildings, two survivors of which, the polygonal church of S. Lorenzo and the basilica of S. Simpliciano, are a link between the architectural styles of Rome and Ravenna. Remains of this early period are very scanty so that those in Rome are of exceptional interest.

As well as creating Byzantium the new capital of the Empire Constantine, his son and successors honoured the Shrines of Christendom. As in the Holy Land, they erected in Rome numerous churches, of which three are renowned even today although much altered – St Peter's in the Vatican and St Paul's outside the Walls celebrating the martyrdom of the Apostles and St John Lateran, the Mother Church of Christendom. Each of these is of the greatest importance, St John's, the first to be built, and St Peter's for their influence on European architecture, and St Paul's as a record of the design of Old St Peter's. The basilica of S. Maria Maggiore is notable for its rare series of late fourth-century mosaic narrative pictures. They are all basilicas in plan and were built on a magnificent scale with either double or single aisles separated by arcaded or trabeated colonnades. The clerestories consisted of large round-headed windows beneath the tiled timber roofs (2). The single vaulted apse at the "east" end of St John's was surrounded by a low ambulatory and there were no transepts. St Peter's was designed as a martyrium and St Paul's, when rebuilt half a century later, was modelled on it. They differed from the usual basilica in having a separate hall across one end of the aisled nave, like a T. On the side of this transept opposite the junction with the nave was the apse, which at St Peter's surrounded the shrine of the Apostle.

The basilica is the prototype of the majority of European churches, but the centrally designed or circular building is also important. Such concentric buildings were not uncommon in classical times in both East and West Europe. In Rome itself, this form of structure was developed with great variety and success, the Pantheon being the best-known example of all. The form was readily adopted for certain kinds of church of which the baptistery and sepulchral chapel are the most common; in the fifteenth century it was to be considered the ideal for church design. S. Costanza in Rome is a notable round memorial church of the fourth century which may have also been a baptistery, and there was originally a vaulted round baptistery beside St John Lateran. The baptistery was not always circular; it was a simple rectangular room at St Paul's, Rome, and at St John Lateran and Ravenna in the fifth century it was polygonal. All three forms were copied in later centuries. Some early churches also were polygonal in plan, like S. Lorenzo at Milan and the sixth-century S. Vitale at Ravenna. That many "Churches of the Holy Sepulchre" should be circular is due to their being modelled on one of Constantine's greatest foundations on the site of the Holy Sepulchre at Jerusalem.

It is recorded that St Peter's and St Paul's were extensively decorated. In S. Maria Maggiore is visible evidence of the didactic decoration of these early basilicas. On the "triumphal arch" and in the apse are symbolic representations from the Apocalypse and of the Apostles and the Redeemer; the plain wall-space between the colonnade and the clerestory windows was divided into panels filled with mosaic pictures of stories from the Old and New Testaments. At the end of the fourth century the Vulgate text of the Bible as defined by St Jerome was not yet entirely accepted, and many of the stories depicted in S. Maria are now relegated to the Apocrypha and in some instances are very little known; they derive from obscure Hellenistic traditions. Therefore, while showing the early manner of decoration, these pictures are not part of mediaeval Latin Christian iconography. Mosaics were also used to decorate the external wall of the main façade of the basilicas. Though few fourth-century pavements are known, that at Aquileia serves as an indication of the work of that time.

During the fifth and succeeding centuries the economy of the peninsula, artificially stimulated under the Emperors, declined rapidly and suffered heavily from the marauding barbarian armies. The Emperors had to cede much of their authority to the invaders, retaining for themselves little more than a title. Authority in Rome was vested in the Senate and the bishop. Only Ravenna, for long an important naval port on the Adriatic coast, was suitably placed for defence and for communication with the Empire in the East. As an Imperial residence from 409 the city rapidly acquired an outstanding political and artistic importance which lasted for nearly 200 years. For several centuries Byzantine power maintained an unsteady footing in Italy by its control of the Ravennate, a province lying round the northern Adriatic coast from Ancona to Istria. Roman life and manners, already strongly Hellenized, had been transferred to the Bosphorus; Ravenna was but an outpost reflecting the civilization developed east of the Adriatic and, after its decline, was succeeded by Venice as the chief link between East and West.

Theodoric the Great and his Ostrogothic followers brought a temporary halt to the disturbances of the fifth century of which the repeated sacking of the Eternal City had been, in contemporary eyes, the most terrible manifestation. The eastern emperors, weakened by severe losses in every province, and by internal intrigue, were powerless to resist his usurpation of their authority. Under Theodoric's strong rule civilization was fostered; Ravenna became his capital and some of its finest monuments were begun in his reign. He is also reputed to have built and restored extensively in many other Italian cities. The Ostrogoths were Arians and their control of State and Church, intolerable to Catholics, created a schism. The accession of Justinian the Great in 526 inaugurated a period of Byzantine reconquest which assumed the character of a crusade against the heretical barbarians. When his generals had won back most of Italy, soon after the death of Theodoric, the re-establishment of the orthodox faith was reflected in the intensity of his church-building programme in Italy which matched that in Constantinople and other parts of his Empire.

The century from 450 to 550 was a remarkable period in the history of architecture in Italy. The massive structures of late Imperial Rome no longer served as models; a new tradition had been established. Whereas the fourth and early fifth centuries are represented by the great churches in Rome and by a few rare examples elsewhere, in the late fifth and sixth centuries there was a new flowering of architecture and the decorative arts of real freshness and charm. The instability of the Constantinian churches in Rome, in which the suitability of materials was sacrificed to ambitious scale or economy, was avoided. Typical churches of the period were spacious but not grandiose, enriched by colourful mosaics internally and sometimes externally, and lit by large alabaster-glazed windows. Variety was obtained by the use of antique varicoloured marble columns and imaginatively carved capitals, rarely marred by misfitting fragments. In the finest examples, S. Apollinare Nuovo in Ravenna, S. Apollinare in Classe (4) nearby, and Parenzo, in Istria, the characteristic proportions of the nave and aisles are due to the simple relationship of the width and height to the overall length of the church. There are no deep recesses with heavy shadows, nothing is ponderous or ornate, yet there is no severity of line or form.

The primary features of the "Ravennate" churches are readily recognized. They were built of warm-red brick with marble columns, bases, capitals and the "pulvin" of the Byzantine school. Perhaps the columns and certainly the capitals were imported from Salonika and elsewhere in Greece. The capitals differ markedly from classical types. The ingenious variety of their deep-cut designs form a veil of tendrils and foliage with occasional birds and beasts. The weight of the high walls above the arcade is relieved from the fragile capitals by the use of the pulvin, or impost block, a solid simply-shaped secondary capital. The pulvins were made locally and often inscribed with the monogram of the bishop of the time.

The east end of the nave is terminated by a high apse, usually polygonal externally but semicircular within and lit by three or five ample windows; the side-aisles are square-ended. The floor level was uniform from end to end. The clerestory and aisle windows are large and round-headed in the Roman manner, and placed one to each of the nave bays; they were often glazed with alabaster sheets or occasionally filled by stone tracery (5). Externally, the basilican church is not imposing in appearance, the walls have simple lines and the roof-line is unbroken. To give structural strength without disturbing the simplicity of the interior there are external buttresses in the form of broad shallow arches which also serve to relieve the plainness of the long walls. The church was preceded by an atrium, an open courtyard surrounded by a colonnaded portico. A baptistery was situated either to one side of the church as at Ravenna cathedral or opposite the west entrance to the church, which led to some curious arrangements – Aquileia, Torcello. At Parenzo, which is exceptionally well-preserved, the characteristic sixth-century ensemble is complete with both an atrium and a polygonal baptistery at its west end (*41*).

Contemporary with the churches of Ravenna are remains of similar buildings elsewhere in the peninsula. The first cathedral of Naples, S. Restituta, though rebuilt in the fourteenth century, is preserved in plan and attached to it is the fifth-century baptistery. Similarly, in other places typical capitals and fragments of mosaic survive as a record of the widespread activity of Justinian's builders, particularly in Apulia.

Perhaps the most accomplished period of Byzantine mosaic picture painting was during the fifth and sixth centuries. Mosaics were used to cover every wall and cupola of the greatest Byzantine churches and a remarkably complex iconography based on Biblical and apocryphal teachings was elaborated. In Italy, this was only equalled in scope in the mediaeval mosaics of St Mark's, Venice, which were based on the splendid examples of Justinian's reign in Constantinople, like those of S. Sophia. At Ravenna, however, there is a rich and important series of such pictures, notably in S. Vitale and S. Apollinare Nuovo. The Basilica Ursiana, the original cathedral of Ravenna, was decorated in similar fashion, and in the adjacent baptistery mosaics are combined with delicate stucco reliefs. The symbolic representation of the most sacred subjects, the Redeemer as the Lamb, the Holy Ghost as a dove, the Apostles as sheep for example, continued in use alongside pictures of the Imperial Court attired in the most gorgeous jewelled habits. It is, above all, the colour that distinguishes the mosaics of this period. The subtle tones of rich colour were obtained by the technique employed in laying the little glass and marble cubes to catch the rays of pale light diffused through the yellow alabaster windows.

THE "DARK AGES"

WITH the rest of Europe, Italy suffered severely and continuously from the turmoil of invasion and civil strife during the so-called Dark Ages. This is clearly reflected in the general debasement of art and architecture that left these centuries so bleak. The beautiful work of the Ravennate school was itself a symptom of the decline of the Late Empire; it was all on a very small scale and largely depended on direct Imperial patronage for its success. Once this patronage had been withdrawn, from the mid-sixth century onwards, there were no outstanding Christian monuments newly created in the whole of Italy until the turn of the millennium; there was one exception, the early ninth-century original basilica of St Mark, at Venice. The poverty of the age is revealed by the evidence we have of buildings and their adornment.

Certain notable events in this period most affected the history and life of the peninsula. In 751, the Exarch of Ravenna, the resident Byzantine governor, lost control of his territory to the Lombards who came into possession of the greater part of the country by the end of the sixth century. From then on Byzantine rule was limited to Sicily, Apulia and the Salernitano in the south. The Lombards exercised the rights of conquerors over the inhabitants, who possessed little Roman culture for them to emulate. At the instigation of the Pope their kingdom was in turn overthrown in 774 by Charlemagne, the Frankish king. In spite of religious differences between the Papacy and the iconoclastic eastern emperors of the eighth century, there was no suggestion of the Church disputing the nominal secular authority of the emperors until the conquest of Italy by Charlemagne caused a change of front. The direct result was that Byzantium was repudiated and Charles was crowned Emperor of the West in 800 at Rome. About this time the so-called "Donation of Constantine" was brought to light as evidence for the papal tenure of the "Patrimony of St Peter", the Papal States of later centuries, which the Church held, or claimed as subject to its temporal authority. The Papal States were to be of crucial political and economic importance to the mediaeval Papacy and the cause of endless dispute with secular powers, but direct patronage by Rome influenced many important artistic projects within their confines.

The "Golden Age" of Charlemagne's reign was of little benefit to Italy, but at this time the Saracens were establishing their power in Sicily. This was momentous for the history of the island and the adjacent mainland, since they introduced a culture that was to become inseparable from the history and character of the area. The Saracens and Byzantine Greeks lived together and, when in due course they succumbed to Norman domination, their several contributions to the Siculo-Norman civilization formed its most brilliant and enlightened elements. Late in the ninth century, the emergence of the small maritime republic of Amalfi and the growth of Venice were signs of a return to the prosperous life of earlier times, though the process was to be long and hard.

One church must be taken as representative of early Lombard work. This is the former cathedral of St Peter at Tuscania, a building which is dated in large part to the early eighth century and is attributed to a Comacine master from the region of Como (43). It is a far cry from the beautiful work of the sixth century. The basic form of a basilica is employed but the proportions are radically different. The walls depend on semi-massive construction for stability, the nave arches are clumsy in shape and irregular in size. The external prospect of the east end is relatively imposing with its single tall apse coarsely decorated with shallow arcaded cornices running round the walls. This motif, sometimes supported by flat pilasters or half-shafts, but often without either, is a common feature of minor Lombard decoration that curiously persists from this early date throughout the Middle Ages. But of greater significance is the fact that this primitive building is constructed of dressed stone and incorporates a form of transept that does not project outside the aisle-walls. In such work as this are seen the roots of the Romanesque style of architecture.

In Byzantine Sicily, during the seventh century, the Greek Temple of Athena at Syracuse was transformed into a Christian basilica. The walls of the central "cella" were pierced to make a rough arcade, and the colonnades were walled up to provide aisles. A similar conversion was made of the Temple of Concord at Agrigento, and in Rome several temples were dedicated as churches in the seventh and eighth centuries. They were lying idle, largely despoiled of furniture and were as much the haunts of crime as superstition. The Church was not averse to employing such pagan relics for Christian use. Gregory the Great had recommended St Augustine to make use of pagan groves and shrines of the Saxons for his churches and not to despise the traditional places of religion.

Among the lagoons of the northern shore of the Adriatic, vigorous communities had begun life anew after leaving their mainland homes menaced by barbarian invaders. The settlers in these lagoons developed a profitable maritime trade and relations with Byzantium without losing their independence. On the islands of Torcello, one of the earliest of the new settlements, the simple Ravennate form of the seventh-century cathedral is apparent, but so too are the differences: the high placing of the clerestory windows, the tall apse of the narrow nave and the rejection of the pulvin.

The characteristic exoticism of Venetian architecture is directly due to the close bond with the East. St Mark's has always been the monument to this relationship. The ninth-century predecessor of the present church seems to have been a single-aisled basilica, probably of the Ravennate type, built on a scale unparalleled by any contemporary new structure in Italy and unequalled since the sixth century. It was a fitting shrine for the Evangelist and patron saint. Beyond the probability that this early church was as long as its successor, all that is known of it consists in the materials re-used in the eleventh century.

There were two important architectural innovations introduced in North Italy during this obscure period: the crypt and the campanile or bell-tower. In the first half of the seventh century, a crypt was inserted in Old St Peter's, the floor level of the apse was raised as a platform above the shrine of the Apostle and the principal altar placed directly over it. By means of a semicircular ambulatory, beneath the platform and against the apse wall with, on the axial line, a straight passage, the shrine remained accessible from the rear and visible through a grille in front. This model was naturally imitated and many churches were altered in this way in the provinces, as for example some in the Ravennate, as well as a number in Rome. The altar was in this way raised a step above the nave floor, whereas hitherto it had been on the same level. Later churches were planned to include these modifications and there were striking developments of the crypt in Italy with peculiar liturgical implications which may be contrasted with the division of greater English churches by the choir screen or pulpitum (71).

The earliest campanili are found round the northern shores of the Adriatic and perhaps the earliest of all, those in Ravenna, date from the late ninth century; some were square in plan, others circular and almost all stood free of the church. The bell-tower became an essential adjunct of every church and considerable talent was shown in design. Perhaps the finest of all are those in the Lombard cities; in Rome and its vicinity is another notable group, while in the southern provinces towers are adorned with a bizarre medley of Norman, Saracen and Gothic forms. The massive Lombard and Tuscan campanili are usually detached from the church, singly or in pairs, at the east or west end. The slighter towers of the Roman school generally stand on an angle of a façade; the Normans in Italy typically favoured pairs of massive towers closely tied to the structure of the church, which emphasized their sturdy appearance.

Symptomatic of life during the "Dark Ages" was the primitive nature of decorative art. The strong influence of Byzantine art at Ravenna up to the sixth century was only perfunctorily effective except in Rome, the Veneto and the southern provinces for the succeeding four centuries. Little material survives from the seventh and eighth centuries, rather more from the ninth and tenth centuries. Marble panels rudely carved in low relief with birds, beasts and foliage designs are found in most northern areas and, as may be seen at Tuscania and Torcello, these served as enclosure walls for the sanctuary and other chapels. But these panels are also found at later dates and the poorest craftsmanship is not necessarily attributable to this earlier period. Pictorial representation in colour has rarely survived the improvements of later centuries, and even in Rome the survival of painting from these times is rare and usually constitutes an "archaeological find".

THE "ROMANESQUE" PERIOD

Towards the end of the tenth century a new era in European history was opened. There was a "Renaissance" in which intellectual and spiritual life recovered from the blight of the Dark Ages. During the succeeding two centuries intellectual studies rapidly developed in the church schools and advanced to the founding of universities, the earliest of which were in Italy, as at Salerno and Bologna. There were notable advances in the development of canon and civil law, and a renewed study of classical texts, preserved by the Arabs and Byzantines, encouraged philosophical and scientific learning. Not least impressive was the renewal of artistic activity, not solely represented by the adoption of Byzantine practice as in mosaic picture work and manuscript illumination, but manifested also in the skill and imagination of native genius, above all in sculpture and ecclesiastical and civil architecture.

Contemporary with this Renaissance in art and learning was a parallel economic expansion. Trade flourished between the Orient and the West and the ports along the Adriatic and Ionian coasts of Italy were among the most favoured points of embarkation for merchants, pilgrims and crusaders. But the most significant factor lay in the rise of the maritime republics, and their activity encouraged the industrialization of inland cities. Increased wealth strengthened demands for independence from the feudal claims of land-owners, and political autonomy stimulated competition. As the most fortunate cities acquired a measure of independence they were established as privileged communes. From the eleventh to the sixteenth century, the political history of Italy turned on their problems and ambitions, the rise and fall of popular governments, the succession of petty despots and the feuds between neighbours.

Independence, once gained, was affected by relations with two principal conflicting forces: the Papacy with its authority over the Church States and its spiritual supremacy, and the Holy Roman

Emperors with their idealistic but potent claims to temporal authority in Italy as in Germany. One state alone, the Norman kingdom of Sicily and South Italy, held its own against these powers for the greater part of the eleventh and twelfth centuries.

The history of the Papacy in this period is marked by its bitter struggle for political independence and effective authority. The increasing strength of European kings, the clamours of the Roman populace and the perpetual claims of the German Emperors to be the rightful guardians of temporal power threatened to undermine the authority of the Church. Individual Popes, like Gregory VII, Alexander III, Innocent III and Boniface VIII with their personal vigour and sacerdotal idealism, opposed secular participation in Church matters. By strenuous litigation and diplomacy they strove to acquire a position of strength from which their spiritual functions could be effectively exercised in a world of turmoil. The rise of the communes and republics was of paramount importance. On the one hand it increased the number of irreconcilably independent and semi-independent powers in every part of the peninsula, and encouraged anarchical dissension among them. These problems were unmitigated by any equivalent to the centralizing authority of sovereign rulers which existed in England, France and Sicily; the papal and imperial forces only aggravated factious differences. On the other hand the pride of the citizens stimulated community life, and economic activity was matched by cultural competition. Every city is a lasting monument of its own history, and the cathedral in particular was, as a matter of course, endowed with the best the citizens could bestow. The growth of the communes depended on several factors. The earliest to attain independence were those that depended on their maritime trade and strength. Amalfi and Venice both grew up as vigorous communities in the ninth century. While Venice, secure in its impregnable lagoons, continued to prosper, Amalfi was supplanted in importance by Pisa in the eleventh century. Pisa in its turn had to face the growing competition of its greater rivals, Venice and Genoa, but held its own until forced to meet the threats of its inland neighbour, Florence. The trade of these sea faring republics was carried the length and breadth of the Mediterranean. Their depots and colonies were established in all the leading ports around its shores, and their great wealth was won from the transport of oriental luxury goods and in the service of the inland industrial centres.

Venice holds a unique place in European and Italian history. Even during the "Dark Ages" it was an outpost of the East in the West.

6　CIVITA CASTELLANA: "Cosmatesque" façade by Jacobus and Cosma, dated 1210

7　ROME: St John Lateran. "Cosmatesque" cloister by Vassalletto and his father, 1220–28

8 ASSISI: an Umbrian façade and campanile of the twelfth
to thirteenth centuries

9 LUCCA: the façade showing
Tuscan sculpture of about 1200

10 PALERMO: porphyry
tomb of the Empress Constance
(†1198)

From the eleventh to the thirteenth centuries the Serene Republic's fortune rose to the point of greatness. An autocratic government kept it free from mainland politics until the end of this period and encouraged successful merchants, so that wealth from the Orient flowed into the city and with it the produce of its colonies and spoils of war; the most striking example of this process was in 1204 when the Venetians provided transport for the Crusaders, only to plunder the treasures of Constantinople.

The ancient cities of the Lombard plain were among the earliest to recover from the vicissitudes of the "Dark Ages", and in succeeding centuries were flourishing centres of industry, as they are today. This was their strength. The interests of the merchant-banker and artisan classes led to the expulsion of noble rulers, while the sympathy between the clergy and the nobles in their conflicts with the burghers forged a ready tool for the Emperors in their endeavours to control the Church and Papacy. The famous epithets Guelph (the papal party) and Ghibelline (the imperial party) were once closely identified with the struggles in these factious cities, but the meaning was lost in the maze of pacts and leagues between one city and another which were made and broken. The traditional Italian political anti-clericalism was a formidable obstacle to the satisfaction of papal needs. The Papacy could indeed maintain relatively strong ties with those communes within the Church States, but those beyond, in Lombardy, kept up a fierce resistance against external authority of any kind. Throughout the Middle Ages, the independence of the communes was the outstanding factor in the history of North Italy. The greatest among them strove to gain mastery over their neighbours, which were absorbed into city-states, whether republics like Florence, Siena and Venice, or despotic states like Milan and Verona. Unity of action against a common enemy was rarely attained, and the Lombard Leagues set up to oppose the German emperors broke up as soon as the immediate danger had apparently passed. Resistance to military invasions came to depend on the strength of individual States like Milan but invaders succeeded by their diplomacy more than by trials of strength. Milan has always been the capital of Lombardy and Florence could claim to be pre-eminent in Tuscany. The industrial interests of such inland cities brought them great wealth which was increased by their merchant-bankers who were capable of subsidizing kings and popes.

The impact of the Normans on South Italy and Sicily created political conditions quite different from those in the north. It is interesting to compare the effects of Norman rule in Sicily, Normandy, England and the Kingdom of Jerusalem respectively. In each country the northmen arrived as raiders or mercenaries and stayed as rulers. They governed with a hard efficiency and employed the forms of feudalism for their despotic ends. In the eyes of contemporaries they had a singular tolerance for the established customs of their conquered subjects. Wherever they settled, the Normans turned to their own advantage the best in local custom: in Normandy the nascent feudalism of the French kingdom; in England the administrative organization of the Saxons; into Sicily they imported the forms of feudalism, adopted the theocratic principles of the Byzantine monarchy, developed a high standard of administration with three official languages and encouraged cultural interchanges between Greeks, Saracens, Latins and Normans. In no other mediaeval state in Europe were diverse elements so harmonized or culture so broadly based. Much is owed to the Normans in Sicily for that transmission of classical literature from the Eastern Mediterranean to Western Europe which was so significant a part of the Renaissance of the eleventh and twelfth centuries. The art and architecture of Sicily in this period are evidence of the energy of the Norman kings, the Byzantine character of their regal pretensions and their fusion of three cultures in one.

The Norman kingdom on the mainland comprised Apulia and Calabria; the latter has always been stricken by poverty, but the former was once quite otherwise. The cities of Apulia prospered under Norman rule as they had in Roman times. This was largely due to their situation near the coast on the all-important land and sea route for travellers between Western Europe and the Levant. The Normans conquered the mainland territories more rapidly from the Byzantines than they did Sicily. But while the life of the combined kingdom was continually broken by feudal discord, the urban life of the area flourished. As a result, in due course numerous towns from the "heel of Italy" to Manfredonia proudly possessed a fine cathedral.

The most splendid periods of Norman rule were the reigns of Roger II (1101–54) and Frederick II (1198–1250). The subsequent neglect of the well-being of their subjects by the Angevins and Aragonese brought about an economic and artistic decline which lasted until the nineteenth century. This decline was aggravated as the crusading fervour lapsed, Venice came to control the Adriatic and Mediterranean trade routes and, finally, Eastern trade slowly waned after the discovery of the Americas.

From the eleventh century onwards the resurgence throughout Italy in every field of activity was matched by the development of the

Romanesque style in architecture. Great numbers of churches, large and small, were built throughout Europe and especially in Italy. The finest cathedrals of the period were naturally in those cities which had acquired the greatest wealth and power, but so magnificent were many of these projects that the resources of the most willing were severely strained, and the work was prolonged over periods sometimes amounting to centuries. Along with the active process of rebuilding went the intensive restoration and embellishment of the old basilicas. Restoration work was marked by a faithful adherence to traditional practice, and the most venerated ancient buildings were given a new lease of life.

The great basilicas in Rome were already many centuries old and had suffered from frequent fires, from general dilapidation and, not least, at the hands of the Normans who sacked the city in 1084. The restoration of these lingered throughout the twelfth century and there was little large-scale building, so that little stylistic development was made. Additions were made like campanili, porticos and cloisters that today remain a characteristic feature of the basilicas in Rome.

The forms of building and decoration in Rome spread over a wide area outside the walls, towards Tuscany, Umbria and especially southward into Campania. Campanili, for example, are built of brick with cornices, pilaster-strips and superficial decoration of marble discs and panels; the several stages are pierced with large round-headed lights in pairs, and the roofs are almost flat. This style of bell-tower is widespread outside Rome; mild variants occur in Umbria where stone-building affected the general design (8). The stylistic influence of Spoleto was locally strong, and the lofty bell-chamber of its massive campanile (16) is even found on brick towers in the neighbourhood. The narthex or portico across the façade was given greater importance with the neglect of the atrium.

The inexhaustible supply of precious marbles conveniently at hand in both classical and mediaeval buildings was ransacked for materials for the characteristic mosaic decoration; shafts and blocks were sliced up for discs and panels. Mediaeval Roman mosaics, unlike those of the Sicilian school, were made up of the most elementary shapes, squares and circles, set in a base of white marble; the patterns were highly stylized, especially for pavements. Although much of this kind of work showed little imagination in design, the so-called Cosmati workers, active during the twelfth and thirteenth centuries, set a new standard following the introduction of glass-paste *tesserae* between 1160 and 1180, which were applied in combination with carved ornaments.

They were, however, responsible for only a limited quantity of such work. The success of their technique was effectively demonstrated in all forms of furniture, choir screens and stalls, ambos, pulpits, baldacchinos and altars. They also entered the field of architecture, erecting porticos as at Civita Castellana (6), and cloisters like those of St John's in Rome (7). Their range in sculpture was limited to stiff floral motifs and a number of animal forms. Towards the end of the thirteenth century, the arrival in Rome of Arnolfo di Cambio, whose experience in the school of Nicola Pisano at Siena had shown him to be one of the leading sculptors of the time, brought fresh life and a vigour to Roman art which had hitherto been lacking. He collaborated with Cosmati workers like Pietro Oderisio at St Paul's and fused their mosaic technique with his sculptural and architectural sense. For large-scale pictorial mosaic work, artists from Venice were widely employed in the twelfth century. These were closely in touch with the developments in technique and changes in iconography current in the Byzantine world, the style of which pervaded the representational art of Italy in this period. In the following century, however, native craftsmen like Torriti attained a high degree of skill in this medium.

Though there was little architectural development in Rome itself during the period, its historic buildings were a standard source of inspiration elsewhere. The form of the basilica, of which the transept had become a standard adjunct, determined the design of new work and the principal features of the new style, whether in Salerno and Sicily, to the south, or Aquileia and Pisa, to the north. The Lombard school of architecture has been claimed to be the cradle of North European Romanesque architecture, but north of the Alps, in Germany, France and England development was so rapid that it would be arbitrary to assert the whole truth of this. A primary distinction between North European and Lombard architecture is that, whereas the former is based on stone construction, the latter is almost invariably carried out in brick and the different forms developed are, in part, attributable to this fact. Stone and marble were employed in Lombardy for wall-facings and sculptural work, which was executed with increasing skill. Fresh marble, readily available in Tuscany, was used from the eleventh century onwards to decorate inner and outer walls with bands of alternate light and dark colours and multicoloured inlay; from the Florentine baptistery to Pisa, Siena and Orvieto this was to become an inseparable feature of Tuscan church architecture. The whole course of Romanesque development can be followed in work of the Lombard school. Intense activity, particularly in such important centres as

Milan, naturally fostered experiment in building technique, proportion, height and span of vaulting, lighting and decoration. Much of this development took place in the eleventh century, but it is noteworthy that a large number of the finest buildings incorporating newly developed forms date from the first decades of the twelfth century; the effects of an earthquake in 1117 necessitated extensive rebuilding in many towns. It is clear that experience acquired by that date taught the master builders how to build on the grand scale. From then and even earlier we find the names of some master-builders and other craftsmen on record, and their work can be traced from city to city. The conception of Pisa cathedral was reputedly due to Buscheto, whose career may have begun in Rome, while developments in Lombardy are marked by the masterpieces of Lanfranc, architect of Modena cathedral.

Even while the new characteristic Romanesque forms were being elaborated the influence of classical and post-classical models kept Italian mediaeval architecture outside the North European movement towards the Gothic style. Pisa cathedral clearly demonstrated this persistence of the sense of proportion and space that had pervaded classical Roman work. The principal features of the basilica, the colonnades, the timber roof and the short apsidal-ended presbytery were preserved even when vaulting, for example, was contemplated. Transepts were frequently contained within the lines of the aisle-walls (69) or, when projecting, followed the model of St Peter's in Rome in having one or more apses flush with the east wall. In the twelfth century the presbytery was frequently extended beyond the transept (73) and an octagonal cupola was raised above the main arches of the crossing. Such cupolas are a distinctive feature of Lombard churches and were given additional prominence in Tuscany (13). The drum was encircled inside and out by loggias and often pierced by lights. The cupola had a simple, low, ribbed vault internally, with a low-pitched roof (cf. 11, see p. 174).

The elevation of the North Italian church, unlike the trans-Alpine, is low; the emphasis is laid on horizontal line and carefully regulated mass rather than height. The matroneum, or triforium, was not much favoured in Italy, possibly because it was not a feature of classical basilicas. It was employed indeed in a number of Romanesque buildings but frequently it is found to be "false", that is, it merely serves a decorative purpose and opens equally into the nave and aisles (cf. 71, 87, 97, but 75). The balanced proportions between main arcade, triforium and clerestory were rarely worked out so carefully as north of the Alps; a bold nave arcade usually dominates the elevation with noble effect.

The timber roof of the ancient basilica continued in use, in spite of the development of vaulting in stone and brick at the turn of the eleventh century. It was not possible to employ heavy vaulting while slender marble columns were still favoured for the nave arcading, but side-aisles were frequently given a simple groin-vault, as had always been used for apses. The massive low vaults of churches at Milan and Pavia belonged to a local type in striking contrast to the relative lightness of such timber-roofed churches as Modena.

A necessary concomitant of the erection of high vaults was the strengthening of the supporting structure. A step in this direction was the introduction of "diaphragm arches" which also strengthened the walls and roof. These arches traversed the nave at intervals of two or three bays at clerestory level and rose from stone piers of coupled half-shafts alternating with columns of marble or freestone. The practice necessary for constructing high vaults had hardly been acquired by 1100. The earliest ribbed high vault in Europe is that of Durham cathedral, begun in 1093 and vaulted in about 1130. One of the aesthetic problems involved in erecting such a vault while using half-round arches, is how to arrange the cross-ribs so that the centre line of the vault should not undulate between each bay. At Durham this was resolved by the use of the pointed arch for the main transverse arches. At Parma, in Lombardy, where the plans were laid soon after 1117, an alternative solution was employed so that, the transverse arches being semicircular, the cross-ribs are depressed (75).

The treatment of the exterior is well represented by a number of examples whose design has not been much altered in more recent centuries, with the result that the principal features may be readily distinguished. The broad wall-surfaces, whether of bare brick or faced with stone, are relieved by tall blind-arcades, or panels framed by projecting half-shafts (70) or by pilaster-strips (78), and by the shallow loggias of free-standing arcades with colonnettes which distinguished most large churches between Pavia and Ferrara. The loggias are disposed in one or two rows along side-walls, transepts, round the apses of the east end, and especially across the façades. These motifs spread rapidly and were developed locally with extraordinary variety (see Tuscany, Apulia).

The shape of arches and vaulting ribs in Italy has always been simple, and the typical moulded form developed in northern countries was rarely introduced. Even where the direct influence of France and

Spain affected the general design, the Italian craftsman rarely abandoned the square-cut section. This traditional form continued even during the Gothic period. The moulded orders of northern Romanesque and Gothic were never to Italian taste; in this respect Genoa and Ferrara cathedrals are exceptional and the buildings of the later Angevin School, in the Kingdom of Naples, quite alien.

The treatment of the façades of the earliest Lombard churches was unpretentious and followed the simple outline of the nave and aisles. But during the thirteenth century it became increasingly common for the façade to be given a separate identity with high gables and broad lines of cornices and loggias. The façade generally had three sections boldly marked by prominent, unstepped buttresses at the junction of the nave and aisles. The central and side gables were emphasized by a moulded cornice, and, in some cases, a single gable with a loggia following its line united the whole west end (*11*). Windows were small as a rule but were utilized for their decorative effect in groups of up to five lights. The same pattern was applied to transeptal façades. There were usually three doorways in the façade (*11*, *78*), but even in large churches occasionally there was only one (*see* p. 171). It was usual for these important entrances and some side-doors to be embellished by a porch. The arches, the doors and the porches were decorated with sculpture in high and low relief (*9*); the porch was supported by columns on recumbent lions or griffons with, in some cases, a second storey containing statues of patron saints, Evangelists or Prophets.

The use of sculpture was to acquire particular significance since it is in the plastic treatment of wall-surfaces that Italian mediaeval and Renaissance architects were most accomplished. Modena cathedral was an important contribution to this development. Its early twelfth-century internal and external sculptured decoration was largely due to Wiligelmo and his school. He developed as a motif the series of low reliefs found on churches of the eleventh century like S. Michele in Ciel d'Oro at Pavia. He carved narratives from the Old and New Testaments in a personal manner that also reflected the continuous influence of classical models. In the twelfth century the fullest development of this application of reliefs was attained by Antelami with particular effect in the baptistery at Parma. At the same time capitals and corbels, both internally and externally, were richly carved with figures and scenes of a traditional nature; the seasonal occupations of Man, the Arts and Crafts, and the stories of the Bible. Contemporary sculpture in the south of France was matched by figures in full relief or free-standing, placed round porches and in niches. The sources of stone for facing the Lombard churches were chiefly in the foothills of the Alps round the "Italian Lakes". The experience gained in working stone by the local craftsmen of that area was in general demand throughout the province. These "Campionese masters" were active throughout the twelfth, thirteenth and fourteenth centuries, as at Modena, Milan and Pisa. They were capable carvers and produced a prodigious quantity of figured sculpture and small architectural pieces like porches, but they rarely ventured away from their set habits of expression. The increasing use of sculpture was given a new and invigorating impulse by the example of Nicola Pisano, who is first recorded as active in Pisa in 1254. His presumably South Italian origin may explain the freshness of his style, for it is without parallel in the northern provinces. Although his own contribution was chiefly confined to his celebrated pulpits (14, 54), his disciple, Arnolfo di Cambio, and his son, Giovanni Pisano, were among the most prominent architects at the turn of the thirteenth century.

The pulpitum of monastic and cathedral churches in England is unknown in Italy, but there is a comparable arrangement by which the choir and nave are virtually separated from one another, an elaboration of the confessio in Roman churches. The crypt introduced in the seventh century was developed into a principal part of the structure during the eleventh century, as at Modena and the earlier church of S. Miniato at Florence. Partly owing to the nature of the site of many churches the crypt could not be excavated far below the main floor level; to allow head-room, the presbytery above was raised up some ten feet and joined by a flight of steps to the nave. Two variations of this form are common: either there is a broad flight of steps across the nave (75) with entrances to the crypt in the aisles, or the crypt is open to the nave with steps down to it and steps in the aisle lead up to the presbytery (71). The latter gave scope for elaborate sculptured schemes on the parapet wall of the *pontile* and for supporting columns and arches. The crypt attained truly vast proportions, extending beneath the presbytery and transepts. This division of the body of the church altered the requirements for furniture. In place of the traditional ambos, a pulpit was erected abutting on the *pontile* of the raised presbytery (44, 71). The altar was made of stone or marble and occupied the traditional place west of the chord of the apse, in which stood the episcopal throne.

Detached Lombard campanili are a spectacular and characteristic

11 PIACENZA: a mid-twelfth-century façade with porches of the late thirteenth century and campanile of 1333

12 MONREALE: the nave and presbytery begun 1174; the mosaic-work well
advanced in 1182

landmark to be seen in every city from the western Alps to the Adriatic. Massively built of brick and stone, they reach impressive heights of up to 250 feet. Towards the end of the eleventh century and throughout the succeeding century they were given refinement; their sides were gently graded upward and the height accentuated by light pilaster strips rising at the angles and on the faces to lofty bell-chambers, with groups of three, four or five lights increasing in number upwards; overall rode a conical spire (11, 76) or, as added later in the thirteenth century, a daring octagonal lantern and spire (70). The campanili were usually erected in a free-standing position on the north or south side, but in the eleventh century at Ivrea two were attached to the apsidal east end, and at Parma two were intended to flank the west front.

Even in the twelfth century the traditional baptistery continued to be an essential adjunct of the cathedral, as is shown by the imposing examples at Pisa, Parma and Cremona, all modelled on the Florentine baptistery.

Venice is unique in Western Europe as much for its architecture as for its canals and way of life. For the greater part of the Republic's history, Venetian interests lay eastward and inclined towards the splendours of Constantinople, the capital of the Eastern Empire. The eleventh-century basilica of St Mark's has a unique place in European architecture. Its affinities with contemporary local architecture are few. The whole nature of the structure and its decoration are explained by the developments in design and decorative iconography in Constantinople and other Levantine centres, but the class of building to which it belongs is also rare in the East, where it was the product of the patronage of the Imperial Court. The Greek cross plan of St Mark's (47) with cupolas over each arm and the crossing, and a vaulted narthex round the sides and front of the "nave", is considered to have been designed in emulation of the Apostolion, the Church of the Apostles, at Constantinople. This church, founded by Constantine, was rebuilt by the Emperor Justinian between 536 and 546. The historian Procopius called the Apostolion the moon to the great S. Sophia; both these churches were the work of the same architect, Antemios of Trales. Justinian's Apostolion was modified from 913 to 961 under Constantine Porphyrogenitos, especially in its decoration but also, it seems, to some degree structurally; this tenth-century church served the Venetians as a model for their new ducal chapel in 1063. To vindicate the comparison with a building no longer existing, it should be added that another of Justinian's basilicas, St John the Evangelist at Ephesus, the plan of which has been exposed, was described by Procopius as "very like and in every way equal to the Church of the Apostles". Though St Mark's was not completed until the sixteenth century, its main structure and the greater part of its decorative scheme are eleventh and twelfth century in date, as may be seen in the mid-thirteenth-century mosaic picture preserved in an arch of the main façade. Its design had virtually no influence on Italian architecture, but the iconostasis and side-apses, derived from the usage of the Eastern rite, are also found in churches nearby at Torcello and Padua, which came under the direct influence of Venice.

The traditional forms of architecture in the Ravennate survived into the eleventh century at Torcello, Murano and Aquileia, but by the following century the Lombard style had asserted its dominance, as is shown by the construction of Ferrara cathedral and the sculptured ornament of part of the façade of St Mark's itself.

The place held by Venice as the leading centre for the dissemination of Byzantine ideas was paramount in the field of mosaic picture decoration. Its resident artists, probably Greeks, were summoned even to Rome, and the characteristic Byzantine iconography and colour pervaded Italian art until the latter asserted its individuality at the end of the thirteenth century. The vast series of mosaics in St Mark's indicate the variety and changes in Byzantine practice which, contrary to general opinion, was by no means static. The hieratic formality of ritual and the mystic element in Eastern religion are strong elements in the conservative expression, but the best work exhibited a rare delicacy of tone and restrained movement. Byzantine representational art had continued to live while Europe suffered under the pall of the "Dark Ages", and only receded before the impact of the new tradition of naturalism that gained ascendancy in the West in the fourteenth century.

The architecture of the Norman kingdom stands today a vivid record of the splendour of the Royal Court and the integration of the several diverse cultures it patronized. The Normans here, as elsewhere, interpreted in grandiose terms the natural resources of the territory they governed. The three principal zones in which this new force acted most vigorously, the coast between Naples and Salerno, referred to here as the Salernitano, Apulia and the Capitanata, and especially the island of Sicily, preserved their distinct identities.

In the Salernitano the cathedrals follow the style of Roman basilicas with transepts, colonnades, timber-roofs and shallow eastern apses. The arcades of the churches and atriums were stilted and the walls ornamented with coloured and inlaid plaques in the Moorish fashion.

Exotic decorations were applied, for example, to campanili (*93*), and the Siculo-Norman school of mosaic workers and carvers adorned the furniture with bright colours and ornamental sculptures.

The most numerous church buildings of the Norman period are in Apulia. S. Nicola at Bari was begun in 1087 and cathedrals in a local Romanesque style were erected throughout the province in succeeding centuries; they were little affected by Gothic forms until the second half of the thirteenth century. The Apulian Romanesque style developed rapidly from the eleventh century with a strong individual character, and in its sculpture it was somewhat in advance of the Lombard school, from which it derived a degree of inspiration sharpened by Saracen and Byzantine contacts. The Apulian churches were built of freestone in an imposing manner, if not on a large scale. The short colonnaded naves are almost invariably timber-roofed and the single aisles commonly have simple ribbed vaults. The transept at the east end with one or three apses extends slightly beyond the aisle walls, but by a curious local trick the overall plan of the church was sometimes made rect-angular by the addition of a screen wall across the apses, over which were built a pair of towers, and deeply recessed arcading along the sides of the aisles (*100*). This arcading, possibly inspired by some Roman gate or aqueduct, gives added height and the impression of great strength. The triforium was in some cases "false", and in others a gallery, but, either way, the aisle roofs were raised to a level little below the clerestory. The general lofty appearance was accentuated by making the height of the transept equal to that of the nave, and by high façades with "dropped shoulders" over the aisles. Over the junction of the transept and nave a cupola was sometimes raised and campanili were placed on each side of the apse or attached to the west end. In the Capitanata round Foggia and Troia the churches surpris-ingly exhibit all the characteristics of the Pisan Romanesque style.

The early development of sculpture and the important work of bronze casting (*104, 117*) gave a wealth of plastic decoration to these churches. Byzantine, Saracen and classical decorative motifs were mingled with subjects from mediaeval folklore, such as gargoyles, and stories from the Bible. In the second half of the twelfth century, some years in advance of the Lombard sculptors, naturalistic sculpture was already well developed (*98*); it cannot be a coincidence that the patronymic of Nicola Pisano shows he came from Apulia early in the thirteenth century.

Of the earliest Norman foundations in Sicily both the plan and elevation are preserved only at Messina, and there almost complete reconstruction has taken place. The greatest Norman cathedrals were begun between 1131 and the end of that century at Cefalù, Monreale and Palermo. In these grandiose buildings is embodied the fullness of the Siculo-Norman civilization. In design and decoration they are distinctive in every way. The naves have colonnades with Saracen, not Gothic, pointed arches, and a highly placed clerestory; only Palermo had a triforium, possibly at the instance of its Anglo-Norman arch-bishop. The east end was designed after the Greek *trichorae*, a tri-apsidal ended model that gives the high box-like form to the presbytery and its aisles (*110*); the colonnades give way in this part to walls pierced by arches. The grandeur of this rare plan was given a typical Norman boldness by the erection of a pair of massive towers flanking the western narthex or portico; at Palermo two towers were added to each end. The external walls have Saracen interlaced arcading round the apses on the façade and, at Monreale, in the cloister; the pointed windows have broad patterned jambs under continuous blind arcading.

The magnificent pretensions of the Norman kings caused them to emulate the Imperial pomp of Byzantium in their Courts. They adorned their churches with mosaics on a sumptuous scale. The finest of the series of mosaic pictures in Sicily are at Cefalù and in the Cappella Palatina in Palermo; the most complete and gorgeous are those of Monreale where every wall and arch is faced with pictures of the Old and New Testament while the Pantocrator, the Redeemer, looks down from the main apse; the lower walls are faced with sheets of veined marble. The furniture of the same cathedral, the choir enclosure, the royal and episcopal daises, like its renowned cloister, are also adorned with delicate mosaics and carvings. The Siculo-Norman school of mosaic workers far exceeded the Roman in its skill in preparing a wide variety of shapes in glass and precious marbles, and in applying them in the Byzantine manner with an additional quality of naturalism. The ability of the royal craftsmen to work porphyry is a striking demonstration of the technical skill commanded by the Normans. Red porphyry was found only in Egypt and used in great quantities in Ancient Rome. The skill to cut massive columns and complicated figures was inherited by Byzantium. There are still in Constantinople several massive sarco-phagi, formerly the tombs of the Emperors, and the Norman kings adopted this form of Imperial dignity for themselves. Such tombs stand today in the cathedrals of Palermo and Monreale (*10*).

13   SIENA: begun 1226. Thirteenth-century campanile and cupola. Lower half of façade by Giovanni Pisano, 1284; upper half concluded after 1377

14　SIENA: pulpit by Nicola Pisano and his assistants, 1265–69. Staircase and
plinth added in 1543

ITALIAN GOTHIC

WHILE Venice expanded landward and continued the bitter struggle with its rival Genoa during the fourteenth century, the republics and communes of Lombardy and Tuscany increased in strength amid continuous strife, yet made important contributions to their cultural heritage. While the Popes were in "Babylonian captivity" at Avignon, Rome lay neglected. The Kingdom of Naples after the fall of the Angevins was possessed by the House of Aragon, which was entirely careless of the well-being of the State. North of Rome architecture continued to flourish in this period, but in Rome itself there was little or no activity, whilst in the south what little there was depended on the work of the Angevins and their Spanish successors. The architecture of this period was in the "Italian Gothic" style.

On one score in particular the northern visitor to Italy, experienced in the appreciation of mediaeval architecture at home, must be prepared for a rude shock. Churches designed in terms of glass and stone, flying buttresses and lofty nave vaults found very little favour; the Gothic style in architecture was never taken seriously in Italy. The glories of French and English building in the High Middle Ages are rather mocked by the forms in which they are reflected in Tuscan and Lombard buildings. Gothic architecture in Italy is a contradiction in terms; its forms were employed for decoration. The traditional Lombard Romanesque wall-mass continued to be the basis of structural design and before all else was placed a concept of space and plasticity that was quite different from that current north of the Alps. The elements of Gothic architecture were first introduced in the first half of the thirteenth century in Cistercian churches erected under the supervision of French monks; their use by Italian craftsmen began some fifty years later and they were radically adapted to the local idiom as imaginative decoration. The pointed arch, as a technical advance in structure, differed from the rounded arch in permitting a greater relative height in the arcades, as in North Europe, or a greater span as in Italy; it also had the effect of lightening the appearance of the wall-surfaces. In North European Gothic the essential structure is visible externally as well as internally; the flying buttresses are the key to the internal parts. In Italy the contrary is rather true; the Italian artist treated the interior and exterior separately. The massive walls and small windows of the Romanesque style were rarely discarded; the rounded arch and window were used simultaneously with the pointed, as at Florence and Siena, and there was a continuous use of classical motifs. These distinctions are fundamental to an appreciation of the Italian Gothic style.

The very name of Rome rejects the influence of Gothic; one church alone, S. Maria sopra Minerva, was built in a Gothic manner, and that by Tuscan architects. The adoption there of insignificant though charming details such as the cusped and pointed arch for minor works like tombs, furnishings and picture frames emphasizes the failure of the new style to establish itself (*33*). Particular encouragement was given to Tuscan art by the Papacy. While resident in Rome, the Popes had patronized artists there or in the adjacent papal provinces like Umbria, but once removed to Avignon, they ignored Rome in favour of Tuscan and French artists; it was expedient to concede to the interests of the merchant-bankers on the one hand and their neighbours on the other. The choice was not misplaced.

The finest flower of Italian Gothic sprang up in Tuscany. A new internal spaciousness and an exuberance of decoration is found in its churches. The outstanding monuments of this school and the master-craftsmen to whom they are owed are justly celebrated. The years that saw the completion of Pisa (*49*) were those of the commencement of Orvieto (*1*) and Florence (*17*) and of the extensions at Siena (*13*). The transition in style was evolved in the hands of Nicola and Giovanni Pisano, of Arnolfo di Cambio and Lorenzo Maitani. Florence cathedral has a severe and spacious interior while its exterior is colourful and enhanced by carefully executed detail, with a façade (originally de-signed by Arnolfo di Cambio, although never completed) of statue-filled niches and richly carved porticos (*65*). The great sculptured façades of the Tuscan cathedrals have an incomparable richness; Pisa with its snow-white marble loggias, Siena with the elaborately carved portals and innumerable statues by Giovanni Pisano and his followers, and Orvieto with its exquisite gabled front decked with mosaics and the low reliefs by Lorenzo Maitani and his school. In spite of the use of the pointed arches for arcades and vaulting, the vertical elevation is denied the dominating value it has in northern Gothic; there is no triforium and in its place runs a corbelled cornice; the clerestory has little visual significance. The windows are tall and slender, mere slits in broad wall surfaces, and buttresses are shallow and unstepped, rising from massive plinths. The hexagonal cupola at Siena, erected in the second half of the thirteenth century, was a remarkable innovation in its plan and scale; it was a considerable advance technically over the small octagonal cupolas of Lombardy. Its construction was of a different order from that of the Florentine baptistery, for example, and must have been in Arnolfo di Cambio's mind when he proposed so large an octagon for S. Maria del Fiore. But the prominence of this octagon in the plan of the church bears a remarkable resemblance to the Church of the Holy Sepulchre in Jerusalem.

In Lombardy the traditional breadth of line and surface was tenaciously preserved, but the more immediate influence of trans-Alpine models, interpreted with the greater seriousness of the northern character, produced a Gothic style sterner and more substantial than the Tuscan. While Bologna was on the fringe of the Tuscan school and Genoa was served by French masters, the northern edge of the Po valley developed independently; the styles formed in Venice, Verona and Milan have their own distinctive character (cf. 15).

Though the cathedral of Milan was faced in marble, elsewhere deep-red brick and terracotta were used internally and externally with fine effect. The lofty brick walls and façades of the churches of I Frari in Venice, of S. Anastasia at Verona and of the cathedral at Cremona are adorned with moulded tabernacles and cornices, tall slender lights and great wheel windows. The spacious interiors with their high piers and broad arcades tied with massive beams in the Byzantine manner (15) have no triforium and only diminutive clerestories. The fretted sky-lines of the façade of St Mark's, Venice, and of the parapets of Milan cathedral form an unusual fantasy, in contrast with the general mass of the walls.

It was in the thirteenth century that sculpture emerged a fully integral part of European architecture; nowhere more than in Italy. In the eleventh century there had been some experimental application of sculpture to parts of buildings but little beyond the simple carving of capitals and occasional primitive low reliefs. In the twelfth century greater confidence brought an increase in quantity and quality and the Lombard and Tuscan schools applied sculpture increasingly, enriching porches, façades and interior parts. Recesses, salients and sculpture were combined to form the texture of the wall-surfaces moulded in varicoloured stone and marble; contrasts of light and shadow were strengthened, and play on the brilliance of strong sunlight. To the eye it is logical that the base of a building should be solid and broken as little as possible; it was Italian genius that conceived a compensatory lightening of the upper stages of façades (49 and 78). The most intricate formula was employed in the Tuscan churches (1 and 13) in which the façade became a screen created by sculptor architects. The most remarkable experiment is the fourteenth-century treatment of St Mark's, Venice; the apparent inversion of the masses of the Romanesque façade was obtained by piercing the originally blind arches of the atrium, and over-burdening the upper parts with a lace-work crown of arcades and pinnacles as a foil to the bulk of the outer cupolas which reflect the bright sunlight above the cool shadows of the base. This inversion is shared by the adjacent Ducal Palace and the long porticoed sides of the Piazza di S. Marco, "the finest ballroom in Europe", a unique assimilation of a fine church in an extraordinary setting.

The thirteenth century was one of significant development in the stature of the individual in all walks of life, not least in the creative arts; Nicola Pisano in sculpture, Cimabue and Cavallini in painting and mosaic work. The succeeding generation, including Arnolfo di Cambio, Giovanni Pisano, Giotto and Dante Alighieri, was one of the most significant in Italian history when, in a short space of time, the cathedral of Florence was begun, the cathedral at Siena given its façade, a new freedom instilled into painting, and the *Divine Comedy* composed. While the greatest activity was in Tuscany, the artists were able to disseminate their work in other parts of Italy by personally undertaking commissions or, indirectly, through their numerous disciples. The Tuscan spirit had begun to dominate the field of art even before 1300. Arnolfo di Cambio's best years were spent in Rome, Giotto worked extensively in Assisi, Padua and Rome, and the disciples of the Pisano family were active in every major centre in Italy from Venice to Genoa and Naples.

The communal spirit of the cities in the fourteenth century was apparently disturbed by the individuality of the artists they commissioned for the greatest projects. Advisory councils were established to adjudicate on the design of every detail. Every effort was made to oblige successive masters to adhere to models made to incorporate their conclusions, as at Florence and Milan. The designs they considered and adopted were often by craftsmen of such trade gilds as the goldsmiths, carpenters and miniature-painters, as well as masons; the criterion was a sense of design, not an ability to build.

The greatness of these men lay in the originality and personal nature of their art. Interpretation of observed expression and movement in life displaced the strong formalism of Byzantine influence which had been a barrier to the expression of individual personality. Representation of nature came alive in sculpture and painting. The influence of St Francis cannot be ignored in such a context, and indeed his life was the theme of Giotto's sympathetic frescoes in the Franciscan church at Assisi. But the skill to express the subtle living form in marble was derived from direct imitation of ancient classical models, of which an example preserved in the cathedral museum at Siena was undoubtedly used by Nicola Pisano, notably in his pulpit in the Pisan baptistery (54) (the panel concerned is in the baptistery at Pisa, cf. also Siena). Giovanni Pisano absorbed the practical lessons learnt by his father and something of the variety of French Gothic sculpture, while ignoring any prettiness in it. In mastering the most impelling expression and in modifying the representation of perspective, he gave renewed life to the stories of the Bible (53). Arnolfo's sculpture was more robust than that of the Pisanos. He did not despise the stolid form of the Romanesque style but captured a new freedom in his treatment of drapery on free-standing figures and a masterly sense of group composition. In Rome, his architectural work in Old St Peter's has been almost entirely lost, but some fine statuary is still preserved there and at S. Maria Maggiore. The ciborium of the High Altar of St Paul's well shows how he combined sculpture with the work of Roman mosaicists and utilized for purely decorative purposes the cusped and pointed arch. Sculpture in this period is known as Italian Gothic, but the classical tradition so far pervades its finest and most typical products that this is quite misleading and is a yard-stick which may only lead to a false evaluation of its remarkable merits.

The traditional use of mosaic for the decoration of buildings continued through the thirteenth century but gave way to the advances in technique in fresco painting early in the following century. Several artists, like Cimabue and Cavallini, towards the end of the thirteenth century, worked in both media, and the influence of painting is apparent in the relaxation of the formal stiffness inherent in the technique of mosaic design. Painted fresco was predominant from the early fourteenth century and in the new-found freedom of this medium a great example was set by Giotto. Elements of the characteristic technique in mosaic, like the stiffness of draperies and the small box-like frames by which changes of scene were kaleidoscopically presented, continued in fresco work. These boxes were used by Giotto at Padua, while later at Assisi he enlarged them for greater freedom.

These great artists overshadowed the activities of their contemporaries in the provinces where their influence was felt. In Lombardy the traditions of Romanesque sculpture, perpetuated by the Campionese masters, were strong, and continued throughout the mediaeval period. Nevertheless, during the thirteenth century a greater richness, encouraged more by trans-Alpine than Tuscan practice, is apparent in the deep carving and more complex design of doorways, porches and arcading of Lombard churches (Modena, south porch) combined with the decorative effects of Gothic forms. But the influence of the Pisa

63

school on sculpture was powerful and is evident in many Lombard centres.

Preserving a continuous tradition, decorative mosaic work continued to tell its story in St Mark's throughout the Middle Ages; the chronology of its development can be pieced together from the work of its masters employed elsewhere, especially in Rome, but its harmonious effect is only to be seen complete in Venice. In North Italy generally, mosaic was displaced by fresco painting, the nature of which is indicated by the decoration of the baptistery at Parma which shows the persistence of Byzantine style even in the fourteenth century.

The political situation was responsible for the imposition of a strictly alien style of architecture on southern Italy. The Gothic style had little effect in South Italy before the Angevin succession in 1266 brought an abrupt end to the brilliant Siculo-Norman civilization; Romanesque architectural forms were firmly entrenched in the area. The transfer of the capital from Palermo to Naples reorientated the life of the area and the foreigners brought with them their own architectural preference, the French Gothic style. The chief centre of new activity was naturally Naples and some fine churches were erected there (though the cathedral was built by the Angevins, it was remade during the fourteenth century). Lucera cathedral, where Charles of Anjou is buried, was built for him by 1311; it is a harmonious work, though severe, and is the most complete Angevin church in South Italy. In other parts this school is represented by the multiple-moulded orders of doorways with rich floral carving as in the sacristy of Palermo cathedral. The anarchy and neglect that prevailed in South Italy under the Aragonese kings effectively prevented the establishment of any particular school of art; lack of local talent meant the employment of craftsmen from elsewhere, especially North Italy, throughout the fourteenth century. This backward state persisted generally on the mainland during the succeeding centuries (though see p. 219), but in Sicily, in the first half of the fifteenth century, there was a revival when a local school, which exaggerated Gothic forms by combining them with debased Byzantine and Moorish motifs (see p. 250), achieved a vigorous and independent success.

THE HUMANIST RENAISSANCE

THE humanism of the fifteenth century in Italy may have been overrated by common judgment, but the expression of the individuality and versatility of the leading figures of the period has left an indelible mark on European life and manners. The continual bickerings and changes of alliance between the innumerable petty communes and despotisms did not halt the course of art.

The outstanding powers were Venice, Milan, Florence, Naples and the Papacy. Venice, after defeating the Genoese fleet in 1381, recovered her possessions on the mainland and eventually extended her dominion towards Milan in the sixteenth century, her period of greatest wealth. The city-states of Milan, under the Sforzas, and Florence, under the Medici, reached the height of their fame in the riches of their industries and bankers and in the brilliance of their almost regal courts. In Naples lay festering the claims of the Spaniards and French. The papal court, after its return to Rome, was preoccupied with the re-establishment of its territorial power in the Church States which degenerated into the baneful secularism and blatant corruption of the Borgias. When the Emperor Charles carried his claim to Italy against Francis I of France into the peninsula itself, Italy was riven and Rome sacked. By this terrifying event the country was shaken out of its petty jealousies only to fall into the ignominy of foreign dominion; here lay a sharp cæsura in Italian life from which it recovered only in the nineteenth century. Far more significant than political rivalry was the patronage of the potentates whose favour gave opportunity to the artist and craftsman and whose ambition demanded that high quality for which they indubitably had a superlative taste.

Though classical learning has been invoked as the source of Italian Renaissance architecture, its fullest influence was not effective until the sixteenth century, when the canons derived from a study of the Roman writer Vitruvius forced architectural practice into a strait-jacket. The influence of classical art, as has been already indicated, never entirely failed in Italy, even during the darkest centuries. The closer observation of antique Roman remains in the fifteenth century and the use made of classical motifs and proportions was subject to the archi-tectural practice of the different provinces; thus there is little affinity between the Renaissance style of Lombardy and Tuscany, where its forms took shape. The most important differences between the highly individual styles of Brunelleschi, Alberti or Bramante are, in fact, due to the traditions inherent in their respective spheres of origin.

It must be remembered that in the fifteenth century numerous ancient buildings, of which today there is no trace, were still standing almost complete in the provinces, as in Rome; they are often recorded in sketch books preserved from that time. In Rome, for example, whole temples were utterly destroyed for the sake of materials for building St Peter's. Once the conscious observation of classical architectural forms had begun there was a wealth of material to be studied. But, whereas the literary humanist preferred the arid expression of Ciceronian Latin, the contemporary artist combined observation with his practical experience. The imaginative ideals that were developed as theories were put into practice as opportunity offered. Leonardo da Vinci could advocate the perfection of a centrally designed church but Bramante and Michelangelo not only upheld that theory, they grasped the chance of proving it in St Peter's. The great strides made in every field of human activity during the Middle Ages encouraged the development of technique and design until, in the fifteenth century, the artist had complete confidence in his ability to build what his imagination conceived. It was a technological innovation that heralded the Renaissance in architecture. Brunelleschi's solution of the problem of raising a cupola over the octagon of Florence cathedral facilitated the erection of cupolas and vaults with spans, and at heights, not possible before without immense labour and expense (17). He rejected the "tower", hitherto indispensable for such a purpose, and used "centering" set up on geometrical principles above the drum of the cupola. He also perceived the aesthetic advantage of a "double-skinned" cupola to provide a harmonious effect externally as well as internally, and successfully executed it in brick and stone. On the other hand he was not concerned to dispense with the customary "Gothic"-shaped ribs.

The rapid dissemination and absorption of the geometry of perspective coupled with the advance from traditional constructional methods lay behind the new approach to design in the latter half of the fifteenth century. The contemporary solution of representing perspective was made in the frescoes of Masaccio and the bronze reliefs of Ghiberti. The activity of the finest sculptors was intense, and many minor architectural features were undertaken by them as a matter of course. The sculptor was not merely a carver of beautiful figures, a purveyor of garlands and putti; the setting for such work was also his concern. The proper relation of sculpture to the spatial context was as characteristic of Renaissance work in Tuscany as it had been of Gothic, the decorative nature of which paved the way to the light and sensuous forms of the new style. In Lombardy where there had always been less fantasy, decoration was sober and often severely limited, but supremely elegant in line and in proportion of space. The ornamentation of the fifteenth-century buildings, though so often delightful and refreshing, had a tendency to be tritely repetitive and, where not carefully applied, it ran to monotony. As in mediaeval work there was a combination of secular with

16 SPOLETO: façade dated 1207 with portico of 1491.
The belfry was added to the Romanesque campanile in 1461

15 COMO: the late fourteenth-century Gothic nave
and late sixteenth-century apse

17   FLORENCE: a view from the south showing the baptistery, Giotto's tower and the "Gothic" cathedral with its cupola erected by Brunelleschi in 1420

religious motifs in all ecclesiastical buildings. But a delightful virtuosity was attained in the carving and painting of natural forms; the naked body, swirling gowns, delicate plants and flowers with animated birds and beasts were liberally applied as decoration. The motifs of "heroic" humanism, war-trophies, armour, garlands and heraldry were placed next to laudatory scenes of patronage of the arts and sciences (*83*), or pictures of the Holy Family and saints in the guise of familiar figures of the age; portraiture, too, had its place, whether of the patron or the artist. Such exquisite carvings in low and high relief were frequently enriched with colour.

As the movement towards the full re-creation of classical architectural style gathered way, the free use of columns, pilasters, entablatures and pediments acquired precision. The study of precedents led away from the freedom of creative imagination. Michelangelo, assimilating all, made his superhuman effort in the last years of a long life, moulding the new St Peter's in the likeness of his own *terribilità*, and left the world of architecture vainly striving to match his power when the last word had perhaps been said in the vigorous formulation of strict classicism. During the Renaissance, however, not more than a few works attained the rank of masterpiece, though the liberal endowment of secular and religious buildings and the exceptionally fertile imagination and expressive skill of so many artists of the time were conducive of a general high standard of artistic decoration. The delightful style of their prolific genius was essential to the manners and life of the time. The greater part of architectural production was secular; in the ecclesiastical field innumerable chapels were added to existing churches, and many churches of a moderate size were erected. The few new cathedrals built were important like St Peter's in Rome (*23*), and the cathedral of Pavia (*85*), both conceived on the grandest scale, and others of lesser size but considerable charm like Pienza and Mantua; the Tempio Malatestiano at Rimini was only made a cathedral by command of Napoleon.

The Florentine, Filippo Brunelleschi (1377–1444), may be called the first architect of the Renaissance, since he was the first to apply to architecture the principles of classical perspective and proportion newly developed in the other arts towards the end of the fourteenth century. The skill he acquired as a goldsmith placed him second only to Ghiberti in a competition for the bronze doors of the Florentine baptistery. After this he pursued his studies in Rome where he acquired his knowledge of construction and was free to observe the classical monuments. Once he had overcome the considerable opposition to his scheme for erecting the cupola of S. Maria del Fiore his resounding success was heralded throughout Italy. His other work, in which he was preoccupied with the problems of geometrical design and the use of classical orders, preserved the light spaciousness of Florentine architecture. Lorenzo Ghiberti (1378–1455) was appointed his assistant for the completion of the cupola without being allowed much scope because he was too "Gothic" minded. Ghiberti's first design for the bronze doors of the baptistery showed his true worth and his reputation was crowned by his superb "Doors of Paradise" for the same building.

Also to the forefront of the new movement was Leon Battista Alberti (1404–72), who was as well known in his own day as a church organist as for his treatise on architecture, De Re Aedificatoria. This was the first of a number of works in the history of architecture outstanding for their influence on the canons of classical design. Among Alberti's few buildings are the incomplete campanile at Ferrara (78) and the Tempio Malatestiano (84), now the cathedral church of Rimini. These structures show the robust nature of his designs in contrast to the light harmony of Brunelleschi's. But they have in common a fine simplicity to which the proportions of all parts great and small are essential. He was the first to use, not just the forms of classical architecture interpreted in terms of the new geometry, but the structural principles as well, and for the façade of the Tempio he adopted the Roman triumphal arch as his model. The economy of decoration on the exterior of the Tempio is entirely consonant with Alberti's own dictum that "every part should be concerted in such a way that nothing can be added or taken away unless for the worse". In so far as there may be superfluous decoration in the carving of the frieze on the plinth and in the soffits of the window jambs, it is to be attributed to the resident architect Matteo de'Pasti, who carried out the design of the master. But this was the penalty he paid in maintaining the new and momentous view that "an architect should preserve his reputation by limiting his activities to an abstract directive function". Bramante's work was to suffer for the same reason.

While maintaining a regular correspondence with de'Pasti on the subject of the Tempio, Alberti was busily engaged in Rome on the new project of rebuilding St Peter's, promoted by Nicholas V. In collaboration with Bernardo Rossellino, with whom he also worked on the cathedral at Pienza, a plan was drawn up and work begun; but little progress was made before a grander project was proposed. A slighter architectural innovation made by Alberti was a "scroll" on the façade

of the church of S. Maria Novella at Florence, unifying the nave and
aisles; a motif to be widely adopted in succeeding centuries. In contrast
with Alberti's economy of detail was the manner of his executant
architect, de'Pasti, who was also responsible for the interior (*83*) of
the Tempio at Rimini. De'Pasti was a Veronese medallionist and his
architectural style combined the floridity of Veronese Gothic with the
uninhibited use of Tuscan decorative sculpture; just as Romanesque
structure had once died hard, so now did Italian Gothic.

The Lombard style remained distinct from the Tuscan during the
fifteenth and sixteenth centuries when "foreigners" were much des-
pised and any opportunity to denigrate their work was taken. Though
Il Moro, Duke of Milan, surrounded himself with the finest scholars
and artists he could find, they could only be put to work in the face of
local opinion. Amadeo, Dolcebono and Solari, although disciples of
Bramante, were unhindered by these petty antagonisms of the craft-
gilds; Bramante himself and Leonardo da Vinci were only grudgingly
accepted until their exceptional brilliance answered all criticism. There
is no doubt that Leonardo da Vinci had considerable influence on those
who came in contact with him but he was not, in fact, responsible for
the architectural work attributed to him. His design for the cupola of
Milan cathedral, for example, was not accepted. Bramante, on the other
hand, was the inspirer of the Lombard Renaissance style that was
maintained with its particular flavour into the seventeenth century. He
was not directly affected by his friend Alberti's style. The highly
personal principles he developed were impressed on his disciples, and
thereby an understanding continuation of his schemes was ensured as at
Pavia; he subscribed however to the Albertian view of professional
dignity. His nobility and independence of thought were made clear by
his bearing at the discussions on the proposals for the cupola of the
cathedral at Milan (*see* p. 189); after stating the essential principles for
the work, solidity of construction, conformity of style and beauty of
form, he pointed out that he had expected so many celebrated and
capable engineers both local and foreign to be able to provide the
answer, but that they could not; after indicating the faults in the design
of his pupil Amadeo (*81*) he recommended its acceptance in preference
to his own. Though fully occupied in Milan, Bramante was also sent by
Il Moro to Pavia where his design, probably for a Greek Cross plan,
was the pattern for the fine cathedral continued by Amadeo and
Dolcebono (*85*). Though only the crypt and eastern apse were carried
out by him they do exemplify the broad simplicity of mass and the grave
elegance of carving characteristic of his work. In the spacious interior,

allowance being made for the stilting of the arches in the seventeenth century, something may be understood of the harmonious conception of his plan for the new St Peter's. When this design, with which he won the competition organized by Julius II, was begun the nucleus of Michelangelo's masterpiece was established; here again only part is owed to Bramante, namely the crypt and the core of the massive piers of the main crossing, but round these were centred all his successors' proposals.

The Lombard Renaissance style is dominated by the traditional features of the region's mediaeval architecture, as it passed through the Romanesque and Gothic phases, interpreted in classical terms by Bramante. The harmony of simple delicate line, defined in shallow relief on open wall surfaces between broad spaces, is often left to speak for itself in the subtle tones of natural stone, as at Pavia; or else the same forms are richly adorned with coloured patterns within the economical architectural frame; but most characteristic of all, along the whole length and breadth of the Po valley, are the humble reddish brick cornices, pilasters, portals and windows against a whitish stucco ground. Whatever the colours, the texture and tone have always a pictorial quality, limpid and clear. Curiously persistent, rising over church after church, is the loggia-encircled outer drum enclosing the favourite cupola. Almost as common are the internal loggias and richly coffered barrel vaults. The dual vernacular tradition of low-built Romanesque churches in Milan and the tall-built work of the Veronese Gothic gave food for equivalent lines of development which were fully exploited in classical terms (15).

St Peter's, the most magnificent project contemplated in the history of architecture, stands a monument to the ambition, both personal and public, of the Popes of the Renaissance period, and to the skill of their artists. The ancient Constantinian basilica had, with periodic restoration but with little material change, withstood the vicissitudes of nearly twelve turbulent centuries. There is no doubt that its structure was in poor condition by 1450 when the idea of rebuilding was first broached, and Alberti was commissioned to draw up specific proposals. Little was done until Julius II seized on the idea of erecting on the site of the Church of the Apostle a mausoleum worthy of himself and of his aspirations for the Church. The competition he opened excited the imagination of the most distinguished artists of the time; the central design by Bramante was chosen and the foundations which alone were laid in his lifetime were the nucleus of the finally completed building. Circumstances in Rome changed rapidly in the sixteenth century and a succes-

18 LECCE: the north
façade in the Baroque
style of G. Zimbalo
(1659–70)

19 BOLOGNA: the nave
designed in 1605 by
F. Ambrosini

20 NOTO: a Sicilian Baroque façade of the eighteenth century

sion of exceptional artists, with strong personal views on the most appropriate form for such a scheme, got nowhere. After the Sack of Rome in 1527, in spite of further artists being commissioned, again virtually no progress was made until Michelangelo was given full authority by Paul III to carry out the work in his own way. For seventeen years, until his death in 1564, he laboured on his greatest architectural concept. In the spirit of his time Michelangelo turned from his lifelong pursuit of the ideal expression in sculpture and painting of the grandeur of Nature as created by God and expressed in the human form, to the abstract conceptions of architecture. The comprehensive genius of Michelangelo mastered the complete system of classical architecture as it had been propounded by the theorists of the late fifteenth and early sixteenth centuries.

The evolution of design during the fifteenth century was controlled by the application of geometry and the forms of classical architecture; the entablature, columns and pilasters of the great orders, the arcades and attic storeys. Nurtured in the building traditions of the different provinces, the architects of the period manifested the influence of their local background. When Bramante moved to Rome from Milan in 1500, he acquired a new experience among the classical remains abounding there. Whereas until that time the scale of Renaissance architecture was small Bramante enlarged it, confident in his knowledge and judgment and moved by the grandeur of the Eternal City. His plans for the Vatican palace and the new St Peter's were on an unprecedented scale; where Bramante enlarged, the greatest master of the Roman Renaissance, Michelangelo, aggrandized. Others had been appointed to further the project, like Raphael, Peruzzi and Sangallo, who produced plans radically different from the original design. Michelangelo condemned them in saying: "to set aside Bramante's design was to set aside the truth, for he had conceived it not full of confusion, but clear, simple and luminous". Where his predecessors had favoured the Latin Cross plan, a significant indication of the persistence of mediaeval custom, and elaborate schemes full of deep recesses and imaginative vistas, Michelangelo preserved the Greek Cross, the broad wall surfaces and spaciousness of the first design. But where Bramante's style was light and poised in its geometrical rhythm, he expressed the whole *terribilità* of his nature as he had in sculpture. He himself attributed his mastery of architectural form to his experience as a sculptor; "he who has not been or is not a good master of the nude, and especially of anatomy, cannot understand the principles of architecture". His innate sense of proportion and space charged the heroic scale of his greatest architectural work with harmony in every part, great and small. The grandeur of the arms of the cross and their colossal pilastered piers make no concession to puny mortality moving beneath the majestic cupola. The hemispherical cupola which he intended, perfect in its geometrical profile and lower than that actually erected, was an integral part of the whole. In St Peter's, Michelangelo consummated the highest attainment of the classical Renaissance in architecture and left his successors an unenviable legacy.

Michelangelo did not accept the view of such men as Alberti and Bramante before him that the architect should maintain the dignity of his profession by deputing the building work. He was his own "clerk of works" and supervised every detail of provision and construction personally and unremittingly for the last seventeen years of his life. It is as organizer as well as sculptor, painter and architect that he is to be remembered.

THE COUNTER-REFORMATION AND THE "BAROQUE" PERIOD

THE invasions of Italy by the armies of France and the Empire leading to the terrible Sack of Rome in 1527 seemed to set a term to the Renaissance. Of the great figures dominating the first decades of the century in Rome only Michelangelo, towering above all others, lived on. Great political and religious events altered the life of Europe during the sixteenth century. The growth of Protestantism was answered by the Counter-Reformation in the Catholic Church. From the Council of Trent emerged a new religious discipline and intolerance characterized by the spirit of the Inquisition in Spanish lands; in 1559 began the Spanish domination of a large part of Italy that was to last 150 years, and to impress itself on Italian life and manners. The bright light of the Italian Renaissance was suddenly eclipsed and replaced by a long-drawn-out period of stagnation. Only the Venetian territories preserved independence from this blight, but their life-blood, too, was being sapped by the costly war with the Turks and then by the heavy losses suffered in the mid-seventeenth century; Venice, too, degenerated. By the Peace of Utrecht, in 1713, Italy was delivered from the Spaniards into the hands of the Austrians. A few years later the Spaniards returned to stay as Kings of Naples and Sicily until the nineteenth century. The Austrians remained in possession of Italy north of Rome until driven out by the French revolutionaries, but only to return after Napoleon's fall. Such was the fate of a divided Italy.

The intolerant spirit of the sixteenth century that produced both

Protestantism and the dogmas of the Counter-Reformation, seems to have deprived church art of all spontaneity. Few architects were able to do more than look over their shoulders at the past which their fathers had made so brilliant. The humanist was no longer the arbiter of taste; his place was taken by the ardent churchman who, like S. Carlo Borromeo, Archbishop of Milan, could in about 1572 condemn the circular building as pagan and recommend the invariable use of the form of the Latin cross. Although the frank delight in classical subjects exhibited in Renaissance art was identified with the disrepute into which the Church had fallen and was attacked for its secular paganism, classical architectural motifs were inseparable from the building of the period. But, whereas hitherto these forms had been an integral part of structure, they were now commonly divorced from it and served a superficially decorative purpose. An increase in the dissemination of exact knowledge of classical buildings hardened by the authority of the printed book diminished imaginative interpretation. Architecture became an exercise in the application of academic formulae which were blurred by a profusion of irrelevant decorative detail and polychrome patterns. The example set by Michelangelo in St Peter's stands apart through his mastery of proportion and space. His successors did not possess the power of the man who "placed men nearer to God than had any other". His achievement stretched their imagination beyond their capacity and their work is laboured and "mannered".

The new invention of printing facilitated the dissemination of the theories and work of such architectural writers as Alberti and Palladio who, like Raphael, finding the Roman Vitruvius a valuable but insufficient guide, studied the classical models at first hand. Though their writings were critical commentaries on the text of Vitruvius enlightened by personal experience, their readers accepted his canons as they accepted the new dogmas of the Church. The consequent uniformity in style spread throughout Italy. A standard structural formula for ecclesiastical architecture was established to serve as a base for the tedious repetitive embellishment that persisted from the late sixteenth century with rare exceptions until the nineteenth century. These exceptions were brilliant but occurred in only limited spheres, principally Rome, where the masters of Baroque rose above the prevailing mediocrity.

After the Council of Trent, no ancient building was safe from the hands of restorers and well-meaning modernizers. The example set in Rome by reforming popes was emulated everywhere by denigrators of the barbaric Middle Ages. From the end of the fifteenth century there had been a conflict between those who, possessed by the urge to build anew, did not hesitate to despoil the ruins of antiquity, and others who, recording them in detail, appealed for their preservation. Compunction had rarely been felt in any period about using materials from ancient buildings, and now the practice was given fresh impetus. Few mediaeval churches remained untouched; they were cleared of most of their mediaeval furniture and given a new look. Of the great papal basilicas, only St Paul's remained unaltered and that because it was lying neglected, a feeding ground for cattle.

A large part of the architectural output of the century was sponsored by the popes, and their domestic projects were to change radically the face of Rome. The activity of the architects of the period is only represented to a minor degree by their ecclesiastical work. The new movement in Rome was effective before the death of Michelangelo in 1564, and he was invited to contribute designs in furtherance of its principles. His successors as architects to St Peter's, Vignola and Pirro Ligorio, continued the great design, but only in 1588 was the cupola actually begun by Giacomo della Porta. Then followed the tenure of this office by Carlo Maderna who, in the spirit of the reform movement, was commissioned to add to Michelangelo's Greek cross the great nave and the imposing façade. This act destroyed the values of the mighty cupola and typified the carelessness of the period for "pleasing the eye" when an inflexible religious principle was at stake. Maderna's work may be respected for its continuance of the details of Michelangelo's design, but the aesthetic damage was irreparable. Other work in Rome was done by Domenico Fontana whose monotonous Lateran Palace and the Cappella Sistina in S. Maria Maggiore were the capable work of one more accomplished as an engineer than as an artist.

In Lombardy, the architectural influence of Bramante's school persisted into the following century (15), but the personal intervention of S. Carlo Borromeo left its mark. He concerned himself not only with the suitability of architecture for the new liturgy but with the whole field of taste. Demanding modernity in all things, he studied designs in every detail, chapels, tabernacles and inscriptions. His favourite architect, Pellegrino Pellegrini, was responsible for extensive work in Milan cathedral from 1567, where his ponderous designs characterize Borromeo's attitude. In so far as the term Baroque can be applied to Lombard architecture, it continued throughout the seventeenth and eighteenth centuries suffused with the strong local characteristics of the school (19). In Piedmont the style suffered from the heaviness of

Guarini (90) but was enhanced by the refreshing contribution of Juvara.

The reconstruction of Rome after the sack of 1527 was largely due to the vigorous patronage of Popes Paul III and Sixtus V in the sixteenth century, and of Urban VIII and Innocent X in the seventeenth century. The new look given to the City was governed by the aspect of the great palaces which today give the streets and hills their impressive vistas. To match the monumental façades of the palaces, churches were treated in similar fashion. The simple exteriors of scores of ancient buildings with, in many cases, their interiors, were faced anew in the style of the time. After Fontana's new Lateran Palace and north façade of St John's came the façade at St Peter's by Maderna. The ardour for rebuilding was the breeding ground of the Roman Baroque style in which a reaction to the formalism of preceding generations was expressed. Two outstanding architects, Gian Lorenzo Bernini and Francesco Borromini, were the greatest exponents of this new attitude to architecture. Architecture has always expressed in its forms and atmosphere the spirit and manners of an age. Where the Renaissance is full of elegance and of the breadth of humanistic endeavour, the Baroque reflects the gorgeous pretensions and theatricality of the seventeenth century courtly classes. In the period when Monteverdi and the melodramatic opera brought a new era to music, classical architecture was reshaped with flaunting lines and interpreted on a note of tense vigour.

The pre-eminent favour Bernini enjoyed at the Papal Court won him commissions for the embellishment of St Peter's. His remarkable bronze baldacchino for the High Altar and the theatrical setting for the Throne of St Peter are the product of an amazingly fertile imagination interpreted with a masterly sculptural and architectural sensibility. Whereas Michelangelo proposed quite a small canopy, Bernini had to create a terminal piece for the immense vista along the recently added nave. The interplay of rippling lines and surfaces with the light that streams through the windows of the cupola and apse are, with the religious symbolic motifs, the most theatrical exhibition of his versatile genius. Bernini's carefully controlled extension of geometrical principles in planning, and his novel sense of space and vista are incomparably exhibited in the glorious sweep of the mighty colonnades of the elliptical piazza. He also provided a design for the east prospect of S. Maria Maggiore which was, with little alteration, completed by Carlo Rainaldi; here, he made the most of a hill site surrounded by a broad open space.

Borromini, more daring and fluent in his designs than Bernini, sought infinite variety in the geometrically calculated counter-rhythms of broken surfaces and line. His most interesting new churches were contrived on irregular sites and, though not one of his best creations, the interior of the ancient basilica of St John Lateran was converted by him in this new idiom. He was able to give fresh interest to the method of renovation used by Fontana at S. Maria Maggiore; he closed alternate windows with panelling and converted the unstable colonnades into alternating piers and arches, yet retained a suggestion of the ancient decorative zones of the wall-surfaces under a new pattern of syncopated and rephrased lines.

Although the movement continued in the eighteenth century, there were few works of exceptional merit. However the finest individual façade of a Roman church, designed on the customary lines, is, perhaps, the west façade of St John Lateran by Alessandro Galilei (27). A few years later, in 1743, the Florentine architect Ferdinando Fuga erected the west façade of S. Maria Maggiore (35), certainly his best single work and outstanding of its kind. Fuga's style deteriorated when he passed into the service of the Kings of Naples and assumed a very cold quality (21).

The architects of the Baroque period had been thoroughly grounded in the customary classical formulae, but they emphasized minor deviations such as were made even in the mid-sixteenth century. Where Michelangelo had used curved and broken pediments, now the straight lines of even the most important architectural members, the entablatures and cornices, were curved, details were contorted and elaborated and deep contrasts in light and shade were created by the studied arrangement of recesses and modulated wall-surfaces. But in the best hands restraint was ably exercised so that a lively and picturesque style was created. Sculpture was generously applied to embellish the architectural work. Statues wrapped in swirling drapery which served to increase the impression of wind-blown ornament were placed on porticos, as at St John's and St Peter's in Rome, Salerno, Lecce and Syracuse in the south.

In South Italy the prolonged Spanish dominion had marked influence on Baroque art. For the most part, the seventeenth and eighteenth centuries produced an abundance of garish superficial decoration which was applied to churches of all periods without any regard to its suitability and it rarely deserves attention. But in certain centres there was work of good, and sometimes excellent, quality even though it was anonymous in expression. The principal areas where it flourished were round Lecce, in Naples and its vicinity, and in Sicily. The Spanish rule made for curious contrasts. In some places the Baroque is notable for its extreme flamboyance, while elsewhere there is a cold severity unmitigated by colour or freedom of line. At Lecce there was, from the mid-sixteenth to the eighteenth century, an isolated school of sculptor-architects whose work was made possible by the admirable properties of the local freestone. This could be easily carved when fresh and hardened on exposure to the air, so that rich decoration (18) that has endured weathering could be applied to exteriors. Local traditional details, survivals from the Romanesque period, continued in use throughout the period, but there was also an access of direct Spanish influence from which was evolved an exuberant style of sculptural decoration applied to both ecclesiastical and secular buildings, though with little regard for architectural propriety. Where the churches were newly built they were architecturally undistinguished and followed the standard structural forms common in the whole peninsula. In Naples the contrast of severity and flamboyant decoration is particularly apparent and occurs wherever Neapolitan architects were employed. The competent but severely renovated interior of Salerno cathedral (92) may be compared with that at Amalfi (95), which is richly and not unattractively faced with polychrome marbled stucco, panelled walls and coffered ceilings.

Sicilian Baroque has a distinctive and attractive flavour. During the seventeenth and eighteenth centuries there was widespread activity in new building and renovations. The new town of Noto was built entirely in Baroque style at the end of the seventeenth century, and has a cathedral with a pleasant façade at the head of a magnificent flight of steps (20); in a similarly effective manner is the façade of the cathedral at Syracuse (107), a few decades later in date. During the second half of the seventeenth century a florid style prevailed at Palermo in which brightly coloured, ornately carved architectural details were combined with sculptures and elaborate inlay (115), but it did not survive long. In 1761 the desire for modernization of the cathedral led the archbishop there to request the services of Ferdinando Fuga who was comfortably established at the royal court of Naples. Fuga was undoubtedly the best architect in the kingdom, but the promise he had shown in Rome (21) seems to have failed him. His work in Palermo, as in Naples, is bare and inexpressive, and reflects the parsimony of his royal master; his competence was not enhanced by any real personality.

MODERN TIMES

THE late eighteenth and nineteenth centuries were notable in Italy, especially in the north, for the activity of numerous local Academies of arts and sciences. The denial of political activity to the upper classes led them to devote their energies to study. An admiration for the past pervaded all subjects from languages to architecture. The discoveries of the eighteenth century, for example at Pompeii, sharpened the taste of the period for archaeology and an epidemic of neo-classicism broke out. The completion of Pavia cathedral, for example, was projected in 1811 with a façade and cupola designed in close imitation of classical monuments, but with none of the characteristics that had long distinguished Renaissance and Baroque style from the classical. Yet while academic bodies were advocating the reproduction of ancient monuments there remained a body of capable craftsmen and architects who were able to continue incomplete projects like Milan and Pavia cathedrals in the style of their early builders. It is also interesting to observe that in Italy, as in England, during much of the nineteenth century it was felt necessary to perfect the methods of the past and to invest such a building as St Paul's in Rome, when it was rebuilt after the fire of 1823, with a grandeur and mechanical perfection it never had before (2 and 22).

Since the end of the nineteenth century there has been constant restoration of the ancient churches of Italy. By this process many fine churches have had their early structure and decoration revealed by the removal of "Baroque" decoration and the accumulated "improvements" of several centuries. Orvieto cathedral was thoroughly restored in 1890, Syracuse in the 1920's and Bari cathedral before the Second World War. The devastation caused by military operations throughout Italy in that war has been largely made good so far as those churches not completely destroyed are concerned. The Tempio at Rimini (83), Ancona and Vicenza cathedrals have now been completely restored. Work is continually in progress on such monuments as St Mark's, Venice, where the mosaics demand constant attention. The skill and care devoted to such laborious work of restoration ensures the preservation of many of the greatest treasure-houses of European art for the world.

21 PALERMO: the interior remodelled by F. Fuga in 1781

22 ROME: St Paul's outside the Walls. The façade
rebuilt by L. Poletti about 1850, seen from the
atrium by the brothers Vespignani and by Calderini

23   ROME: St Peter's. Prospect of the nave. *An engraving from G. B. Piranesi's "Vedute di Roma", c. 1750*

Some Italian Cathedrals
Described

Rome

ROME is the most remarkable store-house of architectural and artistic history in Europe, the product of two thousand years of intense activity. Its atmosphere is charged with the spirit of the classical Empire and the traditions of the Christian Church. The urge to preserve traditional sites has been so strong that the present aspect of a majority of churches in Rome conceals a primitive plan and structure. The loss of many noble and venerated churches may be regretted but they have ever given way to new and no less admirable examples of human creativeness and imagination. The proximity of innumerable monuments and ruins of strikingly diverse character in the styles of so many periods can be overwhelming to the visitor.

The four Papal basilicas hold a particular place in the history of the Church. St John Lateran is the Cathedral of Christendom, the Mother of Churches and the only truly Patriarchal church in the West. The Lateran was the principal palace of the Popes until the fifteenth century when they transferred the administration of the Church to the Vatican City while planning to rebuild St Peter's, the shrine of the first of the Apostles. Just outside the ancient city walls, to the south-west, is the basilica of the Apostle Paul, and near the heart of the City, is S. Maria Maggiore, one of the earliest churches dedicated to the Virgin Mary.

ST JOHN LATERAN

THE Lateran Palace, once the property of an ancient Roman family of that name, was acquired by the Empress Helena, wife of Constantine the Great, who made over part of it to the Church. The two churches of S. Croce in Gerusalemme and of the Redeemer, to whom St John's was first dedicated, with its baptistery, were erected among the great halls of the palace at the command of the Emperor in about the year 320. During its long history, St John's has suffered repeatedly from fire and dilapidation yet, in spite of the thorough transformation carried out in the seventeenth and eighteenth centuries, parts of the original fabric are still incorporated in its walls. It was first built as a four-aisled basilica without transepts and there was at the end of the nave an ambulatory with a broad, shallow apse pierced with seven lights. The walls were brick and the nave and aisle arcades were supported by marble shafts; the thirty-six nave columns had Ionic and Corinthian capitals. The length of the church remained unaltered until the apse was enlarged from 1877 to 1890. This church is not only known as the Mother of Churches but was also in effect the prototype of the standard Christian basilica.

When, at the end of the ninth century the timber roof collapsed owing to the weakness of the high walls, the building was restored and, probably at the same time, the transept added (24) after the model of St Peter's and St Paul's. During the twelfth and fourteenth centuries the campanili were added, and from 1220 to 1228 the magnificent cloister was built (cf. St Paul's). The cloister (7) is square in plan and measures 120 feet each way. Along each side of the arcade of the groin-vaulted lower walk are twenty-five arches with coupled pairs of colonnettes grouped between piers and standing on a high plinth wall; in the middle of each side is an entrance from the garth, and overall runs an architrave with corbelled cornices. This is one of the finest architectural works by the Roman craftsmen Vassallettus and his

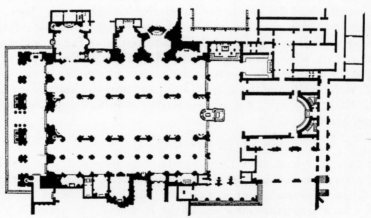

24 Rome: St John Lateran, begun c. 320.

father, whose names are praised in the inscription round the architrave. They combined a strong taste for classical forms with a fine decorative sense; they applied colourful mosaic to the varied shapes of the coupled shafts and to the architrave and effectively carved the capitals, corbels and cornices.

The principal alterations to the interior of the basilica were begun in 1597, when Clement VIII undertook the renovation of the transept. The design of Giacomo Della Porta is simple in line though ornate in detail; the garlanded walls are faced with panels of marbled stucco and painted with seventeenth-century scenes of the life of the Emperor Constantine ranged in two tiers beneath the heavily coffered and gilded wooden ceiling. At the north end was erected the Altar of the Sacrament made out of antique bronzes, and at the other the ornate organ (1599), by the Pope's organist Luca di Blasio da Perugia.

Innocent X had the rest of the basilica transformed by Francesco Borromini for the Jubilee of 1650. Borromini's remarkable skill in endowing with a new and individual form the most irregular sites did not fail him here. Though the basilica is not to be rated among his finest works, the treatment of the great space of the nave and four aisles is fine and harmonious in spite of the rigid frame of the Constantinian plan and elevation which he conscientiously followed. The ancient marble colonnade remains embedded in brick covered with a veneer of white and grey veined marble. The wall-surfaces of the nave are given a strong rhythm by the alternation of the solid panelled piers which are emphasized by the tall coupled Corinthian pilasters. The bold arches are each surmounted by a window of handsome and original design. A counter rhythm is set up with the recesses of the arches between the projecting green and grey marble niches below, and the windows between the shallow, painted and wreathed panels above (26). The nine-feet-high statues of the Apostles in the niches are of the early eighteenth century, and have an obvious place in the decoration of the Cathedral of Christendom, though they are not of great artistic merit. The proportions and the elevation of the Constantinian nave (cf. 2) are subtly recalled by the panels in sharp relief set between the heads of the main arches. The mid-sixteenth century coffered ceiling, richly carved with the emblems of the Passion and the arms of Popes Pius IV, V and VI, all gilded and coloured, spans the great width of the nave. In contrast are the gracious vaults and delicate carved decoration of the aisles, and also some of the side-chapels added in the seventeenth century as part of the new plan.

Even though much of the mediaeval furniture and decoration (some of it is now in the cloister museum), was discarded during the transformation, certain notable things were preserved. The main "eastern" apse of the basilica was preserved until, in the nineteenth century, Pius IX and Leo XIII extended it eastward and inserted an additional bay for the presbytery; as a result of this rebuilding the decoration of the apse is only a copy of the original. The pointed lights inserted in the thirteenth century, when the fourth-century ambulatory round the apse was removed, were preserved. The mosaic pictures were faithfully reproduced, but they are sadly cold and lustreless. They preserve the design completed in 1291 and signed by Jacopo Torriti, assisted by Jacopo da Camerino. Torriti himself perpetuated the style and symbolism of the fourth and fifth centuries, though it is improbable that he merely made a thorough restoration of the original work and some additions. His skilful use of mosaic indicates the accomplishment of many contemporaries of Cimabue and Giotto. On a gold ground the figures of Saints Paul and Peter and the Blessed Virgin Mary on the left side, and Saints Andrew, John the Evangelist and John the Baptist on the right, are half turned towards a central Cross surmounted by the mystic Dove. Naïvely inserted between these are miniature figures of St Francis, St Antony of Padua and Pope Nicholas IV, and at their feet the four Sacred Rivers fed by the waters of Grace are symbolically represented issuing from the Dove; there are also Jews, Gentiles and Catechumens and, between the windows, other saints. From above, the head and shoulders of the Redeemer in Heaven, surrounded by angels, dominate the scene.

Over the High Altar, reserved for the celebration of Mass by the Pontiff alone, is the grandiose ciborium erected by Urban V (1362–70) in the Gothic style, with mediocre sculptures but excellent painted panels of the fifteenth-century Sienese school. In front of the altar is the confessio. The unusually fine mosaic and marble pavement was laid down during the pontificate of Martin V in 1425.

From the exterior of the basilica only a faint idea of its mediaeval appearance can be gained. The small fourteenth-century campanili above the transept eaves, and patches of the brickwork, visible from the cloister, are the only evidence. Two monumental porches contribute greatly to the dignity of the church. That at the south end of the transept is the work of Domenico Fontana; built in 1586, it is characteristic of his regular designs which amount to monotony in the adjacent palace. The narthex and loggia by Alessandro Galilei at the west end (27), dated 1737, with their splendid proportions and the depth of the composition form perhaps the finest of all Roman façades.

25 ROME: St. John Lateran. The nave as remodelled by Borromini (1650)

26 ROME: St John Lateran. The west façade by A. Galilei, 1737

Galilei's work contains part of the columns and entablature of the twelfth-century portico by Niccola d'Angelo. Of the five doorways from the narthex into the church (*see* introduction, on p. 28) the central one contains the great Roman bronze doors enlarged and transferred by Alexander VII from the ancient Curia in the Forum Romanum.

27 Rome: Lateran Baptistery, 5th century.

Of the mediaeval Lateran palace little but the *Scala Santa*, the apse of a great hall, the *Triclinium*, and the baptistery remain. All else was largely destroyed during the sixteenth century. The baptistery (27), on the site of a Constantinian circular building, was given its present form perhaps by Sixtus III (432–440) and restored in exemplary fashion by Urban VIII in the seventeenth century. Within its octagonal walls the central peristyle of light porphyry columns and architraves in two tiers with a cupola above surrounding the octagonal marble baptismal basin. The columns, the restored Ionic capitals, the classical architraves and fifth-century bronze doors are all of excellent quality. The trabeated doorways open into side-chapels and the round-ended narthex. The narthex is decorated in mosaic with the symbolic Lamb and Dove and floral motifs in delicate green and gold on a deep blue ground. In the oratory of St John (461–468) the mosaics show the persistence of the classical tradition, while in the seventh-century oratory of S. Venanzio the ninth-century pictures of Christ giving His Benediction with figures of the Virgin and saints, are similar in style to those in the apse of the basilica. These mosaics are only partially preserved but are valuable evidence for the history of mosaic iconography in the "Dark Ages".

ST PETER'S

THE venerated shrine of the first of the Apostles, St Peter's, is second only to the Holy Sepulchre in Jerusalem among the churches of Christendom. Ever since its foundation in about 322 by Constantine the Great and its substantial completion in 337, it has been a centre of perpetual and devoted pilgrimage. It was given new importance in the fifteenth century when the Papal Curia was established in the Vatican, which became the centre of the administration of the Catholic Church. As a consequence of this primacy, both the old and the new basilica have had exceptionally strong and widespread influence on the development of church design. In the embellishment of the old and the construction of the new basilica many of the greatest Italian artists played a part; the former was a treasure house of the relics of Christianity in Rome, the latter is the outcome of a deliberate attempt to create the most imposing Christian temple of all.

Few churches have since exceeded Old St Peter's in size, and its dimensions may be compared with those of the slightly later basilica of St Paul's outside the Walls (*q.v.*). A major feat of engineering was involved in preparing the hillside site and recent excavations have revealed the remains of the pagan cemetery of the second century over which the foundations were laid. In this cemetery was the shrine, firmly held in the fourth century to mark the burial place of the Apostle. Even though no firm proof of the ultimate truth of the tradition can be produced, it has been shown that the shrine now beneath the High Altar existed as early as about the year 170. The customary rituals of the fourth century for commemorating the dead were an important element in determining the plan of the new church. It comprised two great halls forming a T-cross orientated with the shrine at the west end. The main hall was a basilica of the traditional Roman type with a nave and four aisles, and the other, at the west end, was long and narrow with, in the middle of one

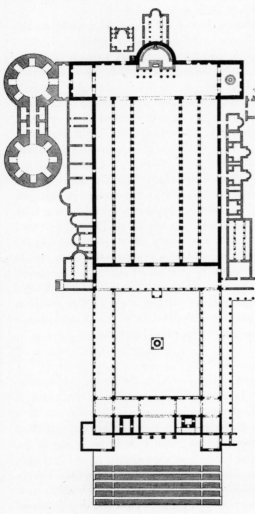

28 Rome: Old St Peter's, begun c. 322.

side, a single apse in which stood the shrine (28). These two parts may have been separated by a screen beneath the triumphal arch; the "transept" was sacred to the shrine and the other hall was used for commemorative banquets; when these were abandoned the altar was placed in it for the Mass. This distinction between the body of the church and the chapel containing the shrine became normal during the Middle Ages, especially in North Europe. By the seventh century, the altar had been moved and placed on a raised platform over the shrine, which was probably protected by a grille in front and was made accessible through an ambulatory contrived beneath the platform (introduction, p. 28) against the wall of the apse. Over the shrine was a baldacchino and before it seems to have stood a screen of strangely twisted columns, one of which now stands in the chapel of the Pietà, brought according to ancient tradition from Solomon's Temple in Jerusalem. In the reign of Innocent III the shrine was given a more imposing setting; a larger altar, enclosed in that of today, was erected above the earlier one and encased in panels of Cosmatesque mosaic work.

In spite of the ambitious scale of the project, it was carried out in the greatest haste with a jumble of materials taken from classical monuments. The main structure was of brick with eighty miscellaneous marble columns in the nave and aisles. The nave colonnade was trabeated with a miscellany of pieces of classical architraves and cornices, whereas between the aisles there were arcades. The clerestory consisted of large round-headed windows, and the great low-pitched roofs of the nave and transept and the single-pitched roof over each pair of aisles were of timber open-work construction (cf. 2). At the east end of the basilica was the atrium with open arcaded porticos having more than forty columns round the four sides. In the middle of the atrium were placed the classical bronze *pigna* or pine-cone, now in the Belvedere court of the Vatican Palace, a large bronze fountain of the sixth century and the venerated bronze statue of St Peter. The church had five doorways (for the fifteenth-century doors of the central one by Filarete see p. 101), and the triple entrance to the atrium stood thirty-five steps above the level of the piazza.

The early decoration of the interior and of the atrium included mosaic pictures which, restored from time to time, notably by Innocent III, were preserved until the apse was finally razed in 1592. The mosaic in the apse represented, in the style of the fourth century, Christ in Majesty with Saints Peter and Paul on either side; above was the Agnus Dei between twelve sheep, the Apostles and the cities of Bethlehem and Jerusalem. Another scene, on the triumphal arch, included an inscription recording Constantine's foundation. A mosaic representing St Peter walking on the waves, believed to have been formerly in the atrium and said by some to be by Giotto is now in the seventeenth-century narthex. The frescos with which the nave walls were painted in the ninth century seem to have survived until the end. They were in two rows of panels above the architrave, and there were standing figures between the clerestory windows. These frescos seem to have been largely obscured by the accumulation of grime on the walls, the upper part of which began leaning outwards in a perilous fashion during the Middle Ages.

Though numerous tombs and altars were erected in the basilica, chapels were for the most part erected outside the aisle-walls, which were pierced by only small doorways; there were also several small basilicas, oratories and monasteries built all round the church (28). The most notable of the chapels were the two chapels of S. Petronilla and St Andrew (later known as S. Maria della Febbre) which were joined together by a corridor, the former being directly attached to the south end of the transept. Each of these was a mausoleum, and in S. Petronilla were buried the Emperor Honorius and his wife and possibly Theodosius II, during the fifth century. St Andrew is known to have foundations of the second century; both were circular in plan and had concrete cupolas of the type constructed in Imperial Rome. These and other chapels were destroyed for the new work and their titles removed to chapels in it.

It is quite certain that by the fifteenth century the ancient fabric of St Peter's was seriously decayed and this may well justify its replacement. But, in any case, the confident spirit characteristic of the Renaissance of the fifteenth and sixteenth centuries had no fear of failing to provide a worthy successor. The most celebrated artists and architects of the day prepared complete plans and models to meet the grandiose schemes of the Popes, not only while the project was in its infancy but even when the work was under way– so far did the possibilities fire their imaginations. Two schools of thought were bitterly opposed on the question of the most suitable plan for the greatest of all churches; the one insisted on the perpetuation of the traditional plan, the Latin cross, the other pursued the ideal of a perfect geometrical form, the Greek cross, or central plan. Not even when the work had begun for Bramante's central design were the hopes of the traditionalists dashed, and eventually they had their way, when Michelangelo's intentions were set aside and the nave added by Maderna.

The new project was first conceived by Pope Nicholas V in 1450 and plans were prepared by Alberti and Rossellino (*see* introduction, p. 70). The work proceeded so slowly that little had been accomplished by the end of the century. But Julius II (1503–13) seized on the scheme as a worthy memorial to himself and the Church of St Peter and vigorously applied his energy and resources to its promotion. Bramante prepared the plans for a Greek cross with a dome resembling that of the Pantheon; medals were struck to celebrate the laying of the foundation stone in 1506 and work was begun on the crypt and the great piers destined to support the cupola. A chapel was specially built to protect the shrine during these operations, and it should be remembered that a great part of the old basilica and the atrium remained standing and in use until the end of the sixteenth century when the site was finally cleared for the nave and façade.

Julius's only memorial here is his initiative in promoting the scheme, for even the magnificent tomb which he commissioned Michelangelo to make was not completed and its parts must be looked for elsewhere, in Rome, Florence and Paris. In spite of the successive appointment of Giuliano di Sangallo, Raphael and Peruzzi as architects by Julius's successor, Leo X, little further progress was made. The Sack of Rome in 1527 put a stop to everything until Paul III called on Antonio di Sangallo and Giulio Romano in turn to act as chief architects. Death intervened and, finally, in 1547 Michelangelo at the age of 72 was induced to take on the task for which he was conceded the free hand and full responsibility he demanded. His appointment was confirmed by Paul's successors in the face of strong opposition from other artists, and Michelangelo devoted the last seventeen years of his life to his architectural masterpiece. He lived to see the completion of the three arms and the great drum but not of the cupola itself. After his death, twenty-four years elapsed before the cupola was undertaken in 1588 by Giacomo della Porta, who completed it in less than two years. Della Porta was also responsible for a large part of the internal mosaic decoration of the walls and pavement and also for the crypt and the Cappella Clementina (*see* below). Paul V (1605–21) appointed Carlo Maderna to add the nave and the façade; the nave was completed in 1612, the narthex and façade two years later. The great baldacchino over the High Altar, the Throne of St Peter in the main apse and the colonnade of the Piazza alone remained to be erected by Bernini later in the seventeenth century for the greatest cathedral in Christendom to be, in its principal features, as it is today (*23, 29–31*). The noblest part of this masterpiece is the work of one man, but the whole is composed of the successive contributions made by the finest Italian artists during nearly two centuries.

That St Peter's should be the largest church ever built seems surprisingly irrelevant to us on first entering it. We are not oppressed by an over-awing sense of size but are drawn into the grandeur of perfectly proportioned space. The actual scale of the whole is revealed by the superhuman figures of the cherubs supporting holy-water stoups just within the entrance, or by the reliefs on the piers of the nave arcade. The massive arcades and the broad, coffered semicircular vault of the nave carry the eye forward unhindered to the crossing, directly illumined by a flood of light from the cupola above. The nave leads us gradually to the shrine, denying us the immediacy of the abrupt admission to the sanctuary planned by Michelangelo. The central space of the crossing is flooded with light from the great windows circling the drum of the majestic cupola and from those in the apses of each arm. The giant fluted pilasters and Corinthian capitals and the massive entablature create a pattern which firmly controls the perspective of the greatest and the smallest parts in the sweeping vistas. So broad and lofty are the arcades that a fresh and new vista is to be had in any direction from and into the furthermost chapels and recesses.

Michelangelo's plan for a Greek cross with the equal arms radiating from

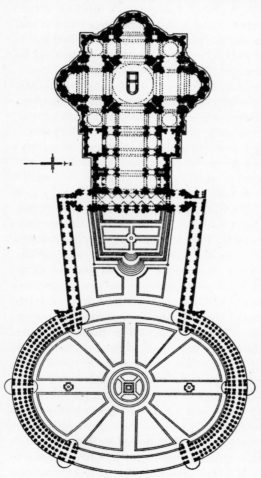

29 Rome: St Peter's, begun 1506.

the central area covered by the cupola, also included circular chapels inscribed in the square between each arm (29). Between these corner chapels and the main arms the piers of the crossing are tied to the outer walls by double arches or barrel vaults. These vaults are essential to the structural cohesion and strength of the brick-built basilica. His system for the main arches and the pairs of giant Corinthian pilasters on each pier, which rise to the entablature and support the mighty coffered vault, was continued unaltered by Maderna in the nave of three bays. Maderna made no original contribution in this respect, being content to maintain the unity of the interior. He was, however, obliged to add windows on each side of the nave vault. The nave is six feet wider than the arms of the cross, and the vaulting of each aisle bay is elliptical in plan. Off the first bay of the nave, next to Michelangelo's work, that is the third bay from the west front, Maderna erected on either side a large rectangular chapel; that on the north is the Chapel of the Sacrament, through which there is access from the Vatican Palace, and that on the south is the Choir of the Canons. The four smaller side-chapels vary little in their elevation; above the pedimented altarpiece is a window in the head of the containing blind arch. The principal side-chapels and the aisle bays are vaulted with a cupola which is raised on a drum ringed by windows and pairs of Corinthian pilasters beneath a projecting entablature. The lantern over these cupolas admits light from a well in the outer roof. Between the pilasters of the colossal piers of the crossing (30) are two tiers of apsidal niches framing giant statues of St Veronica, St Helena, St Longinius and St Andrew below, and above a balcony with a pediment supporting twisted columns, like those of the baldacchino. The High Altar beneath the centre of the cupola is covered by the magnificent gilded baldacchino designed by Lorenzo Bernini and completed in 1633. The four columns of this stupendous bronze canopy were modelled on the twisted columns that formed a screen in front of the shrine of St Peter in the old basilica (see p. 93). The singular voluted crown with its angels and putti is surmounted by a cross and orb, ninety-three feet above the pavement. The Chair of St Peter filling the great western apse, also by Bernini, was not completed until 1666. The ancient marble throne encased in ivory is placed between the four Fathers of the Church below the Glory and symbolized by the Dove diffusing the rays of light of the Spirit among foaming clouds and the happy souls of the Blessed. This sumptuous and theatrical creation in gilded bronze is illuminated by brilliant light from the window behind.

The whole interior is completely faced with marbled stucco veneer and mosaic pictures, all colour and gilt, set off by the white and grey of the applied structural pattern. The mosaic pictures are copies of paintings by great masters in the Vatican collections; they occupy the altar-pieces, the spandrels and panels of the cupola. This polychrome decoration of the walls and the vast inlaid marble pavement were first begun under Della Porta's supervision and largely completed by Bernini. Around the walls and chapels are monumental tombs of popes and others, some of which were transferred from the old basilica, but even these do not seem to diminish the scale of the architecture.

The High Altar, at which the Pope alone celebrates Mass, faces the nave across the confessio designed by Maderna. Behind the grille beneath the altar, is the upper portion of the second-century shrine of the Apostle as it was encased by Constantine. That this should be possible is because the floor of the confessio directly overlies the pavement of the Constantinian basilica. The crypt, designed and built by Bramante, surrounds the site of the shrine which stood above floor-level in the ancient church. The crypt was, naturally enough, constructed along with the foundations of the great piers of the crossing which were planted round the shrine; the ambulatory of the crypt runs round the outside of the Constantinian apse, the walls of which still stand as high as the new pavement of the basilica, and the crypt extends as far as the eastern limit of Bramante's proposed church. There is no normal access to the shrine, but within the crypt there are closed galleries leading to it, one on each side, and a third, the Cappella Clementina, designed by Della Porta, on the axial line of the building by which the shrine is approached from the side opposite the confessio.

The old sacristy was replaced by the extensive new structure on the south side of the nave and transept to the designs of Carlo Marchioni in 1776–80 to house the great treasure and the models made at various stages in the development of the basilica. From the vast elliptical piazza or forecourt only the upper part of Michelangelo's cupola can be seen above the monumental façade. Just as the internal design conceived by Michelangelo was repudiated by the addition of the nave, so the same prolongation by Maderna and his high façade cancelled the effect of the cupola (31), which may now only be seen entire from a distant viewpoint. The giant order of columns and pilasters supporting the heavy entablature and central pediment with the attic above create a barrier between the approach and the church. The Egyptian obelisk, transferred by Domenico Fontana from the south side of the basilica in 1586, and the fountains are surrounded by Bernini's magnificent

30   ROME: St Peter's. The crossing and cupola seen from the north arm, by Michelangelo (1547–64)

31   ROME: St Peter's. View of Maderna's façade (1612–14) and Michelangelo's cupola seen from the Piazza of Bernini (1656–67)

elliptical covered portico of quadruple colonnades (1656–67), the most splendid forecourt of any building in Europe.

Between the façade and the east wall of the church is the wide narthex, with a vestibule at either end. The northern vestibule opens beyond into Bernini's remarkable Royal Staircase which leads upwards to the Vatican apartments. Of the five doorways into the basilica that at the extreme right is the Holy Door which is only unsealed for the Jubilee Year celebrations (*see* p. 28). In the centre doorway are the bronze doors made for Old St Peter's in 1440 by Antonio Filarete and restored in the seventeenth century; they are an important example of the Renaissance artist's treatment of sacred subjects and secular decorative motifs.

Michelangelo's masterly treatment of scale and the relation he intended for the drum and cupola to the main body, are veiled internally by the decoration and from the east by the façade. The true nature of his design may be seen in unaltered state from the south and west. The walls are faced in the attractive local Roman stone in which so much of the finest architectural work of the sixteenth and seventeenth centuries was carried out. The angles and the great curves of the apses are given proportion by the stately couples of flat giant pilasters supporting the architrave which projects over them; below the architrave in each apse are two tiers of windows. Between each couple of pilasters are great pedimented windows with balconies, and in the interval of each pair are three tiers of narrow lights and niches. Maderna continued this system along the nave and carried the attic, above the architrave, across the façade at the same level.

The erection of the drum of the cupola was accomplished in Michelangelo's lifetime. In it he prepared the way for raising the cupola, which springs from a level 240 feet above the pavement over a space 138 feet in diameter. The main wall of the drum stands on a ring based on the crown of the main crossing arches and the pendentives between them. It is pierced by sixteen windows which, internally and externally, have applied pediments alternately triangular and segmental. The entablature above the windows projects over the solid buttresses, faced with coupled columns, which were designed to absorb the thrust of the cupola. When the cupola was erected by Della Porta and Fontana, the design left by Michelangelo in a model was altered by raising the centre to greater height "because the curve looked better". Because one of the three iron chains used to strengthen the structure broke, it was necessary to add five more in 1743, and others since. It may be suspected that the alterations made by

Michelangelo's successors were responsible for these structural defects. The cupola has a "double-skin" divided inside and outside into sixteen segmental compartments between stone ribs which rise up to meet the lantern. On the lantern stands the great cross nearly 450 feet from the ground (*31*).

The exceptional problems of this great engineering undertaking were resolved by Michelangelo himself. In his capacity as architect he undertook the duties of clerk-of-works and personally supervised every operation. So conscious was he of the quest for perfection that he even rebuilt the vault of one transept that he found imperfect. His successors had a relatively easy task in their continuation of the work; the whole definition of space, line and proportion and the preparations for the cupola, the loftiest of all, were the work of the most powerful artist of the Italian Renaissance.

ST PAUL'S OUTSIDE THE WALLS

THERE are three principal phases in the architectural history of this basilica. The first building was comparatively small and was replaced by a greater one within sixty years of its erection by Constantine. In spite of subsequent misfortunes, this second church survived largely until 1823, when a disastrous fire almost completely destroyed it. Reconstruction was undertaken immediately and the noble proportions have been restored to us, even though much else has been irretrievably lost.

By a happy survival of evidence in inscriptions, it is known that the second basilica was begun in 386 at the command of the Emperor in the East, Theodosius, and consecrated in 390 by Pope Siricius and that the architect was probably one Cyriades. This work was no restoration. The Constantinian building faced westwards, like St Peter's, but the new church was completely reorientated so that the principal altar is now at the east end (*see* introduction, p. 27) though on the same site, the traditional place of St Paul's burial. The new work was so much grander that the transept alone was larger than the whole of the earlier church. The dimensions are imposing in every way (*32*); it is worth remembering that there is here the means of visualizing Old St Peter's which was only little larger than St Paul's. Though the

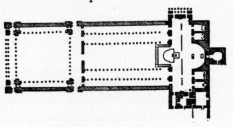

32 St Paul's outside the Walls: begun 386, rebuilt after 1823

total length is only 350 feet, the nave 73 feet wide and 270 feet long, and the overall breadth of about 196 feet, it was rarely equalled, let alone exceeded in size during most of the Middle Ages. The unbroken length of the nave (2), lined by massive columns and arches, is a splendid example of the Imperial basilican form. Comparison alone cannot serve to convey the scale, but the total internal width of the nave and aisles of Westminster Abbey is actually less than that of the nave alone of St Paul's. Even late in the fourth century the magnificence of Imperial patronage continued to be felt in Rome.

The nave and four aisles had colonnades each with twenty shafts; those of the nave were fluted and had Corinthian capitals. Over the aisle arcade was a secondary arcade supporting the low-pitched open-work timber roof. The nave walls, 95 feet high, were divided into several zones of decoration, the lower comprising a continuous series of busts of the popes; a number of the medallions painted before the time of Leo the Great (440–461) are preserved in the monastery. Above these and below the long range of large round-headed windows were two tiers of panels, separated by pilasters, believed to have been painted by Pietro Cavallini about 1320. The tremendous beams of the main timber roof, destroyed in the fire of 1823, were probably those renewed by Leo the Great after the Sack of Rome by Genseric in 455. The pavement was made up of slabs of marble including a large number of ancient inscriptions.

The transept was built at the same time as the nave in direct imitation, we may presume, of St Peter's, and had the function of martyrium for the Apostle Paul. It differed however in having a double *bema* or aisle separated by an arcade and wall. This feature has not been incorporated in the new basilica. The transept extends slightly beyond the walls of the nave and aisles and has the same width as the nave. Between the nave and the transept is the great triumphal arch supported by two columns 46 feet high with Ionic capitals, beyond which the vista is closed by the single apse. The apse and the triumphal arch are both adorned with mosaic pictures which, in spite of insensitive restoration after the fire, retain their original iconography. An inscription in the mosaic on the arch states that the church was begun by the Emperor Theodosius and finished by his son Honorius and that Pope Leo restored and decorated it at the request of Galla Placidia after the sack by Genseric. The subject of this mosaic is the apocalyptic vision of the twenty-four Elders holding out their crowns to the Redeemer; the scene is set on a flat gold ground with symbols of the Evangelists among token clouds (3). Since, at this period, the

City had fallen into one of its periods of decay, it is likely that the artists for this work were sent from Ravenna, where Galla Placidia was then active, or else from the Eastern Empire. The mosaics in the apse are in a much later style. In about 1218 Pope Honorius III brought to Rome craftsmen from Venice and in doing so introduced the Byzantine style of contemporary Venetian work. Our Lord is shown seated in judgment between Saints Peter and Paul, Luke and Andrew; below the shell of the apse is a frieze of the other ten Apostles with St Mark and St Matthias and two angels. Some parts of these mosaics remain unaltered and the whole picture has not been over-harshly restored. On the eastern side of the triumphal arch are mosaics representing Christ in Triumph with the Virgin and St John the Baptist, along with some fragments from those formerly on the mediaeval façade.

Of the mediaeval furniture in the basilica, only the ciborium over the Pontifical Altar and the Paschal candlestick survive. The Paschal candlestick is richly carved with scenes of the death of Christ and His Ascension, and according to the inscription it is the work of Niccola d'Angelo and Pietro Vassalletto (*see below*). Over the tomb of St Paul, east of the confessio, stands the altar, which is raised on a dais and covered by a ciborium in the customary manner. The ciborium (*33*) is one of the most interesting of its kind. The inscription on it records that it was made by Arnolfo di Cambio "cum socio Pietro" as commissioned by Abbot Bartholomew in 1285; it is one of the few of Arnolfo's works surviving in Rome. The ciborium supported by porphyry columns with admirably carved capitals, is faced with patterns in glass mosaic and Arnolfo's sculptures. In the corner niches stand Saints Peter, Paul and Timothy and the Abbot Bartholomew. As well as other figures in the spandrels, there are angels like classical "Victories" upholding the little rose-windows in the gables. This delightful composition survived the fire with little damage.

Arnolfo's collaborator, Pietro, is an uncertain figure but was probably the Roman marble worker Pietro Oderisio. It seems possible to identify him with Peter Odericus, the Roman, who was sent to make the shrine of Edward the Confessor and the mosaic pavements in Westminster Abbey in the years 1268–69. In fact the details of that shrine and this ciborium are not dissimilar. The decorative use of Gothic pinnacles and cusped arches mingled with classical shafts and capitals and the characteristic mosaic underlines the terms on which the unclassical was acceptable in Rome. It has been said that this Gothic style in Rome was French, and it is significant that Westminster Abbey

34 ROME: S. Maria Maggiore. Cappella Borghese by F. Ponzio – the altar, c. 1600

33 ROME: St Paul's outside the Walls. Ciborium by Arnolfo di Cambio and Pietro Oderisio, 1285

35   ROME: S. Maria Maggiore. Façade by F. Fuga; campanile, 1377

is exceptional for its affinities with contemporary French design. Arnolfo's opportunity to use that style architecturally only came later in his plans for Florence cathedral (*q.v.*).

The damage caused to the basilica by the collapse of the great roof in the fire was quite irreparable. The marble columns were shattered and the paintings and mosaics ruined by the heat, the falling timber and bricks and the collapse of some of the walls. Only the transept escaped the general ruin. The new work, consecrated in 1854, preserved the original dimensions and hence virtually the same proportions, but because of the materials used and the immaculate finish given to every part, the whole effect is of impersonal magnificence, largely devoid of appeal to our sympathy (3). The columns are of implacable Simplon granite with capitals of white Carrara marble. The medallions containing busts of some two hundred and fifty popes ranged round the nave, the aisles and the transept, are poorly painted. The pattern of alternate alabaster windows and panels painted with scenes from the life of St Paul, after the model of S. Maria Maggiore, and the massive gilded coffered ceilings are impressive only in their scale; the coldness of a great part of the mosaics deprives them of all but the interest of their ancient iconography. The spirit of the former basilica has been entirely lost as the architect Luigi Poletti did not have sufficient imagination to replace it, but his work was typical of the age. Of the chapels east of the transept all are of the nineteenth century, except the seventeenth-century Chapel of the Crucifixion – or Holy Sacrament – to the left of the apse; this chapel in a minor work of Carlo Maderna.

Attached to the basilica is one of the oldest and most famous Benedictine monasteries. Before the Reformation, the abbey was under the protection of the Kings of England and the abbey coat-of-arms includes the motto and insignia of the Order of the Garter. The cloister of the abbey is directly accessible from the north end of the transept. It was begun in about 1205 by the Abbot Peter of Capua. On each side there are five bays of four arches with a central arch into the garth. Three sides were completed in a uniform plain style with pairs of elegant columns supporting the simply carved arches. The north side, that nearest to the church, is similar to the cloister of St John Lateran in its form and decoration, and was undertaken a few years later by Pietro Vasalletto. It was finished between 1230 and 1235. The pattern of the other sides is followed but the twisted and grooved columns, inlaid with glass mosaic, the carved capitals, the sculptured reliefs in the spandrels on both faces of the arches, and the coffering of their soffits make a vivid picture. In keeping with this, a frieze decorated with mosaic and sculptured corbelling which runs beneath the eaves, unifies all four sides of the cloister around the garth.

From the cloister are visible the walls of the original transept, undamaged by the fire. The rest of the exterior of the basilica was newly faced with white marble in place of the former bare brick. No concession was made to romantic love of the faded glories of the past, save in the retention of the original roof-line. It is interesting to recall that when first built St Paul's, being outside the walls of the City, was for many years connected to it by a portico 4,000–5,000 feet long, and that in the ninth century the basilica was protected by defences known as Johannipolis. Whilst an atrium with a fountain in the middle originally stood at the west end of the basilica, only a narthex existed at the close of the Middle Ages. The magnificent silver-damascened bronze doors (cf. Salernitano) were ordered from Constantinople by the Abbot Hildebrand, later Gregory VII, in 1070 for the main door-way of the five into the church. They suffered sadly in the fire and are now kept in the sacristy. Over the narthex on the west wall were once mosaics by Pietro Cavallini (about 1321), some of which may be seen on the eastern face of the triumphal arch. These mosaics surrounded two tiers of bold round-headed windows, in place of which there are now only three similar windows with standing figures of the four major prophets in mosaic. Above these in the gable is a scene which represents the mystic Lamb surrounded by twelve sheep, symbolizing the Apostles; they are moving to quench their thirst on the waters flowing from the Mount of Paradise. In the gable is enthroned the Redeemer between the Apostles Peter and Paul. The narthex has been replaced by a monumental atrium (22), conceived by the brothers Vespignani and modified by Calderini († 1916) in the style of many a modern Italian cemetery. The narthex and two sides of this atrium have tall trabeated colonnades in white marble; the entrance opposite the façade has a triple colonnade with arches and corner pavilions. The tasteful porch at the north end of the transept, by Poletti, has a simple trabeated colonnade of twelve columns taken from the old interior. The mediaeval campanile which stood at the north corner of the façade has been superseded by Poletti's unusual tower beside the main apse; its square base is topped by an octagon and a colonnaded cylindrical lantern.

S. MARIA MAGGIORE

THE noble basilica of S. Maria Maggiore is the largest church dedicated to the Virgin Mary. It was built by Pope Liberius (352–366) and restored by Sixtus III (432–440), and in spite of certain internal alterations and additional embellishment of later date, it is not difficult to obtain a reasonably clear impression of its original artistic value. The main structure is of the fourth century and even the mosaic decoration is of that early period.

The mosaic-decorated architrave of the nave (*38*) supported by forty columns with antique Ionic capitals, is unusual for the period since arcading was then in common use (*cf.* St Paul's *but* St Peter's). The line of the architrave was broken in the sixteenth century when the side-chapels were added (*see* below). The walls above the colonnade were originally divided into three zones: first a line of mosaic pictures in panels, then the great round-headed windows and, finally, a series of frescoes between the windows and the wall-plate of the open-work timber roof. These frescoes were cut across by the late fifteenth-

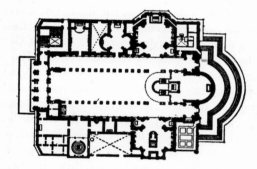

36 Rome: S. Maria Maggiore, begun mid-4th century

century coffered timber ceiling which, it is believed, was designed by Giuliano da Sangallo, and was gilded with the first gold brought from the Americas. This was given by the king of Spain, a patron of the church. The windows, which had hitherto flooded the colourful interior with light (*cf. 4*), and the decoration of the walls were altered and restored in about 1600 by Domenico Fontana, and each alternate window was replaced by a painted panel. The mosaic pictures of the lowest zone, in spite of losses and restoration, are an invaluable survival for only these remain to show us what has been lost in St Paul's and St Peter's. They represent stories from the lives of the prophets, Abraham, Jacob, Moses and Joshua. The pictures are rich in colour, yellow, blue, green and gold, stately movement and variety of expression. They are the work of several artists who, probably active at the end of the fourth century, still showed that influence of Hellenism which had pervaded Roman art for three centuries or more, but some of the individual compositions are monotonous and uninspired. The triumphal arch is decorated on a monumental scale with mosaics of the late fourth and early fifth centuries. The inscription XYSTUS EPISCOPUS PLEBI DEI post-dates the mosaics to the reign of Pope Syxtus, that is 432–40. Over the crown of the arch between Saints Peter and Paul and the symbols of the four Evangelists is a golden jewelled throne, symbolizing the present and Invisible Deity or *Hetimasia*. In the spandrels are panels relating Apocryphal and Biblical stories of the Redeemer; the Cities of Bethlehem and Jerusalem are represented as in the Apocalypse. The principal pictures are quite different from analogous early Christian and mediaeval work and are, therefore, an exceptional record of a rare iconographical system.

The fourth-century transept (36) is obscured by the sixteenth-century vaulting of the side-aisles of the nave, but above this vault are visible the remains of decoration which includes frescoed roundels containing busts of Popes attributed to the hand of Giotto; these are mutilated by the fifteenth-century wooden ceiling. The broad apse was originally surrounded by an ambulatory (*see also* p. 86), but this was removed and its arcading blocked in the thirteenth century when the four Gothic pointed lights were inserted and the mosaics in the half-dome restored. Some elements of the fourth- and fifth-century design seem to have been preserved, for example the coiled vine, but the greater part is by Jacopo Torriti. The centre-piece depicts Our Lord crowning the Virgin; they are seated together on a throne. On either side stand smaller figures of Saints Peter and Paul, John the Baptist and John the Evangelist, Francis and Antony, and the kneeling figures of Pope Nicholas IV and Cardinal Giacomo Colonna, the donor; the Sacred Rivers are at their feet, and below the windows and cornice are scenes from the life of the Virgin. The whole work is finely coloured, dominantly blue, on a gold ground. Mosaics of the period are preserved in the loggia of the façade (*see* below) and there were once others on the external face of the mediaeval apse. The apse is hidden from the nave by the unsuitable baldacchino of the Pontifical Altar; it was designed with columns of red porphyry by Ferdinando Fuga and bronze garlands were added later with little advantage. The pavement is a good example of Cosmatesque mosaic and marble work. It was given in 1198 by Scotto Paparone, a Roman consul and senator, and his son, who are commemorated together on a central slab and depicted as knights in full armour.

The thorough remodelling of the interior was initiated by Pope Sixtus V in 1587; the external restoration was only completed in the eighteenth century. There emerged a noble and elegant building which embodied the principal features and most venerated objects of the ancient basilica in a setting of studied refinement. Presumably, the interior had been for centuries somewhat untidy with brick walls and partially completed mosaics and fresco decoration (*cf.* 2). The modifications to the nave have already been outlined. The aisles were given groined vaults and their walls panelled by niches and doorways, with well-proportioned rectangular tympana between simple pilasters regularly aligned with the bays of the ancient colonnade. The doorways open into side-chapels which were added at various dates by notable architects. The most important are the Chapel of the Holy Sacrament, or the Cappella Sistina, to the right, and the Cappella Borghese to the left, for both of which the nave architraves were interrupted to provide miniature triumphal arches.

The Cappella Sistina was erected for Sixtus V by Domenico Fontana. It has the form of a Greek cross with a cupola suspended over the central space. The fine and deeply-carved details of the piers and frieze and the rich decoration of bas-reliefs and paintings are heightened by the colours of the marbled stucco. Against the side-walls are the monumental tombs of Pius V and Sixtus V, almost identical and both designed by Fontana. In the centre is a pontifical altar surmounted by a bronze tabernacle in which the form of the chapel is reproduced. The base of this altar is that of the *Presepio* or Crib, the work of Arnolfo di Cambio, shifted from the main apse of the basilica by Fontana, whose engineering skill is better known from his removal and re-erection of the great obelisk in the Piazza of St Peter's. By descending into the confessio it is possible to see Arnolfo's sculptured group of the Holy Family and the Magi (about 1300). The Cappella Borghese was erected for Paul V by Flaminio Ponzio, who used the same plan and elevation as those of Fontana's chapel, but far outdid it in the use of rich detail and effect. It contains the massive monuments of Paul V and Clement VIII (1605) and was for long the chapel of the noble Roman Borghese family. The principal feature of the chapel is, however, the grandiose altar, ornately decorated with metals and semi-precious stones as a setting for the much venerated picture of the Virgin (34). The other chapels which open out of the side-aisles are the Cappella Sforza-Cesarini (left aisle) completed by Giacomo Della Porta (after the designs of Michelangelo), the Cappella Cesi by Longhi, and the baptistery (right aisle) by Ponzio. All are works of the Roman school between the time of Michelangelo and the flowering of the Baroque, the so-called Mannerist period; they are designed with architectural forms as decoration which are independent of the actual structure.

The basilica occupies an island site on the Esquiline Hill, and the exterior has been given particular distinction by the designs of Rainaldi, after Bernini, and of Fuga; the unified outline conceals the irregularities of the chapels added to the ancient basilica. Commissioned by Clement IX, Bernini, who is buried in the nave, proposed a grand design for the east end and began the work. This was soon halted by the death of his patron, and the next pope, Clement X, put an end to the disquiet that Bernini's plan had aroused by appointing Rainaldi to modify it, without apparently meeting the objections. The result is a fine example of Roman Baroque; the wings are logically united to the central mass which is dominated by the ample projecting apse. Its grandeur is enhanced by the broad flight of steps sweeping up to the podium from the piazza which slopes away below.

The west end (35) was given its present form in 1743 by Ferdinando Fuga, and is one of his best works. The harmonious composition consists of the arcaded narthex, after the customary Roman manner, with coffered barrel-vaulting and, above, the Loggia of the Benediction. The five entrances through the narthex match the five doorways of the basilica of which one is the sealed Holy Door (*see* p. 28). The central doors, set up in 1950, have fine bronze reliefs by Ludovico Pogliaghi. They represent the principal events in the life of Our Lord. A wide staircase leads up from the narthex to the spacious loggia, the high groined-vault of which was arranged with uncommon regard for the preservation of the mosaics on the main wall of the basilica. This wall was originally unprotected except by a concave overhang beneath the eaves, as still survives at another Roman basilica, St Lawrence outside the Walls. The mosaics adorning it are signed by Filippo Rusuti, a contemporary of Torriti to whom something of the design may have been due. Christ is represented in the act of benediction with the Virgin Mary, surrounded by saints and angels; beneath is the traditional story of the miraculous appearance of Our Lady to Pope Liberius and the Patrician John who together founded the church in her honour.

Towering above the eighteenth-century façade is the campanile, the tallest in Rome, built in 1377 in the reign of Gregory XI. Though in need of restoration it is a fine example of the kind of tower that persisted in Rome throughout the Middle Ages. The several storeys of brick construction are decorated with coloured marble discs round the simple lights, and the whole is topped by a plain pyramidal roof.

The Veneto

THE Ravennate was the last province of the Byzantine Empire in North Italy. After the withdrawal of the Emperors from Rome during the fourth century, the seat of imperial government in the West was shifted from one place to another to meet the threats of invasion from the north. For the sake of security and to facilitate communication with Byzantium the Imperial Court was established in Ravenna by Honorius in 409. In 476 the barbarian Odoacar ejected the imperial forces and established himself in Ravenna where he was killed by Theodoric, who confirmed the city as the capital of the Ostrogothic kingdom. Many of the famous churches of Ravenna were begun in Theodoric's reign and dedicated to the Arian rite. After his death in 526 and the conquest of the city in 540 by Justinian's forces the work continued, but the churches were dedicated or re-dedicated for the Catholic Church. The power of the Exarchs, the governors installed by the Eastern Emperors, continued until overcome by the Lombards in 751; by this time there is evidence of the decline that had befallen the arts as well as affairs of State. Under the rule of the Emperor Justinian, the Exarchate of Ravenna was extended territorially to include the lagoons and northern coasts of the Adriatic; this area is now largely included in the Veneto. This expansion carried with it the work of the Ravennate architects and artists.

There were important cities in the area long before the lagoons of the northern Adriatic coast were populated by refugees, fleeing from the northern invaders. One of these cities, Aquileia, was founded as a Roman colony and was at an early date the seat of a bishop, who in 554 assumed the dignified title of Patriarch. The dangers of the times led to the Patriarch's transfer to the nearby city of Grado in 568. Owing to frequent schisms and other disputes among the ecclesiastics, two separate sees were established by the Pope in 698.

During the mediaeval period the Exarchate was shared between the German Emperors and the Papacy. In the thirteenth century Ravenna itself came into the hands of the Da Polenta family, best known for their hospitality to Dante who on his death was buried in their city. With the expansion of Venetian territorial power in the fifteenth century the whole province became subject to it until, in 1509, the southern part was restored to the Papal States.

RAVENNA

THE city of Ravenna was a naval station of the Roman Empire, whereas today it is four miles from the sea. Like Venice, it was once a group of islands surrounded by marshes at the mouth of the River Po and thus enjoyed a strong defensive position, though it suffered from the ravages of disease. The city, together with nearby Classe, possesses more than a dozen churches and other buildings decorated in the fifth and sixth centuries which, in spite of frequent restoration and considerable losses, are sufficiently well preserved to provide an authentic impression of their original beauty. The most important of these are the early fifth-century basilica of St John the Evangelist and the early sixth-century churches of S. Vitale, S. Apollinare Nuovo, the orthodox baptistery of the cathedral, and S. Apollinare in Classe. The cathedral, begun in the first or second decade of the fifth century and the largest of all the churches in Ravenna, was unfortunately destroyed in the eighteenth century, but it is possible to deduce something of its character by comparison with these other churches and the records left by the architect, Gian Francesco Buonamici, who was responsible for erecting the present Baroque cathedral in its place.

The Basilica Ursiana, so-called from the name of its founder, Archbishop Ursus, was dedicated to the *Anastasis* or Resurrection. It had a nave and double-aisles of equal length, without transepts. Though considerably smaller than the great Roman basilicas of St Paul and St Peter, it was the largest new building of the fifth century in what may conveniently be called the Ravennate style. The important characteristics were the spaciousness of the interior and the simplicity of the structure. The colonnades of fourteen bays in the cathedral had granite and marble shafts with capitals and pulvins, or impost blocks relieving the capitals of the full weight of the walls (37, *cf.* Parenzo and fig. 4). The great apse at the east end was semi-circular internally but polygonal outside; its vault was lightly constructed of shafts of hollow terracotta tubes set in cement (*cf.*5); this technique was widely employed for the vaults of apses and cupolas in this period, especially in the Ravennate. The nave and aisles had open-work timber roofs. The five windows in the apse and those of the clerestory and aisles were

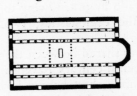

37 Ravenna (*after* Buonamici), early fifth century

38 ROME: S. Maria Maggiore. The nave; colonnade of 352–66; mosaics, before 440; the late fifteenth-century ceiling. The aisles and upper nave walls were refaced in 1587 and the baldacchino erected by F. Fuga in about 1750

39 RAVENNA: Orthodox Baptistery. The interior decorated with mosaics and stucco reliefs in the fifth century; the Romanesque font with a pulpit attached

40 TORCELLO: the interior as reconstructed in 1008, showing iconostasis, altar and elevated episcopal throne

broad and high with plain round-heads, and had unsplayed jambs in the Roman style (2). The size and number of the windows with the simplicity of the main colonnades give these early churches a remarkable luminosity; the brilliance of the light was probably tempered by glazing with thin yellow alabaster sheets such as have survived in S. Vitale. The altar was at first placed in the centre of the nave as it was formerly in Old St Peter's, Rome, and as may still be seen in S. Apollinare in Classe. In the lower face of the altar, enclosed in that of the modern cathedral, is a niche decorated with carved palms, sheep and doves in which relics were preserved. The introduction of the crypt in Rome in the seventh century spread rapidly into the provinces but, by analogy with other churches in Ravenna like S. Apollinare in Classe, that of the cathedral, which still exists, was not inserted until the ninth or tenth century. The altar, by that time situated in the main apse, was raised up on a dais beneath which an ambulatory-crypt ran round the inside of the apse wall, with an entrance to a cell under the altar on the axial line. In 545 the high altar of the cathedral was covered with a baldacchino with ornaments of silver; this was destroyed by French troops in 1512.

When the cathedral was virtually rebuilt in the twelfth century there was apparently no alteration to the essential plan of the building. The great mosaic pictures in the apse as reset in 1112 were still well preserved in the eighteenth century. The delight of the Ravenna churches lies above all in their rich decoration. The interiors and outer face of the façades were often completely covered with polychrome decoration (cf. 39) of mosaics, marble-inlay veneer and stucco. The colours of the mosaics were given brilliance by their being irregularly set to reflect light from all angles and not, as happens today, to form a dull flat surface; the great variety of the lovely shades of green, yellow, blue, red and gold were mellowed by the amber light diffused by the alabaster windows. The customary oriental symbolism of Christian theology and history, the Cross of Christ, the Dove of the Holy Spirit, the Apostles as sheep, was applied to the principal pictures over the sanctuary as in Rome. The use of symbolic animals was extended to the sculptured panels which were produced by the Ravennate school. On the sixth-century marble ambo of S. Agnello (556–569) preserved in the cathedral are small squares containing rather lifeless reliefs of fish, ducks, doves, deer, peacocks and lambs. An innovation due to the direct influence of Byzantium was the depiction of the semi-priestly authority of the Emperors, represented with their sumptuously garbed attendants on the nave walls of S. Apollinare Nuovo, and interpreted on the basis of doctrinal development in S. Vitale. Veined marble sheets and panels, inlaid with motifs found in Imperial Rome, covered the walls of the apse and aisles; stucco coffering was used on the soffits of the arches and for figures in relief as in the cathedral baptistery.

The destruction and replacement of the Basilica Ursiana took place in 1733. Though it was generally desired that the mosaic-decorated apse should be preserved that, too, was razed so that now only the crypt remains. The design of the architect Gian Francesco Buonamici was entirely consonant with the academic modernism of the early eighteenth century. The cathedral now has a vaulted nave and single-aisles with piers and entablature, transept and cupola. The walls and pavement are entirely faced with coloured marble. But the design lacks all distinction.

The campanili or bell-towers in Ravenna are perhaps the earliest in Europe. The first seems to be that of the basilica of St John the Evangelist, and is attributed to the last decade of the ninth century; it is square in plan. The cylindrical campanile of the cathedral was erected during the tenth century in a free-standing position on the north side; the lower part is entirely of that century, for it is known that in 1038 the top two stages were added with blind-arcading which was not used on the early part.

Adjacent to the cathedral is the orthodox baptistery, one of two baptisteries in Ravenna. The other was built next to the church of S. Spirito by Theodoric for the Arians, after whom it is named; it was re-dedicated to the orthodox rite in the mid-sixth century. The octagonal orthodox baptistery, called S. Giovanni in Fonte, is held by some to have been one room of a Roman bath adapted for use and decorated by Archbishop Neon in the mid-fifth century; it is in any case later than the Basilica Ursiana. The brick exterior of the octagon has a single large round-headed window in each face with blind-arcading of a later period above and a low pitched roof. The lower part, with apses projecting from alternate sides, is truncated by the ground level raised ten feet above that of the late Roman period. The internal floor level has also been raised so that the same effect applies to the columns and arcading round the wall. The walls and vault of the baptistery are probably fifth-century work (39). The walls are divided into two tiers of blind-arcading supported by columns with pulvins; the columns of the lower tier are deeply buried to at least half their height, and the floors of the apses in each alternate face have been raised to the mediaeval level and contain early altars. The vault rises from the spandrels of the arcade in the second tier and is constructed in the

Ravennate manner with super-imposed rings of hollow terracotta tubes (5). The token matroneum is comparable with that in the Florentine baptistery (67). In the middle of the floor is a large Romanesque octagonal font made of slabs of marble and porphyry; the semicircular pulpit let into one side is the only part surviving from the earliest font and is interesting as a rare survival of the rite of baptism by pouring water over the head of the baptizand.

The remarkable completeness and variety of the internal decoration is an outstanding example of fifth-century work. In the small arches on either side of each window are stucco reliefs whose architectural motifs are given a hesitant perspective by the use of bent lines; the figures of saints bear a close resemblance to the similar stucco work applied to tombs and mausolea in Imperial Rome during the second and third centuries, but for their period they are a unique and fortunate survival; the vases and acanthus whirls in the tympanum above have been partly destroyed, on the misunderstanding that they are work of the Renaissance. The extensive series of mosaic pictures may be by the same artist as those in the celebrated Mausoleum of Galla Placidia. The pictures are richly coloured with yellow, gold and green on a deep blue ground and, like the stuccos, give a semblance of architectural form to the walls, with a frieze above the arcading and eight segmental compartments in the vault. The symbolic pictures in the frieze represent abstract concepts of the Gospels and the Invisible Divinity; in the vault are the mantled Apostles carrying crowns in their hands, and in the apex of the vault is shown the baptism of Christ. Throughout, the acanthus is curled and wound around to break up spaces and provide frames to individual subjects. The arches of the lower tier alternating with the apses are panelled with marble inlay in stylized patterns. While all these themes are depicted with the classical realism evident in secular Roman work of the late Empire, the iconography and ritual sense are strongly influenced by contemporary Byzantine practice.

PARENZO

THE cathedral at Parenzo, erected between 535 and about 543 by Archbishop Euphrasius on the site of a fourth-century church, is contemporary with the basilica of S. Apollinare in Classe (4) and possibly the work of the same architect. It is an admirable example of the Ravennate style but is particularly important for the survival of its furniture and decorations and for the rare completeness of its ancillary buildings. It is a simple building of brick construction. The nave and single-aisles of ten bays have an arcade of regular semicircular arches supported by marble columns. The clerestory in the high nave walls consists of broad, round-headed windows. The deeply carved capitals of the arcade are relieved by the characteristic rhomboid pulvin or impost block. These pulvins were probably made locally since they are marked with the monogram of the founder. The capitals, on the other hand, seem to have been imported from Salonika or Byzantium itself. They are also rhomboid in shape with flat or curved faces incised with a basket-work pattern composed of tendrils of acanthus, lotus and vines, sometimes entwining figures of birds and beasts; others are designed in the Byzantine composite form. The nave is uninterrupted by cross-arches and, like the aisles, is timber roofed. The apse, polygonal outside but semicircular within, is lightly vaulted with open tubes set in cement (5); the aisles terminate in shallow apses which do not project beyond the outer wall-face and served as sacristies after the Greek custom (41).

The presbytery in the apse was originally raised by only two steps above the nave floor level. Round the wall of the main apse is preserved the hemicycle of marble presbyteral seats with the decorated episcopal throne in the middle against the wall. On the chord of the apse stands the original High Altar of marble in which is a confessio or window (cf. 4). Over it is a baldacchino decorated in mosaic and supported by four columns, erected in 1277. By ancient tradition, though the church is orientated in the usual way, the priest when celebrating mass faces the congregation over the altar as in the papal basilicas in Rome. Of the original parapet wall of the choir and presbytery, only a few carved panels remain.

The whole basilica was decorated with colourful mosaics, stucco and inlay work both inside and on the façade; of this sixth-century scheme a great deal is preserved. The archivolts of the nave arcade are coffered in stucco but the wall mosaics (see p. 117) have been lost. The apse and its triumphal arch retain their mosaics and inlay; there is also a fine pavement. The mosaic picture in the vault of the apse includes an inscription ascribing the foundation of the church to Euphrasius. The theme of the picture is similar to work in S. Vitale at Ravenna. In the middle, in place of the Redeemer, are the Virgin and Child enthroned against a gold ground between saints and angels; Euphrasius also is shown carrying a model of the church in his hand and followed by his archdeacon and an acolyte. Above, the

41 Parenzo, c. 535–43

Almighty's hand stretches down from rose and azure clouds. Though the iconography is not identical with that at Ravenna, it is clearly derived from the same oriental tradition. The mosaics on the arch have been almost entirely renewed by restoration, but they show the Redeemer among the standing Apostles, seated on the orb of the World and holding the Gospels; in the soffit of the arch are medallions containing figures of saints. Between the four windows of the apse below the scene of the Virgin are depicted the Annunciation and Visitation with the Angel Gabriel, St John the Baptist and Zacharias. The wall of the apse is resplendent with a fine inlaid dado of rare marbles, mother-of-pearl and natural glasses, forming patterns of lozenges and crosses in circles as in the presbytery of S. Vitale at Ravenna and in the basilica of S. Sabina in Rome. The mosaics between the three great windows of the west front made a picture of Christ adored by the saints. The mosaic pavement of the nave is inscribed with the names of those who donated parts of it in the sixth century.

The exterior of the basilica has certain features peculiar to the Ravennate school of architecture and rarely found in the East. The basilican form of the church is in the Roman tradition, not that of sixth-century Byzantium; similarly, from what little is known of the fourth-century basilica, its plan with an ambulatory round the eastern apse was derived from Rome (cf. p. 86). Externally the ranges of large round-headed windows in the aisles and nave are contained in a system of shallow blind-arcading that faces the walls; this arcading is quite plain without any capitals, but along the eaves are the arcaded cornices which continue as a characteristic motif in Italian decoration in the Middle Ages (70).

In front of the church are the contemporary square atrium and baptistery. The portico of the atrium is an arcade of slightly stilted semicircular arches with columns, capitals and pulvins of the same type as those in the nave. The three doors into the basilica have marble lintels and jambs which narrow towards the top. The octagonal baptistery (41), analogous in its position with that at Florence, rather than those at Aquileia and Torcello, has been re-roofed in modern times. There are remains of the central basin. The square campanile was attached to the baptistery perhaps as late as the fourteenth century.

The basilica was restored to its present condition in the first decade of this century and a number of accretions were removed, windows unblocked and the mosaics consolidated; some alterations could not, however, be corrected.

GRADO

THE cathedral at Grado was erected by Patriarch Elia (c. 571–586), according to an inscription in its pavement. With the nearby church of S. Maria delle Grazie, the Basilica Eliana is a product of the Ravenna school of architecture but the date of its foundation is later than anything still standing in Ravenna from the sixth century. It has the characteristic features of the school. The basilica (42) has a nave and single-aisles with marble colonnades of eleven bays, supporting plain semicircular arches; a polygonal apse terminates the nave. But the quality of workmanship had clearly declined by the second half of the century. The pulvin was rejected and a poverty-stricken miscellany of capitals and marble shafts was collected; the shafts are of different heights and orders; five of the capitals are classical spoils, the remainder are Byzantine work but probably taken from other sites. (The damage caused by a fire in the Middle Ages was set right by the use of stucco which has since been removed). To support the open-work timber roof, the walls were strengthened by the unprecedented addition of pilaster-strips over alternate columns on the inner and outer faces. The windows seem to have been filled with pierced marble sheets (cf. 5) in place of the alabaster commonly used in earlier decades. None of the mosaics that presumably decorated the apse, if not the plastered walls, have survived and the fresco in the apse is poor mediaeval work. The mosaic pavement, however, is a rare survival. It is exceptionally fine in its workmanship and includes a series of Latin and Greek inscriptions indicating the extent of mosaic contributed by the several donors. It has a stylized pattern of rhomboids and squares laid out in regular rows with current borders of floral design. Some of the sixth-century sculptured panels of the presbytery enclosure are still in use for the same purpose; all other furniture of the early period has been lost. The bizarre twelfth-century pulpit is not unique; there is a similar one in St Mark's, Venice (44). It is hexagonal in plan, with curved panels on which are carved the symbols of the Evangelists, and stands on short columns with Romanesque capitals: the polychrome inlaid canopy with its ogive arches reflects the exotic nature of mediaeval art in the Venetian area.

The exterior is simply designed in the Ravennate fashion with blind-arcading containing the large windows; the polygonal outer face of the apse is undecorated. The atrium that used to stand in front of the basilica is now only marked in outline on the roadway; there is, instead, a crude narthex across the façade with a late campanile built over its south end. Next to the north-east corner of the basilica stands a large octagonal baptistery with a single apse on the side opposite its only doorway; it is otherwise quite plain and probably contemporary with the basilica.

The poor condition of this cathedral is as much due to the damage caused during conflicts with the Patriarch of Aquileia as to more recent neglect. The unmistakable decline in its design and execution, however, marks the end of the brilliant period of Ravennate art.

AQUILEIA

THE history of few churches can be traced back to before the year 312 when the Emperor Constantine embraced the Christian religion and freed it from open persecution. Soon after that year a great basilica was erected by the bishop Theodore (308–17) next to a small third-century Christian oratory in Roman Aquileia. Of this building there survives the splendid Romano-Christian mosaic pavement. The oratory and the basilica were destroyed in the following century, probably by Attila the Hun in 452. In their place were erected two parallel basilicas on a scale only equalled at Ravenna, one measuring 240 feet by 102 feet, the other 213 feet by 95 feet; all that remains of the former are the foundations with its mosaic pavement beneath the eleventh-century campanile. (It is of interest that there are several examples of ancient twin churches accorded equal or nearly equal status elsewhere in Italy – at Trieste, Milan, Pavia and Albenga, for example.) The smaller of the two was restored under the patronage of Charlemagne and again by the Patriarch Poppone (1021–31). The present basilica is in great part Poppone's work, but it had to be restored yet again after an earthquake in 1348 when pointed arches were added to the nave and the fine timber roof erected. There are also remains of three successive baptisteries of which that erected in the fifth century still stands, though unroofed, at the west end of the basilica. The chequered history of this cathedral has not diminished its grandeur but has rather vested it with a particular interest.

The stone-faced exterior of the church has no decoration other than small arcaded cornices and small windows. Against the gabled west front is a low eleventh-century portico with columns, pulvins and massive capitals connecting the fifth-century baptistery to the church. The baptistery is octagonal in plan with niches in the angles of the walls like the orthodox baptistery at Ravenna but, in the Roman tradition represented by the baptistery of St John Lateran at Rome, it had a peristyle of columns surrounding the central baptismal basin. The imposing stone-faced campanile, irregularly four-sided with an octagonal cusp at the top, was begun during the period of reconstruction of the church between 1021 and 1031; work on it seems, however, to have been continued in the mid-twelfth century.

The interior of the church is majestic in its scale: though the proportions differ from those of the majority of Ravennate basilicas, in that the aisles are wider in relation to the nave and the length considerably greater than in other single-aisled examples. The site of the apse was not changed when the tall, long and wide aisle-less transepts were added in the eleventh century. The colonnades of the eleven-bay nave have miscellaneous classical shafts and capitals with pulvins, strangely enough provided by the Gothic restorers for the Patriarch Marquard (1365–81); they were also responsible for the pointed arches of the nave and crossing and the great height of the walls. The fine timber ceiling is in the "wagon" style common in large fourteenth-century buildings of North Italy, and is coffered and painted in yellow, black and white; there are tie beams between the nave walls, below the clerestory of curiously traceried windows and also in the roof. The presbytery and transept are raised well above the level of the nave over the eleventh-century crypt. The front of the dais thus formed was sumptuously embellished in about 1490 by Bernardino of Milan; it has a richly carved balustrade and confessio in the form of an arched recess framed by coupled pilasters and cornices between two flights of five steps. The grille in the confessio shows the sarcophagus of Saints Hermagoras and Fortunatian in the crypt. In the main apse is the eleventh-century patriarchal throne of white marble inlaid with serpentine. In the north aisle of the nave is a curious circular structure of marble with a pyramidal roof and what may be a small altar inside, for which no explanation, liturgical or otherwise, has yet been discovered.

The mosaic pavement of the nave, uncovered in this century, can be dated from before the year 320. It extends across the whole length and breadth of the nave and the greater part of the aisles; it does not completely cover the south aisle since the outer walls and the nave arcade of the fifth-century basilica did not correspond exactly with the earlier work. With the remains of the pavement of the adjacent north basilica, this is the most extensive and admirable of known Christian mosaic pavements of the period. The whole design consists of circular and square compartments surrounded by borders. An inscription says that the great work was completed with the help of the faithful, and it

42   GRADO: the late sixth-century interior

43   TUSCANIA: the early eighth-century nave and presbytery

44   VENICE: St Mark's. The nave and presbytery seen from the gallery at the west end, showing the massive structure and the cupolas; the mosaics begun in 1159 and altered in the early sixteenth century

45   VENICE: St Mark's. The thirteenth-century mosaic over the Porta di S. Alipio: the basilica at that time

46   VENICE: St Mark's. The thirteenth-century mosaics of the cupola-vault over the main entrance in the atrium; stories of Abraham

may readily be believed that the busts of men and women which appear
to be portraits, though broadly impressionistic, are in fact those of the
donors (*cf.* Grado, Parenzo). In other compartments are geometrically
interlaced patterns of acanthus with figures and animals such as the
Good Shepherd with the Lamb on his shoulders in an idyllic setting,
the cockerel fighting a tortoise, geniuses, and various fish, with the
monster of the deep regurgitating Jonah later seen recuperating in an
arbour. This sacred symbolism, like the treatment of the motifs and
the figures, is part of the strong current of oriental Hellenism that
pervaded Italy under the Empire, and which was continued not only in
the Ravennate in the sixth century but throughout the Middle Ages on
account of its mystical connotations.

TORCELLO

TORCELLO was one of the earliest lagunal colonies of refugees from the
barbarian invaders. It was once, like its neighbour Venice, a considerable city built on several islands and canals, but today it consists merely
of a few scattered dwellings, a cathedral church with its campanile
and another smaller church beside it. The cathedral of S. Maria
Assunta was first erected in 639 and the plan of that first church has
been largely preserved in all subsequent restorations and in the final
reconstruction that took place in 1008. The importance of this adherence to the traditional basilican form, basically common to the whole
Ravennate, is that it is typical of the early mediaeval style of the
Venetian area; this was the local tradition in which S. Mark's (*q.v.*)
was probably first built and with which its new Byzantine Greek
cross-form was a complete break. The seventh-century basilica had a
nave of ten bays and single-aisles with one main apse; by analogy with
the basilica at Grado the pulvins on the capitals of the colonnade were
probably dispensed with. Against the west front – it is not known
whether the late narthex replaces an atrium – are the foundations of an
octagonal baptistery with apses projecting from alternate sides, identical in plan with the orthodox baptistery at Ravenna. In 864 the church
was restored and the ambulatory-crypt and side-apses were added. All
other features of the interior and exterior are the work of the early
eleventh century.

The interior (*40*) closely follows the basic elements of the Ravennate style; the timber-roofed nave and aisles, the colonnade and semicircular arches and the high, though small, clerestory and the main
apse, while less polished in their form, reflect the traditional proportions. The fine marble shafts of the colonnade are cut in the same style

as those in Ravenna and St Mark's and the capitals, though varying slightly in pattern and probably imported, are in a fine Byzantine composite style. In place of pulvins, the flat abacus serves to take the weight of the slightly stilted arcade. The high walls were strengthened by the addition of cross-arches in the aisles and tie-beams along the arcade and across the nave and aisles at every alternate bay, after the Byzantine practice. The only windows today are those in the south aisle and clerestory and the single lights beneath the vaulting of each apse; the north aisle has abutting on to it a subsidiary aisle with an apsidal end used as a sacristy which has only a single door into the church. The irregular arrangement of the apses at the east end was not rectified in the rebuilding; the crypt, inserted in the main apse, in the manner found in Rome and Ravenna, with an ambulatory and central corridor, was also given a subsidiary apse projecting from the foot of the main one. The hemicycle of presbyteral benches and the episcopal throne were raised up in the main apse seven steps above the level of the main altar; this arrangement is without parallel in Italy but is found in Eastern churches. The parapet wall round the choir consists of carved marble panels. They are carved with stylized peacocks and acanthus patterns, probably late ninth-century imitations of the sixth-century originals, like some in Venice. Across the front of the choir is an iconostasis on columns with saints painted on panels as icons; this strictly Greek practice is not uncommonly found in the Veneto, as in Venice itself and Padua, but it is rarely found where Byzantine influence was less direct.

The mosaic decoration of the interior is restricted to the apses and the west wall. The main apse contains in its vault the slender eleventh-century figure of the Virgin, standing with her Child in her arms against a gold ground, the Greek *Odegetria*, which appears also in S. Donato, the cathedral of Murano, and in St Mark's. On either side of the single window are standing figures of saints; the lower walls of the apse have a veined marble veneer; in the spandrels of the triumphal arch the Annunciation is represented. The great mosaic picture on the west wall is also work in the Byzantine tradition, but seems to belong to the following century; divided into five tiers, it depicts principally the Last Judgement and the Descent of Christ into Limbo.

The exterior differs markedly in certain respects from the traditional form. The height and narrowness of the nave are accentuated by the tall unbroken pilaster-strips terminating in blind-arcading on the west front. The same method of buttressing was utilized for the lofty square-planned campanile. The flat-roofed belfry has four-arched lights with slender shafts, and is reached by internal ramps rising on each side with steps at the corners. The aisle windows of the church have massive one-piece stone shutters. Round the west front and part of the south side is a pent-roofed narthex on which impinge the foundations of the ancient baptisteries. Within the fifth-century baptistery was later built a smaller octagonal one which seems to be of the eleventh century; this has an octagonal font in the middle.

The adjacent church of S. Fosca has an uncertain architectural history and function. It is held to have been rebuilt in the twelfth century in its present octagonal form with an eastern apse, and that the design for its cupola-vault is derived from a Byzantine model.

VENICE

ST MARK's, Venice, belongs to a fundamentally different architectural tradition from that of other buildings of the Romanesque period in Italy. The first church founded on the site in 828 was a basilica, probably similar in style to other churches in the Ravennate (*cf.* Ravenna, Grado, Torcello), but on a larger scale only made possible in the ninth century by the close interest existing between Venice and Constantinople, the capital of the Eastern Empire. When, in 1063, the present church was begun, Venice had become a strong maritime power and demanded a new church more worthy to be the shrine of the Evangelist and patron saint. It was natural enough to look to the Imperial churches in the East for a model.

When Constantine adopted Constantinople as his new Imperial capital, any new churches so far as we can tell, were built in the basilican style of the fourth century (*cf.* Rome). In the sixth century, however, the Emperor Justinian employed a great architect from Asia Minor, named Antemios of Trales, to build two remarkable churches in the capital; Santa Sofia, which stands today, and the Church of the Apostles, destroyed in the fifteenth century. He combined the traditional stone-building technique and cupola-vaulting of Asia Minor with fruitful observations of such important structures in Rome as the Basilica of Maxentius and the great Imperial Baths like those of Diocletian. From these sources were derived the knowledge

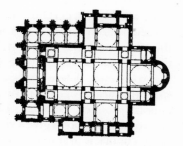

47 Venice: St Mark's, begun 1063

essential for constructing the massive supports for a high cupola of large diameter. The Church of the Apostles, as modified in the tenth century, had certain unusual and unmistakable features according to descriptions and illustrations available and by comparison with the plan of the similar church of St John the Evangelist at Ephesus. It was a Greek cross in plan partly surrounded by a narthex or atrium, with five cupolas supported by piers pierced with arches, colonnades round the arms of the cross and a matroneum with direct access to the Royal Palace at that level. These are the most striking features of St Mark's and, though still hypothetical, a direct derivation from this source seems highly feasible.

The Byzantine cupola looks different and is constructed differently from the type developed in Lombardy in the mediaeval period and eventually adopted from the fifteenth century onwards by architects throughout Europe. In its most ambitious form the circular rim of the saucer-shaped cupola is directly imposed on the crowns of the four great arches and pendentives, the concave spandrels between the arches; there is no intermediate drum and no central lantern. Through the pendentives the entire thrust exerted by the weight of the cupola passes into the massive piers. In the lower edge of the cupola are simple windows lightening, without weakening, the structure at its thickest part.

St Mark's was built as the chapel of the Doges, the annually elected presidents of the Venetian Republic, whose palace it adjoins. Not until 1481 did it become the cathedral of the Patriarch of Venice, successor to the ancient Patriarchate of Aquileia (q.v.). The first church was begun in 828, consecrated in 832, and later restored in 978. This building appears to have been a great colonnaded basilica without transepts. In about 1063 that structure was radically altered by an unknown, though probably Byzantine, architect, so that the earliest walls are almost certainly the core of the present church, which was consecrated in 1094. If this is so, then the church was transformed by the addition of the transepts, to which columns were transferred from the nave, and the insertion of the massive piers at the crossing and at the west end. These piers are pierced by two tiers of arches which span the aisles of the nave and transepts and they support the five cupolas grouped round the crossing (47). The consequent intersecting lines of three cupolas give a visual impression of great magnificence (44). Each cupola is framed by a great half-round arch of square section, rising from the piers, and each arm of the cross comprises a nave and side-aisles separated by tall colonnades and narrow galleries. High up in the walls of the aisles are two rows of windows. The three apses at the east end of the nave and the narrower aisles are circled by shallow niches. The end walls of the transepts are strengthened by chapels and other chambers including the treasury; round the west arm is an atrium, vaulted with small cupolas, the southern part being occupied by the baptistery and a memorial chapel, the Cappella Zen. The whole structure is integrated to counteract the tremendous thrust exerted by the cupola-vaulting.

St Mark's differs from all other great churches not only in the unity of its unusual structure but also in the magnificence of its internal and external decorations (cf. Monreale). The Piazza di San Marco, dubbed by Napoleon the ballroom of Europe, is closed at its eastern end by the façade of the basilica. The brilliant contrast of the coloured marble and mosaic pictures with the strong shadows of the deep recesses, the robust arcades below and the fretted pinnacles and weird onion-shaped cupolas above emphasize the unique place that the basilica holds in European architecture. This exotic decoration is the contribution of three centuries of liberal if buccaneering patronage and artistic activity.

The main external arcading was a series of plain niches until the twelfth century, when the multiple archivolts of the central porch were added and imaginatively carved by Lombard sculptors. Their work comprises one of the most complete iconographic cycles in Italian Romanesque sculpture (cf. Parma). Round the inner arch is an allegory of life, round the middle arch the Months, the signs of the Zodiac, the works of Man and the Virtues, and on the main outer arch the arts and crafts practised in Venice. The rest of the sculptural decoration of the façade and sides includes a rare collection of reliefs of the fifth and sixth centuries; these were in some cases gathered together from the earlier church and elsewhere in Venice, but were mostly procured from other provinces of the Empire, especially from Syria and Constantinople. The tympana of the first, third and fifth porches have small windows, some filled with curiously pierced panels and set with small reliefs framed by a thirteenth-century ogee arch. In the half dome of the niche are mosaics, but only the one in the Porta di Sant'Alipio, at the extreme left end, is of the thirteenth century. This mosaic picture (45), recording the translation of St Mark's body into the new church, is of particular interest as it records the appearance of the church between about 1260 and 1270. Other pictures, one in the right transept of the basilica and Gentile Bellini's painting of a procession in the Accademia Gallery in Venice, record successive stages in the embellishment of the exterior. The mosaics in the other arches were replaced in the seventeenth and eighteenth centuries. The sheafs of marble columns with Byzantine and Ravennate style capitals were despoiled from other buildings on the mainland and elsewhere, and were mostly added in the thirteenth century.

The second-tier arcade with pairs of columns is set back behind the main terrace and its shallow relief is in marked contrast with the lower. Behind the famous Roman bronze horses brought from Constantinople after the Fourth Crusade in 1204, the fully glazed principal arch was formerly filled with delicate marble tracery, which was destroyed, possibly by fire, in 1419. The seventeenth-century mosaics in the tympana of the other arches replace those of the thirteenth century. The colourful picture is completed by the picturesque crown of pierced white marble tabernacles and floridly carved angels and saints set among clusters of foliage round the ogee arches added to the Romanesque work. The north and south sides of the basilica have been treated in similar fashion to the main front and hardly less richly, especially towards the Ducal palace. On top of all stand the fantastic lead-covered outer cupolas surmounted by smaller gilded canopies and crosses.

In the Piazza and the Piazzetta of St Mark, the loggias of the Procuratie, the Palazzo Ducale, the Biblioteca Marciana and the basilica seem to revolve round the magnificent campanile which stands as the vertical hub among the horizontal lines radiating from it (48). After its collapse in 1902 the campanile was faithfully restored to its essential place in this unique setting. Begun as early as the ninth century, its present form is principally due to the designs made in the twelfth century, but the work was not fully completed until the first years of the sixteenth century. The simple pilastered trunk only rises half the total height which, with the belfry and pyramidal cusp, is 323 feet. The ramps originally giving access to the belfry, as at Torcello, have been reproduced. Still today the sonorous tones of its great bell ring out across the lagoon every three hours of the day as they have for centuries.

To enter the church we pass through the narrow narthex. We are obliged to pause here as an act of preparation before entering the church. The central bronze door into the narthex and its pair, the door from the narthex into the Cappella Zen (after 1268), are partly of the sixth century and their network of half-round arches clearly provided a model for those in the lateral doorways. These, signed MCCC (1300) MAGISTER BERTUCCIUS AURIFEX, are open grilles made up of small Gothic arches. The bronze doors of the central doorway into the basilica proper are adorned with saints damascened in silver, and were made between 1112 and 1138 in imitation of those doors of the Byzantine school of the late eleventh century in the right-hand portal of St Clement. Of the great series of mosaics, those of the earliest period (1071–84), part of the first scheme of decoration, may still be seen in the niches of the main doorway into the church, but the cycle of over a thousand stories from the Old Testament covering the entire vault of both arms of the narthex are the most important individual series produced by the Venetian school in the thirteenth century. They depict in utmost detail the stories of the Creation, Cain and Abel, the Flood, the Tower of Babel, Abraham (46), Joseph and Moses.

The interior of the basilica has a rare splendour despite an excessive patina of the marble decoration and insufficient light (44). The sources of light are the great west window, the wheel-window in the south transept, the small round-headed windows in the apse and high in the walls of the aisles, and those piercing the five main cupolas. It has been shown that this disorderly arrangement is far from the original plan, for the rose-window was inserted and the west glazed in the fifteenth century to meet the need for more light. This need arose because the outer cupolas which were added in the thirteenth century, so much increased the thickness of the window jambs in the cupolas that the windows became ineffective as a source of light. Before this, light from these windows served each arm of the building and with the cross-light coming from the windows in the aisles, bathed the whole interior and significantly contributed to the architectural concept. Until the thirteenth century the galleries over the colonnades covered the aisles as a matroneum or triforium, leaving them in shadowy contrast with the nave and transepts. The matroneum was very uncommon before the eleventh century but was an essential feature of the great Imperial churches of the sixth century in the East. It had a particular ritual context in the Church of the Apostles where it was directly accessible from the Imperial palace; it was used for Communion by the Royal Court. The matroneum, reduced to a gallery running round each arm of the church, has panels carved in relief as parapets, the work of Venetian and Byzantine craftsmen from the sixth to the twelfth century. These panels are frequently met as a part of the furnishings of early churches, but such an extensive and fine series is rare. Like these, many of the marble columns and their varied capitals belonged to the earlier basilica. The walls were made of brick with only a few mosaic pictures as adornment until, in 1159, a start was made on the colourful marble veneer. Now some five thousand square yards of glass mosaic in bright colours on a lustrous gold ground cover the immense super-ficial area of the walls and cupolas. This task was finally completed in the fourteenth century. The walls are not only enriched but given a particular schematic pattern by the decoration. Nowhere in Europe is there a more complete "Poor Man's Bible". From the narthex (*see above*) to the sanctuary the essence of the Old and New Testaments and of the teachings of the Church is vividly depicted. The mediaeval iconography has survived largely intact, though some of the pictures were replaced during the sixteenth and seventeenth centuries. Cartoons for these later mosaics were produced by such masters as Titian, Veronese, Tintoretto, Bassano and Pordenone, and skilfully executed by the contemporary Venetian mosaic workers. Their successors have been continuously engaged in careful maintenance.

The principal themes of the iconographic scheme are each confined to a particular arch or cupola. In the apse is Christ enthroned giving his Blessing; in the three cupolas from E.–W. are the coming of the new religion foretold by the prophets, the Church Triumphant and the Preaching of the Gospel; on the soffits of the main arches is related the Life and Passion of Our Lord, whilst over the west end are the two arches of the "Apocalypse" and of "Paradise". In the right transept are the favourite saints of the Venetians and over the Chapels of St Peter and St Clement, at the end of the aisles, is told the work of Saints Peter and Mark with the story of the transportation of the body of the patron saint from Alexandria. With the exception of the scenes of purely local significance, it is believed that this grand design was largely derived from the Church of the Apostles and is therefore an exceptional document reflecting what was lost with that building and comparable with those being revealed today in S. Sofia and the Kharie Djami in Constantinople.

The mosaic decoration continues in the baptistery and in the chapels of S. Isidoro and of the "Mascoli" (the males) at the end of the north transept. The pavement, too, is in marble mosaic in formal patterns but includes a number of attractive figures of birds and animals, such as the delightful cocks carrying a fox on a pole.

The presbytery is raised slightly over the crypt, partly lit by arcading in the presbytery step, and supported by short marble columns. St Mark was solemnly buried there in 1094. The red marble iconostasis which screens the presbytery was made by the two brothers Jacobello and Pier Paolo Masegne in 1394. It has the bronze figures of the Virgin Mary, John the Evangelist and the Apostles on either side of the

48 VENICE: St Mark's and the Piazza. The façade as developed from the eleventh to the fifteenth century; the campanile erected from the twelfth to the sixteenth century and rebuilt in 1908

49   PISA: the Campo Santo, Baptistery, Cathedral and Leaning Tower seen from the west

silver-bronze cross; these show the curious introduction of Gothic style into a Byzantine context.

The High Altar, now containing the body of St Mark, has a ciborium of green marble on which stand thirteenth-century figures of Christ and the Evangelists. The alabaster columns supporting the ciborium are carved with reliefs of the Life of Christ and of the Virgin from the Scriptures and Apocrypha which, though touched up in the thirteenth century, are probably oriental work of the fifth and sixth centuries. The splendid gold reredos, the Pala d'Oro, made in 1345, perhaps by Giampaolo Boninsegna, a Venetian goldsmith, is studded with precious gems and enamels. These last are mostly Byzantine work of the tenth and eleventh centuries, probably brought to Venice in 1204. Of the other mediaeval furnishings in the church the marble ambos beside the screen of the Masegne are quite simple, but the bizarre canopy over that on the left-hand side is very like the lanterns on top of the main cupolas.

Beyond the alterations to the mosaic pictures and some minor details, St Mark's has come down to us, like much else in Venice, intact. It is charged with a deeply moving quality inseparable from the life and history of the Serene Republic, in which it has, for so many centuries, been so profoundly esteemed and venerated.

Tuscany

THROUGHOUT its history, Tuscany has been the centre of a fertile culture. Here are the principal remains of Etruscan civilization; the typical tombs with wall-paintings and sculptures, the cyclopean walls of cities conquered by the armies of the growing Roman Republic. After the series of invasions from the north and the hegemony of the Lombards in the Dark Ages, there emerged a number of vigorous communities like Pisa, Florence and Siena. In the Middle Ages, these great cities were renowned for the wealth of their merchants and bankers and for their craftsmen. Pisa was famous for its builders and sculptors; Siena for its sculptors, painters and embroiderers; Florence could claim to be second to none in almost every visual art. Together the Tuscan communes have an enduring place in European civilization, and among their citizens were numbered many of the finest spirits of the Renaissance of the fifteenth and sixteenth centuries.

TUSCANIA

A LITTLE-KNOWN church of considerable significance is St Peter's at Tuscania (a town once known as Toscanella), which was the cathedral from 852 until the episcopal seat was transferred to the sixteenth-century church of S. Giacomo Maggiore. By the eighth century this part of Italy had been overrun and colonized by the Lombards. St Peter's was erected in the first half of the eighth century and, though partly altered in the eleventh and twelfth centuries, its fabric is an important and rare survival from the most obscure period in the history of European architecture. A so-called Comacine master, Rodperto, was in Tuscania during the reign of Liutprand (712–743) and was probably the responsible architect. Of particular interest are the method of construction and the standard of craftsmanship which differ in so many ways from those of earlier basilicas and from contemporary work in Rome.

Of the eight broad bays of the nave (43 and 50) all but the two most westerly are of the original stone building. The presbytery and side-chapels form an incipient transept between the nave and the east apse, demarcated by a triumphal arch the rough piers of which with half-shafts and contemporary carved capitals are not unskilfully made. The pairs of capitals and shafts of the nave arcade are classical spoils, but the curious teeth on the arches have no analogy elsewhere. The thickness of the walls diminishes towards the top, and pilasters springing from the thicker part of the wall run up to the wall-plate (*see* p. 122). By this means the weight on the arcade is lessened and the weight of the timber roof is carried by strong corbels. High in the nave walls are small clerestory windows. The only parts of the eighth-century furnishings that survive are the panels, carved in shallow relief with birds and beasts, which still serve as the enclosure-wall of the presbytery.

Externally the whole eastern part of the church, built up on a substantial substructure, is of the early period. Irregularly and awkwardly placed buttresses, which may be later additions, reinforce the walls of this part. The two small arcaded cornices decorating the walls are more interesting than their size warrants, for they are a curious link between the building and decorative technique employed in the early centuries in the Ravennate (*q.v.*) and still customary as a typically Lombard feature in the eleventh and twelfth centuries throughout Italy. As well as the small arcaded cornices round the outside of the apse there are vertical pilaster-strips, just like those of Saxon churches in England, and groups of rectangular niches beneath the crown of the apse and the windows. Some of the round-headed windows show that in the eighth century they were all double-splayed slits, whereas, hitherto, no splay had been used at all; those in the apse were enlarged in the eleventh century. The original crypt beneath the presbytery was enlarged when the presbytery and nave floors were raised to their present level. The crypt has now nine bays with vaulting supported by small columns and a variety of capitals some classical but most simple Romanesque work. When the nave level was raised above that of the aisles, the bench wall was presumably added and the main pavement laid, partly in Cosmatesque mosaic work of the twelfth century. In the eleventh century the two westernmost bays of the nave and a new façade with three doorways were added and other restoration work carried out. This façade was altered again about 1200, when the side-doors were blocked up and the central porch enlarged and elaborated. The work of this period, in marked contrast with the rest, is typical of the sculptural work in a number of churches in Umbria. On the portal and its jambs, and round the rose-window above, are reliefs including the symbols of the Evange- lists and a fantasy of Apocalyptic beasts.

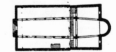

50 Tuscania; eighth and eleventh centuries

An inscription on the ciborium of the High Altar records its erection in 1093, a date which must also refer, by analogy with details, to the general restoration of the eleventh century. By means of this evidence it is possible to distinguish the earliest parts which give this building its important place in the tenuous history of architecture in the Dark Ages. Whence the Lombard builders (the Comacine masters referred to in an edict of the Lombard king, Rotharis) acquired their limited craft, is unknown. The standard derivation from the classical basilica was taken as a pattern, but the work is in stone not brick. This must have determined the divergences from the available models. The robust simplicity inherent in the stone construction was a significant departure from the classical mode and it must hold an important if obscure place in the development of the stone-built Romanesque church in the North. If the Lombard school was really responsible for the dissemination of many typical features of Romanesque architecture in Europe, St Peter's, Tuscania, represents the very beginnings of that movement.

PISA

In spite of its homogeneous appearance, Pisa cathedral was only completed after considerable alterations to its original design and the lapse of some 200 years. The cathedral of S. Maria Maggiore was founded by the citizens, it is said, after a great naval victory over the Saracens in 1063, and it stands a fine monument to their ancient maritime Republic. The traditional date is, unfortunately, open to doubt, and the building was probably begun, in fact, in or about 1089. The name of Buscheto, the architect, is recorded in an inscription and in official documents, in which he is referred to, from 1104 to 1110, as holding a position of authority. In 1118 Pope Gelasius II consecrated

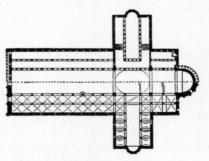

51 Pisa: baptistery, begun 1153–54

52 Pisa: cathedral, begun c. 1089, enlarged in twelfth century

53 PISA CATHEDRAL: the twelfth-century presbytery; the mosaic of the
Redeemer, *c.* 1300; the pulpit by Giovanni Pisano, 1302–10

54 PISA BAPTISTERY: the ambulatory, begun 1153–54; pulpit by Nicola Pisano, 1260

55 PISA BAPTISTERY: a cross-section showing the twelfth-century main arcade and the cupola of 1270 and about 1400

the church, and probably about that time modifications were made to the original plan, followed by further developments in 1150. The work was completed in the last years of the fourteenth century. The individual character of the cathedral's architecture had important and widespread influence at each stage in its development, both on neighbouring cities like Lucca and Pistoia, and on Sardinia, Corsica and even Apulia (*see* p. 152); some of its peculiarities may have been brought from so far afield as Armenia.

The original plan is absorbed in the extensions which preserve and continue its characteristic motifs (52). From the beginning it was strikingly like a Roman basilica, with its clerestory, double-aisles and the simple grandeur of the columned arcades. The addition of the cupola and the long apsidal-ended transepts, and the lengthening of the presbytery and nave gave it the present impressive proportions. The interior (53) is a unique blend of diverse architectural elements which can be reasonably attributed to the masterly conception of one man, Buscheto. His experience must have included a thorough knowledge of classical rather than early Christian Roman buildings and an acquaintance with developments in Lombardy. From the former he adopted the spacious form of the basilica with high nave walls and a timber roof, without diaphragm-arches or massive piers; from the latter he introduced the twin-arched triforium gallery. The use of dressed stone and some marble, in alternate bands of black and white, for the wall-surfaces was local and had taken root in Tuscany where it became for centuries a typical decorative feature (*see 1, 57, 67, also 87*). Most of the columns of the nave and some of those in the transepts are of granite, the others are of marble; all these, with many of the fine Corinthian capitals and bases, were obtained from classical monuments. The double-aisles are groin-vaulted and the minor arcades have slightly-stilted pointed arches, reminiscent of Saracen influence in Southern Italy (*e.g. 12, 91*), with shafts of unequal lengths. The transepts are each separated from the nave by the unbroken line of the main arcade and triforium. The repetition of the arcade and triforium in the transepts gives them the form of separate small churches with their own apses. The rectangular crossing between the nave and transepts is covered by an unusual ellipsoidal cupola which springs from an octagon formed by squinches in the angles of the upper walls. To give access to the cupola an elegant balustraded, double-inclined staircase was later contrived over the triumphal arch (*cf.* p. 156). The main arch between the nave and crossing is pointed in a manner recalling Saracen rather than Gothic forms. The extended presbytery, flanked by small side-chapels, has shallow apses at the end of the inner aisles. The clear-cut, dressed-stone surfaces of the twelfth-century fabric are unblurred, but owing to a serious fire in 1595 some parts towards the west front have been refaced.

The decoration of the interior includes restored mediaeval mosaics in the apses of the presbytery and transepts, but for the greater part it was carried out in the sixteenth century. The mosaic picture of the Redeemer enthroned between the Virgin and St John the Evangelist in the main apse, was made in about 1300; the smaller mosaics in the transepts represent the Annunciation and the Assumption of the Virgin. The outstanding individual work of art in the cathedral is the pulpit by Giovanni Pisano (53) which, with his assistants, he executed between 1302 and 1310. Having helped his father, Nicola, in the carving of the pulpit at Siena (14), he adopted the same polygonal design with supporting columns and carved panels. But the sympathy of expression, the graceful movement in the deeply-cut reliefs and the almost free-standing figures at the corners make this his finest single work of sculpture. The large figures and the panels relating to the Nativity of John the Baptist, scenes from the Life of Christ, and the Last Judgement by his own hand mark an important advance in Italian sculpture. The decoration of the presbytery with painted panels continued throughout the sixteenth century, with notable contributions by Andrea del Sarto and the Sienese Domenico Beccafumi which overlay an earlier scheme by Domenico Ghirlandaio. This pictorial decoration was continued along the aisle walls and was only completed in the eighteenth century. The richly carved wooden choir stalls, damaged at the time of the fire and restored, were begun in about 1470 by Giuliano da Maiano and completed by the end of the century by his successors. Inset in the formally designed inlaid pavement is a panel from the thirteenth-century Cosmatesque pavement which was destroyed in the fire.

The whole group of buildings (49) is justly famous: the cathedral with the leaning tower, the baptistery and the walled cemetery, the Campo Santo, with their white walls. The external grandeur and dignity of the basilica, enhanced by its open setting, are due to the unity of the composition of cornices, continuous blind-arcades and serried loggias. Though the use of arcading on external walls is found in buildings of earlier centuries, notably in the Ravennate, there is such a striking difference in the rhythm and effect that the Pisan form is widely believed to be derived from Ani in Armenia, where the same characteristic inlaid lozenge decoration and arcading occur on the stone-faced cathedral which may date from 1000. If this date is wrong

then, of course, unless Saracen influence may be adduced, the originality of the Pisan architect must be further affirmed. From Pisa this
striking feature spread rapidly throughout Tuscany, Lombardy (70)
and to Apulia. The inlaid lozenges and discs alternate with narrow
windows in the bays of the arcading of all three tiers. The extension of
the presbytery in the twelfth century was modelled on the Lombard
apse ringed with colonnaded galleries and provided the theme for the
façade and the campanile. After the nave had been extended westward
by three main bays, the façade was begun by one Rainaldus, according
to an inscription beside one of the portals. The first stage must have
been completed by the 1180's, since bronze doors were then made by
Bonanno of Pisa for the west front, as well as others for the portal of
S. Ranieri in the south transept. These doors were destroyed in the fire
and were replaced in 1603–4 by the existing bronze doors of Raffaele
Pagni, a disciple of the Florentine Giambologna. Bonanno's surviving
doors of bronze mounted on wood are outstanding in the history of
bronze casting. The impressive simplicity and clarity with which he
relates the Life of Christ, from the Annunciation to the death of Mary,
are entirely different from the work in the Byzantine tradition current
at the time (p. 226, cf. 117). He also made the doors of the west portal
of Monreale cathedral, six years later. The reliefs between the west
doorways and on the half-shafts of the blind-arcade were probably not
finished until the end of the century for they are similar to those on the
baptistery, which can be dated about 1200. The doorways and portals,
typical of the Pisan Romanesque style, have a plain architrave and
jambs and an arched tympanum supported by richly carved columns
with capitals; they are framed by the shafts or pilasters of the main
arcading. The upper galleries with neatly moulded arches, carved
capitals and cornices, shielding the west windows of the nave and aisles,
were continued in the following century. Even this multiplication of
galleries may have been inspired by a classical example, but they are
interpreted with a distinctive grace and charm, and give form to the
façade by their pattern of light and deep shadows. The gallery and
cusped frieze at the springing of the cupola were the last part to be
completed at the end of the fourteenth century.

The leaning tower and the baptistery (49) were both begun in the
second half of the twelfth century. The tower was commenced in 1174
and its belfry set up in 1350. Its style and decoration are uniform
throughout but so early as 1298 it had started to lean, and Giovanni
Pisano was called upon to deal with the problem; whatever his solution
may have been, the inclination of the first four storeys was not

corrected and the work was continued so that at least the upper part should be vertical. The subsidence has increased and the top of the tower is now nearly fourteen feet out of the vertical. Inside the tower is a cylindrical well vaulted below the belfry. There is access to every floor by means of a helical staircase in the thickness of the walls.

The circular baptistery (51 and 55) was begun in 1153–54 and initially designed by one Diotisalvi, whose name is inscribed on the main portal. Two years later, William, son of King Roger of Sicily, made a generous donation towards the work. Within ten years the columns of the internal arcade had been erected and not long after the main floor was completed. The classical style of the sculptured reliefs over the doorways, on their flanking columns and on the capitals of the inner arcade, is assigned to the very end of the twelfth century. Among the deeply cut foliate decoration of these columns the inset panels contain reliefs of David, Christ in Limbo, the Apostles and the "Months", which last are represented by men's perennial occupations. The internal plan follows the ancient precedent of the Lateran baptistery and S. Costanza in Rome in having a central ring of piers and columns, with an arcaded gallery added above; the arches are stilted and the ambulatory cross-vaulted. The pier capitals are carved with foliage and animated figures even including classical centaurs. The arcade of the gallery was once filled with tracery, like that of the Campo Santo. The original project was altered in 1278, possibly by Nicola Pisano, to erect the cupola. The gallery vault was raised, leaving the cross-arches of the original vault in place, and from the inner arcade a conical cupola was erected; this was a rare solution to the problem of covering a circular space for which the Church of the Holy Sepulchre in Jerusalem may have been a model. From outside, this cone appears poking up through the surrounding wooden hemispherical roof, added about 1400. As with the Florentine baptistery, the internal and external elevations differ in their proportions but here the interior is heightened and the external arcading made relatively low. The Gothic gabled loggia of the second tier was begun by Nicola Pisano, though the majority of the half-length figures and corbel heads in the "garland" are by his son, Giovanni – notably the Eternal Father, St John the Evangelist, David and St Luke (copies replace the originals now preserved inside the baptistery and in the Civic Museum) – so also is the tympanum of the east doorway.

The internal simplicity of the baptistery is a foil to the ornamentation of the font, the altar and the sculptured pulpit. The marble baptismal font was made in 1246 by Guido Bigarelli da Como (a master also met at Modena and Parma), according to the inscription on the rim; octagonal in shape, it is approached by three steps. It was kept constantly full of water from a fountain in the middle, on which once stood the bronze statue of John the Baptist now over the main door. A minor font is on each alternate face. On the outer faces are carved complex roses in pairs ornamented with human and animal heads surrounded by a coloured mosaic pattern. The altar is made of twelfth-century carved panels, once the balustrade of the cathedral presbytery.

The pulpit (54) is the first known work of Nicola Pisano and was completed in 1260. Though his full name, Nicola Pietri de Apulia, indicates his family's southern origin, and some motifs he uses such as the roaring lions were common in the south (94), no work of his has yet been identified earlier than this at Pisa. His powerful architectonic and plastic sense was drawn directly from classical models (one is actually preserved in the Cathedral Museum at Siena) and was fully integrated with the few Gothic details he used. Through this masterpiece and his pulpit at Siena, and through the advances made by his gifted pupils, his own son Giovanni and Arnolfo di Cambio (p. 62), Nicola's work had an enduring and all important influence on the development of Italian sculpture. The octagonal pulpit supported by columns and lions provides panels on which are carved scenes of the Redemption of Man, the Nativity, the Adoration of the Magi, the Presentation in the Temple, the Crucifixion and the Last Judgement. The figures are imbued with an essentially human dignity, for Nicola had cast off the inertia typical of the simpler Romanesque schools.

SIENA

THE task of replacing the earlier cathedral of S. Maria Assunta (the Assumption) by one worthy of the Commune and Republic of Siena was begun in 1226, or soon after, when collections were made among the citizens to raise the necessary funds. Within about fifty years a fine Romanesque basilica had been completed. The plan of the east end and transepts is uncertain, but the nave and aisles and the great cupola form part of the present church, which largely assumed its present shape in the early years of the fourteenth century, when considerable alterations were undertaken. It is probable that the nave was originally designed to have diaphragm arches and a timber roof (cf. 71); now it was heightened by the alteration of the clerestory, and vaulted. At the same time, the lower stage of the façade was added, the east end was rebuilt and extended to four bays beyond the cupola, over the top of the baptistery of St John, and the transept enlarged; the baptistery thus became the crypt. In 1339 the Commune decided yet again to enlarge the cathedral. It was planned to erect a new nave at right angles to the old, which was, in this way, to become the transept. The work was begun but could not be completed. So, after this disappointment, the east and west façades were completed and during the succeeding centuries the further embellishment of the interior was continued.

In spite of the alterations to the general plan of the church (56), its parts are in no way discordant. The nave and presbytery are harmoniously matched. The great round-headed arches of the nave are continued with minor modifications beyond the cupola and both parts are drawn together by the pointed arches of the clerestory. The open space beneath the cupola is a bridge between the dark masses of the nave and the lighter tone of the presbytery, while the black and white marble banding of the walls and piers gives an impression of overall continuity; by the greater proportion of white to black towards the east end, what could have otherwise been a pit of gloom, is, instead, bathed in light (57). The nave clerestory is banded in the same way as the presbytery. Light is admitted uniformly by the clerestory and aisle windows which are pointed with delicate Gothic tracery, and the large circular windows filled with stained-glass at the east and west ends. In the earlier work the windows were narrow and round-headed, as in the hexagon, and admitted little light. The nave must have been simple but very imposing in appearance before the clerestory was modified. The great round-headed arches are some 60 feet high. One of the half-shafts of each compound pier, which formerly supported diaphragm arches equal in size to the main arches of the cupola, now supports the quadripartite vaulting. The cupola rose clear above the Romanesque roof and, with its diameter of about 52 feet, was of unprecedented size for a cruciform structure. Whereas the scale of cupolas had been commonly restricted to the width of the nave (*e.g.* Pisa, *fig. 52*), here the space covered includes the width of the aisles. The wooden octagon (1322) of Ely

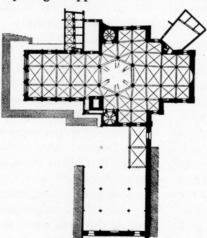

56 Siena, begun 1226, unfinished nave begun 1339.

cathedral is strikingly similar to this scheme. The unequal sides of the hexagon are formed by the great half-round transverse arches of the nave and choir and by the lateral pairs of similar but lower arches, over which are triple lights. In each angle is a squinch, utilized as a niche for the statues standing on the projecting half-shafts of the piers. The shallow twelve-sided drum has a screen of slender shafts beneath the cornice from which the ribs of the cupola spring in a fashion reminiscent of the baptistery at Parma (74). When the clerestory was added and the nave vaulted, the real value of the cupola was lost internally as well as externally; the external arcading of the drum is now visible from within the nave (57).

The most graceful adaptation of Gothic forms in Italy was accomplished by the Sienese school, which applied them almost solely as decoration. In the cathedral this decoration is extraordinarily but attractively ornate. Internally, the fine pointed triple-light windows of the clerestory and the broad-ribbed quadripartite vaults of the nave, presbytery, and aisles have characteristic square-cut members which convey so clearly that the classic "sense" was inseparable even from the Gothic in Italian art. It is, however, the façade that proclaims the value set on the Gothic style by the Italian artist. It has essentially decorative not structural value. The façade has little real structural relation to the building; it is a romantic composition. It must be compared with the similar façade at Orvieto (1), the design of which is admirably unified. Here at Siena, the design falls unmistakably into two parts of different periods. The lower half was undertaken by Giovanni, son of Nicola Pisano, in 1284, but the upper half was not continued until about 1377, that is when the grandiose scheme of extension had been abandoned and the west front had resumed its intended importance. Giovanni Pisano had worked with his father, Nicola, on the pulpit here (*see* below) and on that in the baptistery at Pisa (53). He was subsequently made chief master of the works in 1284 and a citizen of Siena. His masterly design for the façade is an important development in the co-ordination of sculpture with architecture. Nicola's powerful sculpture, based so closely on classical models, is here liberated and invested with vigorous life emanating from a new awareness and observation of nature. Giovanni Pisano shows in his design an understanding of the movement inherent in French Gothic modelling, but he dwelt on the profound human sympathy his father so capably expressed. The three ample portals, deeply recessed between the richly carved piers, reach up to the cornice at the level of the aisle roof. By this delimitation of space, the architrave, frieze and tympanum of the portals, very much like earlier work at Pisa, contradict the principles of French Gothic; the round-headed central arch and the pointed side arches, the triple stiff-leafed capitals and the carved columns were the well-established vocabulary of the Tuscan Romanesque school (*68*). It is the movement of the symbolic beasts, of the statues and the foliate decoration which derives from the northern school; the whole design, like its decoration, is plastic. But out of this mastery of form by the Pisanos grew, in other hands, the weaknesses of excessive decoration. The continuation of the upper part in 1377 or thereabouts confuses the balance of the lower part. It was common even in the fourteenth century for the façade to bear little or no relation to the structure behind, but the advantages of that freedom were squandered. The gables over the rose-window and sides, and the fretted pinnacles and niches are nothing but stock themes applied according to an uninspired formula (*cf.* Orvieto, *fig. 1*).

The general external aspect of the cathedral is greatly enhanced by its high podium stepped on all sides, a miniature of the great block on which the city itself stands. The great mass of the marble-faced church is in contrast with the superb upward thrust of the exceptionally fine thirteenth-century campanile with its carefully graded tiers of lights counterbalanced by the serried bands of black and white. The loss of importance suffered by the cupola when the nave was raised is evident, but the cupola must have originally been very pleasing with its two colonnaded loggias and low roof (*13*).

Standing open on the south side of the transept is the extraordinary spectacle of the New Work, incomplete and abandoned. The decision to reorientate the church was taken in 1339 and work began immediately. The architect Lando di Pietro sought to outdo the splendour of Orvieto and the ambitious plans of the Florentines, but only the shell of the magnificent and imaginative project survives. The five tall and broadly spaced round-headed arches with their relatively slender piers and the aisle vaults convey the spaciousness of the design; the lofty wall of the façade with its daring great window, only reinforced by a single narrow gallery, indicates the height of the nave vault. But Lando di Pietro's imagination outran his technical knowledge and that of his contemporaries too. Although by the fourteenth century, in North Europe, the problems of stabilizing vaulted structures of great height with the minimum of masonry had long been solved by external buttressing, this essential element in Gothic architecture had not been accepted and was indeed not understood in Italy (*cf.* Milan). Lando di Pietro did not appreciate the limitations of the structural principles he

57   SIENA: the interior from the west. The Piccolomini Chapel is in
the north aisle

58 ORVIETO: choir-stalls by G. Ammanati, 1329–57

59 ORVIETO: detail of sculptured marble reliefs on the façade, probably by L. Maitani, begun c. 1310

followed. An advisory committee, including the most celebrated Florentine architects of the time, Benci di Cione and Francesco Talenti, was appointed in 1356 but could not save the project which, for lack of stability, had to be abandoned and partially pulled down for safety. It was, however, a landmark in the development of "Sienese Gothic". The tall narrow splayed windows of the aisle walls, the elaborate doorway in the east wall and the vigorous, abundant carvings of the capitals and corbels, the sensitive arrangement of cornices, friezes and the courses of black and white marble, as in the presbytery, demonstrate the confident care which had been shown for every part from the beginning. It is the more unfortunate for this reason that completion should have proved impossible.

Once this defeat had been accepted, every effort was made to improve the older work externally and internally. Besides the completion of the west façade, work on that at the east end was begun. Because the presbytery had been extended over the lower church of St John the Baptist, there were unusual aesthetic difficulties involved. They were met by the harmonious design of Jacopo di Mino (1423); the three porches leading into the baptistery, included by tradition rather than necessity, the three narrow windows – the central one blind, the other two set high in the wall lighting the aisles of the presbytery and all framed by four unstepped buttresses and intermediate panels – are enlivened with gabled niches and arches.

The essentially decorative nature of Sienese art made the interior of the cathedral the most colourful of the greater Tuscan churches. Not only is there the black and white banding of the walls and the interplay of light and shadow among the deep vistas across the cupola, but the vaults are painted deep-blue spangled with gold stars, the vaulting ribs and arches are gilded and the rose-windows are filled with the deep colours of stained glass (1288). The pavement is unique for the extent and beauty of its rare marble inlay. The use of inlay as distinct from mosaic for this purpose has a tenuous but long history. The developments in technique had parallels in mosaic work, wood inlay and painting. Vasari wrote that Duccio di Boninsegna designed a pavement for the cathedral in the late thirteenth century, but no evidence of this survives. The present work was begun in 1369–70 and was finally completed shortly after 1518. A succession of artists, including Antonio Brunaccio, Domenico di Niccolò, Antonio Federighi, Matteo Giovanni Pinturicchio and Domenico Beccafumi, designed and executed the work. Naturally worn by use, some parts have been restored and three hexagonal panels of the fourteenth century beneath the cupola were placed in the cathedral museum and substituted in 1874 by the designs of Alessandro Franchi. The earlier patterns were symbolic, like the panel recording the confederate States of Siena in the nave, but during the fifteenth century large-scale narrative pictures such as those of the Slaughter of the Philistines, the Siege of Bethel (Betulia) and the Massacre of the Innocents, were laid in the transepts and the figures of the ten sibyls were set in the nave aisles. A new technique adopted by Beccafumi in 1518, employing white, grey and black marbles with incised shading, gives the effect of a cartoon in charcoal, as in the scenes of Moses receiving the Tables of the Law and the Sacrifice of Abraham.

Little of the mediaeval furniture remains beyond Nicola Pisano's celebrated pulpit (14) and that is the most important single work of art in the church. Nicola, assisted by his disciples, Arnolfo di Cambio, Donato and Lapo di Ricevuto and Giovanni, his own son, began the pulpit in 1265 and completed it in 1269. The staircase and the plinth of the pulpit were added in 1543. The sculpture and the architectonic design of the whole in white Carrara marble shows an important maturing of style from Nicola's earlier pulpit in the Pisan baptistery (54). Standing figures, in place of columns at the corners, soften the angularity of the octagon, and like the scenes of the Life of Christ on the panels are much freer in the treatment of the movement of the figures and of perspective. But in spite of greater human feeling in these, Nicola's grounding in classical models is no less apparent than at Pisa. Besides the pulpit, Nicola, or at least his assistants, seems to have carved many of the capitals in the nave with animals and human figures among the classical style of foliage.

Through the fifteenth and sixteenth centuries, chapels and furniture were added by Tuscan artists of the Renaissance. Between 1481 and 1498, the last of the great exponents of Sienese Gothic, Jacopo della Quercia, with the assistance of Donatello and others, made the font for the baptistery of St John (the crypt church). The Chapel of St John the Baptist (in the north transept) was decorated by Giovanni di Stefano and Antonio Federighi with themes of classical and Etruscan origin. Then the delightful Piccolomini library with frescoes by Pinturicchio 1502–09), relating the life of Pope Pius II (Aeneas Sylvius Piccolomini), was given a façade decorated with charming reliefs by Lorenzo di Mariano. The High Altar with its sculptured reredos was designed by Baldassare Peruzzi in 1532. The choir stalls, in their apsidal part the work of Francesco del Tonghi (1362–88), are inlaid after the manner of Ammanati's at Orvieto (58), while the rest is the splendid marquetry of Bartolomeo Neroni (1560–70), though it lacks the lucidity of the earlier part because of its over-heavy total effect.

The problems which arose from the abandonment of the New Work and the consequent embellishment of the original cathedral have made it one of the most richly decorated mediaeval churches in Italy. Only the failure of Lando di Pietro denied the Commune the honour of possessing one of the largest and most imaginative cathedral churches in Italy.

ORVIETO

ALTHOUGH the communal independence of this fortress hilltown was recognized from the twelfth century, its life was continually and closely subjected to Curial influence and it was eventually absorbed into the Papal States in 1354. Several Popes resided in the Palazzo dei Papi next to the cathedral as a refuge from the antagonism of the Roman citizens. To celebrate the Miracle of Bolsena in 1263, which revealed the True Presence of Christ at the Mass to a doubting priest, Urban IV instituted the Feast of Corpus Christi and ordered the erection of the present cathedral of Orvieto.

The work was not begun, however, until about 1290. There is a tradition that Arnolfo di Cambio was the first architect and while this cannot be proved it is not unreasonable to accept it. If it were so, another claimant, Bevignate da Perugia, would have been in charge of the construction. It is recorded that the citizens wanted the new church to be like the basilica of S. Maria Maggiore in Rome (36) and the basilican form with transepts (60), the timber roof, the triumphal arch and single apse may have met their wishes. The design was also based on another Roman building, the (former) Council Chamber of the Lateran Palace, which had tall apsidal niches along its walls. In all other respects the main part of the cathedral is a Romanesque structure with nascent Gothic features such as the bases and heavy, carved circular capitals of the nave columns. The original simplicity of the nave was restored in 1890. The massive cylindrical drums, the high walls above with their tall narrow windows and continuous corbelled cornice, and the aisle walls, curiously broken by the apsidal niches once fitted as chapels, are

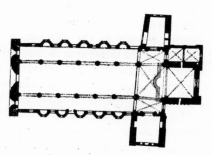

60 Orvieto, begun c. 1290.

all banded in alternate courses of white and grey stone like the cathedral at Siena but with a less heavy effect. The curves of the arches and the spacing of the piers create a particularly satisfying rhythm. The spaciousness of the whole resembles closely that of Arnolfo's church of S. Croce in Florence (*see* p. 158).

In 1310 the Sienese architect Lorenzo Maitani was appointed chief master to rescue part of the building from danger; he remained in this post until his death in 1330. It seems that weaknesses due to the instability of the high vaulting of the transepts had developed. To remedy them he erected a square-ended presbytery in place of the original apse, inserted diagonal buttresses in the walls and chapels, and reduced the window space. The quadripartite vaults of the transept, crossing and presbytery, supported by the elegant compound piers, are pointed in the Gothic style, which by that date was established in Tuscany. The delicately arcaded gallery which rides over the tall tracery-filled east window matches that over the west entrance and is comparable with a similar feature in Pisa cathedral (p. 143). The pictorial effect of the frescos (1370), which divide the end and side-walls into panels, both enhances the sanctuary and contrasts it with the more severe lines of the nave. The pavement of the nave is all pink marble and its only adornment is a set of a score of inlaid concentric octagons each containing a single fleur-de-lys. The choir stalls (58), though much restored (1860–92), are, and were intended to be, among the most precious of their kind. They were begun in 1329 under the direction of Giovanni Ammanati, with whom were employed Sienese craftsmen to carve the full-relief figures beneath the canopies of the stalls and the fine inlaid patterns and figures of saints. Special arrangements were made in 1357 for their care – they were to be brushed only with fox-tails. The former arched entrance to the choir in the same style is now in the museum (Palazzo dei Papi).

The walls of the north chapel of the transept, containing the reliquary of the corporal used at the Mass of Bolsena, were inlaid with marble mosaic by the Florentine Andrea Orcagna in about 1350. The Chapel of the Madonna di San Brizio in the south transept was largely decorated, from 1408 onwards, with the celebrated frescos by Fra Angelico and Luca Signorelli which were to have an important influence on the development of Michelangelo.

Maitani's other significant contribution is the façade (*1*). He did not live to carry out more than the lowest portion himself, but he left designs which, in spite of eventual modifications and tardy completion, are outstanding for their unity of composition. The façade of the cathedral at Siena (*13*) by Giovanni Pisano was an obvious model for Maitani, but the use of detail and the relation of architecture and sculpture in design differ strongly. Pisano's work is dominated by the firm classical lines of the Tuscan Romanesque school. That Maitani was far more directly influenced by Gothic architecture is most clearly shown by the prominence given to the vertical lines of the four moulded buttresses, the pinnacles and gables. The relative simplicity, or rather directness, given by the careful emphasis on the lines of greatest importance and the exclusion of fussy ornament distinguish this work from the contemporary trends in Gothic at Siena. In the architectural setting of arches, gallery, rose-window, pinnacles and gables, the brilliant decoration, combining sculptured reliefs and figures in marble and bronze with mosaic pictures, is only slightly marred in effect by restoration or the replacement of most of the mosaics which were damaged by lightning in the late eighteenth century (the original mosaic from the gable of the right-hand doorway may be seen in the Victoria and Albert Museum, London). The fine balance between the parts remains almost unimpaired.

The unique dado is the most remarkable part of the façade and is, in all probability, due in considerable part to Maitani's own hand. The jambs of the doorways and the great arches containing them are carved and decorated in the style of the Cosmati mosaic workers (*see 6; 33*). The faces of the piers on either side of the three doorways are carved with low reliefs of superb quality and delicacy to a masterly design (*59*). From north to south the themes are: the Story of the Creation including the Fall of Man and the Invention of the Arts; the Tree of Jesse; the Life and Passion of Christ; and the Last Judgement. Maitani's assistants and successors also had great talent; they had acquired much of their experience in the Sienese school. Among them were Francesco Talenti and Andrea Pisano, both to become chief architects to Florence cathedral. Their work included the fine bronze symbols of the Evangelists and the Virgin and Child all of which stand along the principal cornice. The rose-window and its sculptures were carried out by Andrea Pisano and Andrea Orcagna (1354); the main gable was heightened slightly by Antonio Federighi (1452–58) who inserted the horizontal line of niches and statues; the side-gables were finally completed in about 1600.

Standing on its podium, regularly banded on every side with courses of basalt and travertine, this architectural gem, one of the most satisfying of mediaeval Tuscan monuments, dominates the surrounding plain.

FLORENCE

THE ancient cathedral of Florence, S. Reparata, and its baptistery of St John, were both apparently reconstructed during the course of the eleventh century. The baptistery stands today only little altered structurally during successive centuries, though embellished with mosaics and its bronze doors. By the end of the thirteenth century S. Reparata, however, was considered by the Florentines too small and altogether unworthy of their city. It was similar in style if not in detail to S. Miniato al Monte, the only large church of its period surviving in Florence, and to the cathedral of Fiesole (*cf.* p. 50). The new Franciscan churches of S. Croce and S. Maria Novella inspired the Commune to erect a great new church to be known as S. Maria del Fiore and for this Arnolfo di Cambio was commissioned as "the most famous builder of churches" of the time (p. 60). He was the first of the long line of chief masters employed on the project and the essence of his plan, though greatly expanded after his death, was carried through to the end and finally given its greatest glory by the equally celebrated Filippo Brunelleschi, the builder of the cupola.

The foundation of the new cathedral was blessed in 1296 under the aegis of Pope Bonifice VIII and already by 1300 a "great beginning" had been made. The plan (*cf.* 62) was for a nave and two aisles of four bays terminating in an octagon with side-chapels, and a timber roof was probably intended (*cf.* Orvieto). The width of the nave was a little more than twice that of each aisle, the same proportions that Arnolfo gave the Franciscan church of S. Croce also in Florence. What the details of the interior were is scarcely known, nor how it was proposed to cover the

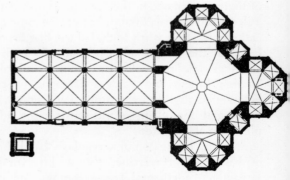

61 Florence: baptistery, probably fifth-century, altered eleventh century.

62 Florence: cathedral, 1296–1426.

great octagon. Work began at the west end and during the first decade
continued on the façade and nave. The external mural pattern for the
three bays of Arnolfo's nave is preserved on the south side. The
equivalent space of each internal bay was divided equally into narrow
panels by flat pilaster-buttresses rising to the original height of the aisles
as marked by the multiple cornice; in each marble-encrusted panel is
a tall, slender, pointed window beneath a gable. The Gothic detail is
delicately fused with the rectilinear panelling. Equally harmonious
was the façade (65), never more than half completed and unhappily
destroyed in 1588. In this part of his work, Arnolfo showed to the full
his devotion to sculpture. He utilized Gothic features for the tabernacle
work of the porches and broke up the intervening spaces with deep
niches outlined by horizontal trabeation and columns. In the niches and
the tympana of the doorways were assembled large statues of the Virgin
and Child, saints and angels, and Pope Boniface VIII (now preserved in
the nearby Museum of the Opera del Duomo), many by Arnolfo's own
hand, and others were added by his successors.

But with Arnolfo's death before 1310 the work came to a halt and
was not furthered at all until, in 1334, Giotto, the most renowned
artist of this time, was appointed chief master and the campanile was
begun. The campanile (17) grew slowly under a succession of masters,
for though known as Giotto's tower, he was in fact only responsible for
the first stage (63); after his death, his assistant Andrea Pisano altered
the design and carried up the next three stages. The upper half, in three
tiers, was designed, differently again, by Francesco Talenti and completed in 1357–58. The gabled and traceried windows piercing each
side of the tower, and the corbelled overhanging cornice of the cap,
match Talenti's decoration of the adjacent aisle walls. Unique in
composition with its octagonal corner buttresses, the distinctive
proportions of its five stages and the gently upward swelling lines to
which the polychromic marble decorative detail is subordinated, it is
the most endearing and striking Florentine monument of the mid-
fourteenth century.

At last, in 1357, work was recommenced on the cathedral with
modifications proposed by Talenti, chief master from 1355 to 1365. It
is probable that he proposed increasing the span and height of the nave
arches (68) to make three bays within the length intended by Arnolfo
(q.v.); the effect was to be more grandiose but less well-proportioned.
The façade and aisle-walls had to be raised as well and the arrangement
of the windows altered. Every detail was lengthily discussed in committee and in public – the height of the columns, the form of the

capitals, the shapes of the windows and arcading – before each part was begun.

In 1365 the whole project was reconsidered by the Commissioners appointed by the Commune. Numerous proposals were discussed and finally plans were settled to which each successive chief master had to swear fidelity. The fourth bay was added and the form of the octagon and its polygonal chapels fixed (62). The work then progressed steadily until, in 1420, the nave was complete, the chapels round the octagon had all been roofed and the drum put up ready for the cupola (17). But the details of how to erect the cupola, 140 feet in diameter, had not been worked out. The problem was great, for nothing so large had been ventured before. The authorities ordered models to be produced for its solution. In 1417 Filippo Brunelleschi made his first proposals, only to have them rejected as insufficient. Then a competition was arranged in which Brunelleschi took part. His plans were treated with derision by both the informed and the general populace. He said he would put up the cupola without centering; a solution inconceivable to his contemporaries. He was allowed eventually to prove his point by building a small cupola for a chapel in the church of S. Jacopo Soprarno. His success led to his immediate appointment as chief master responsible for the cupola, with Ghiberti as his principal assistant. The work began at once (1420) and was successfully concluded fourteen years later. So that the curves of the cupola surfaces should appear well inside and out, he used a double-skin construction. The outer-skin swells more fully than the inner, and the brick panels are tied together between the skins by the twenty-four stone ribs, eight of which show externally. It was a remarkable technical achievement for which Brunelleschi's fame spread throughout Italy. Until his death in 1446 he was responsible for all other work in the cathedral, including the two sacristies and the design of the lantern of the cupola, which was completed by Giuliano da Maiano. In 1588 the marble facing of the exterior had been completed and, at this time, the incomplete façade of Arnolfo (65) was pulled down for the sake of uniformity. But the present façade (63), designed by E. de Fabris, was only completed in 1887. It is a sadly unoriginal design frankly imitated from other parts of the structure; the marble facing is darker and heavier than that of the early period. The bronze doors (66) were added between 1897 and 1903 by Passaglia and Cassioli.

The ascetic quality of the interior (68), well suited to the preaching of a Savanarola, is accentuated by the exotic colours of the exterior. The four giant pointed arches striding along the broad high nave are the

63 FLORENCE: the façade by E. de Fabris, 1887; shows also the side-wall by Arnolfo di Cambio (1296–1310) and Giotto's tower (1334) to the right

64   FLORENCE: a musicians' gallery by Donatello.
Formerly in the cathedral, now in the Museo del Opera del Duomo

65   FLORENCE: the original façade begun by Arnolfo di Cambio *c.* 1296.
Destroyed in 1588. *From a drawing in the Museo del Duomo*

66 FLORENCE: a panel of the bronze doors of the right-hand
portal of the cathedral, by G. Cassioli, 1899

67 FLORENCE: baptistery. The interior from the east side, as modified
in the eleventh century

68   FLORENCE: view of the nave from the crossing and showing the
choir enclosure

most disappointing of all products of Florentine Gothic. This must be attributed to the alterations to the vertical proportions and rhythm of the original plan, and to the depressed vaulting ungraciously starting from the corbelled gallery. All the same, the interior has a particular grandeur borne upon us by its simplicity, the soft contrasts of the whitened walls and brown tufa masonry, the plain surfaces and fretted capitals and cornices. The flat pilasters of the piers are quite plain except for the capitals curiously carved like triple rows of curly kale – a motif to be widely employed elsewhere, especially in North Italy (15). From the capitals the pilasters rise up to the springing of the ribbed quadripartite vault, but they only draw attention to the unhappy combination of the Gothic architectural feature with the indispensable horizontal member, the cornice. The cornice, firmly established in the repertoire of Tuscan design, is here a gallery supported by corbels and runs continuously round the nave and octagon. In the octagon there are two further galleries, at the base of the drum and at the springing of the cupola, above and below the circular windows. The great clarity of the architectural lines of the octagon are the essence of its nobility; the unmoulded arches and lancet windows and the four massive piers between the triumphal arches. The three deep arms round the octagon, each with five side-chapels, emphasise the great height. The easternmost of these was first occupied by the choir and High Altar, but the inadequacy of this was soon realized. Its siting there perpetuated that of the earlier church of S. Reparata, in which the High Altar was raised over the crypt containing the body of Zenobio, an early Florentine saint. His body remains in the crypt which was reshaped by Brunelleschi. The choir and altar were moved, in accordance with the Renaissance conception of the central design, to their place beneath the cupola (68). Brunelleschi designed a choir which after his death was roughly fashioned out of white wood. The circle of stalls with canopies was very soon eaten by rats and condemned. In its place Baccio Bandinelli, in 1555, made the mediocre marble enclosure of today. Over 180 feet above, the octopartite vault of the cupola was painted with the Universal Judgement in fresco by Giorgio Vasari and Federigo Zuccari. This, with the few memorial frescoes in the nave, the reredoses of the altars and the unusually rich coloured glass of the chapel windows, are the only colour in the church. The few sculptures seem particularly fitting in this spatial environment: the Pietà by Michelangelo in the left transept, and the delightful musicians' galleries by Donatello (64) and Luca della Robbia, formerly above the doors of the sacristies in the octagon (now in the cathedral museum).

The vast extent of red, white and green marble-encrusted walls, the white marble gables of the carved doorways, and the red roofs of the nave and cupola, is at first astonishing and discomforting to northern eyes, but once assimilated it holds an indelible place in our affections. The imposing east end and the complex pattern of the polygonal chapels buttressing it on every side are firmly united to the nave by the elaborate cornices which run from end to end; the horizontal lines are relieved by the shallow buttresses, the arcading and the neutralizing circles of the upper windows. But everything is subordinate to the cupola, whose firm curves rise high above to the white marble lantern with its ball and cross. The cupola and nave standing free in the piazza and dominating the city on every side (17) are visible from any point on the surrounding amphitheatre of hills; their grandeur is symbolic of the power and brilliant accomplishments of the Republic.

The date of the Florentine Baptistery is an extraordinary problem defying certain solution. During the eleventh century "S. John the Baptist and S. Reparata" formed a single title; until that time St John had been the city's titular saint. It is improbable that the baptistery was originally attached to the church of S. Reparata and was not on its present site; it may well be compared with Parenzo (41). Recent excavations have shown no evidence of an earlier building and the foundations of the present structure lie directly on those of Roman houses. This implies either that there was an open space here for several centuries or that the existing walls, at least, are of the fifth century, as can be deduced from the classical nature of the interior, and not of the eleventh century. There was in any case a thorough restoration in the eleventh century, when the external marble veneer was added and the rectangular apse replaced the former semicircular one. It was the building thus restored that had such an important influence on the development of the Pisan and Lombard baptisteries in which the dominance of classical influence is so apparent.

Octagonal in shape, like many classical and fifth-century buildings of its kind (61 and 67), it is significantly advanced in the technical accomplishment of its internal architecture. The strength of the heavily trabeated principal order of columns and pilasters beneath the shallower, arcaded second tier, somewhat similar to the Pantheon, convincingly supports the massive vault of the cupola. The accuracy and uniformity of the detailed ornamentation of these members, in particular of the architrave and capitals, encourages the conclusion that they are fifth-century in date. Though it is not necessary to press the claims of such early dating so far as to include the cupola, there are classical analogies for the pointed form of its construction. If, as is more likely, it is mediaeval, it would not have been erected earlier than the first half of the thirteenth century (cf. Parma).

The massive Romanesque arch of the apse unbalances the concentric harmony of the interior. When there was still only a shallow apse for the altar, an octagonal baptismal basin was situated in its proper central position; this basin has since been removed and there is now only a font against the wall. The polychrome marble veneer of the interior overlies the earlier black and white banding of the walls which is visible in the altered window jambs of the second tier, and is in the style of the eleventh and twelfth centuries. The pavement of mixed inlay and mosaic in a quite local style was probably added at the beginning of the thirteenth century. The complete scheme of pictorial mosaics now forms an integral part of the building's character. Those in the apse were begun in 1225 by a Franciscan, Jacopo, who may, too, have started those in the cupola. This exceptional series includes some contributions made by the master painter Cimabue and by Gaddo Gaddi. They were not completed until the early fourteenth century. They include stories from the Old and New Testaments and especially the Life of John the Baptist, the Passion of Christ and the Last Judgement; in all of them the continuous influence of Byzantine style is evident. The pointed vault of the cupola is structurally lightened at the base by a ring of small windows (cf. St Mark's, Venice) and is covered externally by a simple pitched roof. The outer walls have been raised, and conceal the springing of the vault from view.

The exterior has a quite different character because the corner pilasters and the blind arcading, in spite of the three continuous cornices, emphasise the height of the walls. The three doorways and the windows were partly reworked by Brunelleschi, but the greatest glory of this monument lies in the celebrated bronze doors of Andrea Pisano and Lorenzo Ghiberti. Andrea Pisano's doors, dated 1330, were completed six years later in response to the desire of the citizens to have doors equal to those at Pisa. They were first erected facing the cathedral, but were later removed to the south side. A pupil of Giotto, Andrea Pisano shows his mastery of Gothic movement within a framework of classical order. The first doors by Ghiberti, those in the north doorway and the "Gates of Paradise" in the east, demonstrate his progression from a Gothic style to the full vigour of humanistic observation and perfect control of perspective in his medium.

The Lombard Plain

MODENA

THE ancient basilica said to have been built in the fourth century over the tomb of S. Geminiano at Modena was in a state of collapse by the end of the eleventh century, and the present cathedral was begun by the Commune in 1099. It was possible to translate the body of the saint to its new resting-place in the crypt in 1106, but the church was not consecrated until 1184 by Pope Lucius III. An inscription on the façade records the foundation and the name of Lanfranc, the architect of the new church. How much of the work is his is not known. It may, however, be presumed that the plan and principle features are part of his design. Though the building was not completed until the fifteenth century, the twelfth-century work is of particular importance in the development of Lombard Romanesque architecture.

The design was for a timber-roofed basilica with short transepts and three projecting eastern apses. The external walls of the aisles, the façade and the apses have a regular pattern of distinctive blind-arcading which rises to the eaves of the low-pitched roofs. This motif was quite probably derived from Pisa, but was given a new value by the insertion of the continuous loggia of triple arches. The continuity of this theme across the façade counteracts the line of the strong flat buttresses on massive bases, which mark off the nave from the side-aisles. Rising above the plain gable of the nave are two turrets like those over the main apse. Of the three porches in the façade, only the central one, with its simply carved jambs, arch and architrave, seems part of the original design. It is in two tiers, each an arch supported by slender shafts, the lower ones standing on squatting lions derived from an antique model. The great wheel window was inserted in the thirteenth century. On the south side of the church are two other portals of different periods. The small *Porta dei Principi* is similar to the lower part of the main porch, but has the life of S. Geminiano narrated in relief on

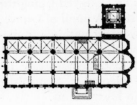

69 Modena, begun 1099.

70 MODENA: the twelfth-century façade with its sculptured reliefs and
the *Torre Ghirlandina*

71 MODENA: the nave and raised presbytery, begun 1099

the architrave and the Apostles figured among entwined tendrils and foliage; the large *Porta Regia* was added between 1209 and 1230 by Anselmo da Campione. This, too, has a double storey but is more imposing. It is of red marble with a single round-headed arch or vault supported by coupled columns; the front pair rest on crouching lions, those against the wall are in pairs, curiously knotted together. The upper tier has a low-pitched roof over three arches also supported by pairs of columns; the doorway itself is deeply recessed with a multiple containing-arch on the colonettes of the splayed jambs. On the north side, next to the transept, is the *Porta Peschiera* which though the smallest, is the most elaborately carved, with the "Months", fables and a rare scene from the Arthurian cycle.

The most important sculptural work is that of Wiligelmo, also named in an inscription on the façade. This artist seems to have been active elsewhere in the second decade of the twelfth century. His set of four panels on the west front are prominent in the early history of Lombard sculpture. Not least remarkable in these reliefs is their reflexion of classical motifs; there is even a naked Genius leaning on a cornucopia. In style they show affinities with contemporary German and south French carving. Stiff and crude perhaps but the beginnings of a native art from which much was to grow, they robustly and vividly describe the Fall of Man from his Creation to the Flood. Wiligelmo and his assistants were also, so far as may be judged, responsible for the fascinating and numerous carved capitals of the external arcading and of the nave and crypt, among which is an infinite variety of ingenious combinations of figures, sacred and profane, saints and tumblers. In the external loggia are traces of frescoes.

The campanile, one of the finest in the Lombard Plain, is known as the *Torre Ghirlandina*; its massive stone-faced walls and spire rise 300 feet from the ground. Though begun in the thirteenth century, with carefully graded sets of lights and arcaded cornices at each of the six stages, the octagonal lantern and spire were only completed in 1319, by Arrigo da Campione.

The interior of the cathedral marks an important stage in the evolution of great Lombard churches. Just as externally Pisan influence is evident, so internally other features probably of Tuscan origin appear. The plan for a timber roof permitted a greater structural lightness here than in other contemporary Lombard designs. The nave arcade has alternate single columns and composite piers giving a typical square embayment, with a double-square in the aisles. From the piers rose plain diaphragm arches across the nave and the subsidiary arches in the aisles to strengthen the walls and incidentally provide some protection from fire – a feature also present in the eleventh-century church of S. Miniato al Monte in Florence. The widely-spaced low arches of the triforium only pierce the wall into the aisle, the ribbed vault of which is supported at a higher level by the double-tier of cross-arches between the main piers and the outer walls. The tall narrow clerestory windows with sharply splayed sills admit light to the whole nave. When the Gothic brick cross-ribbed vault was erected in place of the timber roof in the fifteenth century, the heads of these windows were impinged on, and the blind arcading that formerly contained them was largely obliterated. The effect of the new vault was to render meaningless the special forms introduced in the original design and to lower unduly the ceiling of the main vista. The four double bays of the unfaced brick nave and wide aisles lead up to the presbytery in the transept.

The arrangement of the presbytery and crypt here is not uncommon in North Italian churches, though very rarely found elsewhere (71). The crypt is only slightly below the main floor level and the presbytery and High Altar are raised above it. This was undoubtedly that part of the new cathedral completed in 1106 for the remains of S. Geminiano to be buried in the new main apse. The groin-vaulting of the crypt, which extends beneath the entire width of the transept, is supported by sixty columns with capitals, many in the style of Wiligelmo and his assistants. The presbytery is reached by a flight of steps from each aisle. Across the front is a *pontile* or balcony supported also by columns standing on four lions mauling their prey, and a projecting circular pulpit on columns with very uncomfortable-looking men seated under them. The panels of the *pontile* parapet were carved, between 1170 and 1220, by the resident Campionese masters to represent the Last Supper and other scenes from the Passion. On the panels of the pulpit are carved the Redeemer, the symbols of the Evangelists, the four Doctors of the Church, and Christ waking Peter. Above this parapet and round the sides of the presbytery runs a beam resting on graceful coupled colonettes, a form of iconostasis, and above it hangs a four-teenth-century wooden crucifix. The simple table-altar stands in the middle of the presbytery, surrounded by late fifteenth-century inlaid wooden choir stalls in the apse, which is lit by three single-splayed windows. The early fourteenth-century Gothic arches and vaulting of the transept was probably the last major work before the roof of the nave was replaced in the fifteenth century.

Though not a large church, Modena cathedral is rich in its sculptural decoration and distinguished for the regular unity of its architectural form. Its influence on later work is readily apparent by comparison with such notable buildings as Ferrara cathedral and the important group of Apulian Romanesque churches.

PARMA

PARMA holds a principal place in the turbulent and chequered history of the Lombard Plain. Situated on a Roman highway, the Via Emilia, the city rose to importance under the Republic. During the Middle Ages, as a Ghibelline stronghold, it supported the German Emperor and the cause of several anti-popes, and was in constant conflict with neighbouring communes. As a republic, from the twelfth century it endured the unstable dynastic interests of the Visconti, Este, Sforza and of Pope Julius II until in the eighteenth and nineteenth centuries the Farnese Duchy fell successively under Spanish, French, Austrian and again Spanish princes. Its finest works of art belong to the twelfth, thirteenth and sixteenth centuries.

In 1058 the ancient cathedral of Parma was destroyed by fire and had to be replaced, but its successor was so much damaged by the earthquake of 1117 that it, too, had to be rebuilt. The twelfth-century cathedral dedicated to the Assumption (S. Maria Assunta), the adjacent campanile and the baptistery form one of the most striking and interesting groups of buildings in the region. Structurally the cathedral holds an important place in the development of Lombard Romanesque architecture for it is one of the earliest brick-built churches designed to have a high vault over the nave (cf. Modena). The erection of this was accomplished without loss of the spaciousness characteristic of the style. Those accustomed to the grandiose expansion of the plans of Norman cathedrals in England are struck by the relative shortness of Parma. But, on the other hand, the height and width of the nave and aisles and the proportions of the main arcade with the consequent

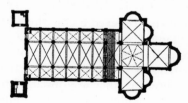

 74 Parma: cathedral, begun after 1117 (side chapels are not shown)

73 Parma: baptistery, begun 1196

breadth of the vistas within this church make for the distinctive nature of North Italian architecture. Here are two breaks with habitual practice, the displacement of the timber roof over the nave and the rejection of the classical columns, whose use still continued further south. From the alternately compound and cruciform piers of the main arcade rise half-shafts to the springing of the vault. The triforium, mutilated in the sixteenth century, originally had a broad blind arch to contain each group of four small arches (75), and the clerestory has simple single lights. The bays of the quadripartite high vault are rectangular between the great transverse arches of the nave, while each bay of the aisles is exactly square. Because the main arches across the nave are semi-circular, those forming the vaulting ribs are depressed to avoid an undulating crest-line between each bay (see Introduction, p. 48). Further features introduced in the first half of the twelfth century were the vaulted transepts and extended presbytery, each with a single square bay, projecting beyond the line of the aisle walls (cf. Modena, Pisa). Over the crossing of the nave and transept is a vaulted octagonal cupola with a drum built on squinches over the main piers. At the ends of the presbytery and transepts and in the east wall of the transepts are tall apses, each lit by three single lights. The presbytery, raised high over the crypt, is reached by a broad flight of seventeen steps from the nave. The vaulted crypt which extends beneath the presbytery and both transepts is entered by steps from the aisles. It is colonnaded with more than sixty varied marble shafts with twelfth-century figured capitals.

The exterior, of unfaced pinkish brick, has a unity emphasized by the almost classical rectilinear walls, the unbroken straight line of the roof-eaves and the continuous loggias round the carefully panelled walls and apses. Round the low octagonal cupola is an open loggia of triple arches in each face and a domical roof, crowned by a small lantern. The façade is a notable example of the type found between Parma and Milan. The heaviness of the broad surface of the wide single-gabled façade (cf. 11) is somewhat relieved by the three open loggias and particularly by the inclined upper one in line with the gables, but it has little of the imaginative appeal of the Pisan treatment of the same motif. The two projecting buttresses on either side of the central doorway are un-related to the interior; they are obscured by the double-decker porch with its columns standing on couchant lions. The simple gable of the upper tier and the reliefs of the "Months" in the soffits of the main arch were executed by the Campionese master Giambono da Bissone in 1281.

Two western towers were planned, but that at the north corner of the façade stands only a few feet high. The completed campanile, 198 feet high, was erected within ten years from 1284 and as a result has a most interesting stylistic unity. It is built of brick with stone-faced pilasters at the corners. The gentle taper from the base to the parapet and the unobtrusive pilasters and cornices of the four faces enhance its dignity. The single group of three pointed lights at the top is unusual, but the finial-cone was common before the introduction of elaborate lanterns, like that of the *Torre Ghirlandina* (70) at Modena.

There is a wealth of minor sculpture inside and outside the cathedral typical of twelfth-century Lombard practice. The earliest pieces are the capitals in the crypt, held by some to be part of the eleventh-century church. The greater part comprises the innumerable capitals and corbels of the nave arcade, triforium, clerestory and aisles, round the external loggias and doorways, carved with a rich variety of frankly secular subjects mingled with Biblical stories and vigorous zoomorphic and floral motifs. On the High Altar of red Verona marble are reliefs of Christ between the symbols of the Evangelists, Apostles and scenes of the martyrdom of saints. In the transept is a panel representing the Deposition of Our Lord sculptured by Benedetto Antelami in 1178, who may also, perhaps, have done the episcopal throne in the main apse. Antelami is one of the most celebrated Lombard sculptors of the late twelfth century and his most important and extensive work is in the adjacent baptistery.

During the fifteenth and sixteenth centuries the chapels opening out of the north and south aisles of the nave of the cathedral were added. Several of these chapels are lit by windows with Gothic tracery; that known as the Cappella Valeri on the north side is a fine example. Each contains tombs of illustrious citizens of Parma and is decorated with frescos of various dates and such minor furnishings as the elegant balustrades and grilles. The combined archiepiscopal and communal status of the cathedral is emphasized by the direct association of these chapels with civic institutions, which is not uncommon in North Italy. In about 1486 the gilded marble ciborium covering the thirteenth-century episcopal throne, and attributed to Alberto Maffeolo, was erected in the main eastern apse. This unhappy inspiration is only mitigated by the admirable bronze figures of the Evangelists by the brothers Da Gonzate (1508) which are placed along the low balustrade.

It is rare to find so complete a scheme of painted mural decoration of such quality in so great a church as this – the walls and vaults are coloured from end to end. The work was begun in about 1490 with the right transept (this part was faithfully redone in the eighteenth century), and continued throughout the sixteenth century. The *tour de force* is Correggio's celebrated Assumption of the Virgin (1522–30) which soars above the crossing in masses of clouds and among gliding graceful figures overriding the architectural form of the cupola. Correggio's personal influence established a Parmesan school of painting which is well represented in the cathedral, chiefly by Lattanzio Gambara who, between about 1560 and 1580, painted scenes from the life of Christ over the triforium arcade and the Ascension on the west wall. The panels of the vaults of the nave and presbytery are filled with heroic figures and variegated patterns, mostly by Girolamo Mazzola Bedoli (1556–70). This grandiose decoration which, by the depth of its perspective and range of colour, is in strong contrast with the Romanesque architecture, effectively augments the impressive grandeur of the interior, though large parts including the Assumption have sadly deteriorated.

The baptistery standing in the piazza at the south-west corner of the cathedral (73) is one of a small group of mediaeval octagonal baptisteries derived from that at Florence (*see* p. 53). Begun in 1196 its Romanesque form exhibits striking reflections of classical influence in the dominance of trabeated loggias and the imposing main arcade. But it has also an element of Gothic "verticality" resulting from the narrowness of the tall internal bays and the Gothic ribs of the cupola, completed in 1260.

The massive brick walls of the irregular polygon are faced outside in stone and inside largely with red Verona marble. The exterior has a curious appearance for a mediaeval structure. The massive ground storey is heavily arcaded on each of the eight sides with three portals deeply recessed in the nine-feet-thick walls. The blind-arcading contains the notable theme that is used throughout the building, the trabeated colonnade. This motif, in all probability derived directly from the Florentine baptistery, is used for each of the four upper tiers of loggias which run between the prominent flat buttresses at each corner (76). The topmost blind-arcade and the overhanging cornice merely face the wall which rises above the springing line of the cupola so as to pin down the outward thrust exerted by the cupola. The turrets at the top of the buttresses have a

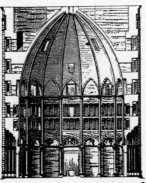

74 Parma: cross-section of the baptistery

similar function. By these means, the Lombard architect could avoid the trans-Alpine practice of using flying-buttresses in such circumstances. Internally the baptistery (74) is sixteen-sided with three irregular narrow apsidal recesses between the broader bays of the doorways and altar. The main arcade formed by these apses is surmounted by two tiers of trabeated loggias with columns in each angle rising from the floor to the springing of the ribbed cupola. Though it cannot be certain that Benedetto Antelami was the architect of the baptistery, the iconography of its rich plastic decoration is clearly due to his active supervision.

A splendid series of sculptures adorns the building both inside and out. In the tympana of the three doorways are represented with extraordinary ingenuity, the Allegory of Life from the "Golden Legend", and the principal scenes of the Life of the Redeemer, with the Last Judgement, and in the other bays are statues representing Solomon and Sheba, King David and Jacob. Round the lower walls is a frieze of creatures as in a bestiary. Inside there is a wealth of representational carving in the capitals and friezes, but most important are the scenes from the New Testament and the Life of David in the lunettes of the main arcade, and the free-standing figures in the first loggia representing the seasonal occupations of the months. All these are the work of Antelami and his assistants, and the carved marble altar is also from his shop. A considerable debt is owed for this iconographical scheme, and something of the style too, to the southern French schools, but Antelami was none the less a notably original artist. Of the two baptismal fonts the larger is double, having a quatrefoil-shaped basin within the main octagonal one. The decoration of the baptistery is completed by an extensive series of frescos occupying the cupola and the niches of the main arcade. They enlarge on the stories of the Old and New Testaments and represent in addition the Apocalypse and the mediaeval conception of the Universe. They seem to be mostly of the late thirteenth century and, while showing the continuance of Byzantine influence, are exhibits of new elements of importance in the development of Lombard painting.

FERRARA

THE city of Ferrara is situated in the delta and on the principal channel of the River Po. In winter the surrounding low-lying land is regularly flooded and frequently covered by dense fogs, while the summer sun turns it to dust. But the city is one of the most delightful in the Lombard Plain. Its mediaeval architecture is distinguished and the elegant accomplishments of its Renaissance rulers, the Este family, are reflected in the palaces and churches. On the death of the last of the Este line in 1598 the Duchy reverted to the administration of the Holy See until the unification of Italy.

The mediaeval cathedral of St George was remarkable for its size and for the strong northern Gothic nature of some of its principal features, but the east end was reconstructed in 1498, and during the early eighteenth century the rest of the interior was completely transformed. The first recorded cathedral of Ferrara stood in the earlier town on the opposite bank of the Po and the episcopal seat was transferred to the new church on the day of its consecration in 1135. According to inscriptions, work was begun in 1113, and the sculptor was named Nicola, a disciple of the "author" Guglielmo or Wiligelmo (see p. 171). What the original interior was like is known from early descriptions and from an eighteenth-century engraving; the noble exterior is well preserved. The church originally had a nave with four aisles and possibly a single short transept. The nave arcade had apparently pointed arches supported by alternate compound piers with attached shafts and single columns, a triforium gallery like that at Parma (75), in which pairs of triple round arches were similarly framed by blind arches; the clerestory was unusual in that it had a double row of four small windows in each of the ten main bays. From the nave piers pointed diaphragm arches rose to the starry blue coffered wooden ceiling. The main transverse arch over the High Altar was adorned with mosaic pictures of Angels and Prophets; one of the latter holds a scroll which records the consecration, sculptor and architect of the church; this is held to be the earliest verse written in colloquial Italian. As at Parma, the presbytery was raised above the nave and reached by a broad flight of nine steps. The form of the east end is not known as it was entirely reconstructed from 1498 to 1500 by Biagio Rossetti, who, as official architect to the ducal family, made of Ferrara "the first modern city in Europe". The semi-cylindrical apsidal presbytery of three bays is typical of his work. Externally, the neat, regular brick work, the elegantly shaped flat pilasters and precisely rounded blind arches with the repetitive stamped pattern of the terracotta cornices show his careful attention to the harmonious balance of each part. The interior was lit by sixteen windows, but four of these were closed at the end of the following century. This alteration was made for the sake of decorating the apse with painted stuccos by Agostino Rossi and Vincenzo Bagnoli in 1583, and an almost complete copy of Michelangelo's frescos in the Sistine Chapel was added by Bastianino. The

75 PARMA: the vaulted nave and raised presbytery, begun shortly after 1117

76   PARMA: a view of the baptistery (begun 1196), the campanile of 1284 and the south side of the cathedral

pilasters and cornice round the presbytery are probably part of Rossetti's work but the transept, which he also rebuilt, with the triumphal arch springing from a triple entablature (*cf. 85*) was altered in the seventeenth century and again in the eighteenth century.

The impressive Romanesque and Gothic exterior is entirely faced with stone (76). The façade and sides are given form and scale by arcaded loggias, almost identical with those of slightly earlier date at Modena. The transept which, by analogy, probably existed before Rossetti's time, did not project beyond the line of the outer aisles, so the apparent length of the nave is notably increased. The first loggia encircled the sides and façade at a uniform height and was part of the first period of building, that is, by Wiligelmo. In the façade are three doorways, of which the central one, in particular, is richly carved and contained by a projecting porch. The doorway is a deep recess with multi-ordered arch and jambs. On its tympanum is a fine equestrian St George and beneath it the architrave is carved with scenes from the early life of Christ. The lowest portion of the porch, banded in red and white marble, shows the hand of a different artist, probably Nicola, and is comparable with other work of his at Verona; the plastic decoration is more advanced in that the sculptured figures project from the surface, whereas Wiligelmo usually set them in recesses or niches, and altogether indicates a broader appreciation of classic models. The pairs of columns supporting the porch are upheld by sturdy caryatids sitting cross-legged on the backs of crouching lions (the originals of these have been replaced in modern times). The other doorways are less prominent but have mosaic pictures on the tympana. The next period of building introduced the Gothic element of the pointed arches which, in the loggias, are exceptionally close to the pure French Gothic form. The original and unfinished scheme derived from Lanfranc's work at Modena is visible along the south side, but it was altered across the façade by the imposition of pointed arches on the earlier Romanesque pattern. A second loggia with small pointed arches was added to the south side at a later date, but the north side still retains its original character. For the completion of the façade towards the middle of the thirteenth century, the original continuity of line with the walls was ignored. The new proportions of the horizontal divisions of the façade are essentially those of the North French School (*e.g.* Notre Dame, Paris), which contributed in addition the sheafs of small columns, deeply recessed arches and pierced quatrefoils. On the other hand, the triple gable with ascending loggias, the strong un-stepped buttresses and the rectilinear form of the upper storey of the porch are in the Lombard tradition. The loggia and gable of the porch are work of the late thirteenth century or early fourteenth century and the sculptured scenes of the Last Judgement indicate the direct influence of the followers of Nicola Pisano (p. 62). The terracotta Virgin and Child in the loggia is by Cristoforo da Firenze (1427). Pieces of another fine portal which, until 1720, stood in the middle of the south side, may be seen in the cathedral museum. They include a series of panels by Antelami (*see* p. 177) with lively scenes representing the occupations of the months.

The foundations and base of the massive marble campanile were laid in 1405 for Niccolò d'Este; work got no further until Borso d'Este had it continued in 1451 to the design of Alberti. Alberti had the satisfaction of giving Ferrara its first classical Renaissance works, the base of the monument to Niccolò III and this campanile. Four stages were completed by 1492 but the fifth and its lead-covered spire, in spite of good intentions, have not been added; hence its unhappy stunted appearance (*78*). Each stage is a cube faced with uncoupled pairs of arches and columns blind on two sides, and, on the other two, pierced by deep tall lights between prominent corner pilasters: the fourth stage is pierced on all four sides; between each is a strong cornice. The whole is a striking instance of Alberti's close study of the details of the classical monumental style.

In 1712, Cardinal Dal Verme, on the pretext that the internal condition of the cathedral was too serious to warrant restoration, determined to modernize it to the designs of one Mazzarelli; only the presbytery and the external shell were spared. The double-aisles were reduced to single-aisles with alternately large and small chapels forming, as it were, three transepts which project incongruously externally (*78*), and the floor was raised so that it was to be entered up six steps from the newly inserted narthex. The original spacious magnificence of the Romanesque cathedral (*cf.* 75) was entirely destroyed by this vast undertaking. The ponderous piers and arches of the nave and the barrel vault have little merit beyond that of size, and the decoration is in the tasteless manner all too often perpetrated in the eighteenth century.

MILAN

THE cathedral of Milan is the greatest Italian architectural project of the late fourteenth century and, with the exception of Seville, is the largest mediaeval cathedral. It was undertaken entirely on the initiative of the citizens and clergy of the city, the foremost in Lombardy. The surly despot Gian Galeazzo Visconti was only with difficulty persuaded to play any part in the great activity and troublesome negotiations that filled the early years. In contrast to this, one hundred years later, Ludovico Sforza, Il Moro, personally attended every discussion on the furtherance of the work. All classes of citizens contributed to the funds; indulgences were proclaimed and supplemented by a moiety of the donations from the whole province for the privileges of a Holy Jubilee made available in Milan instead of Rome. Where money was not to be had or was insufficient, willing bands of townspeople did the work.

On the site of the new cathedral stood several churches and other buildings; the greatest of these was the metropolitan basilica of S. Maria Maggiore, which had been rebuilt after being extensively damaged in the sack of the city by Frederick Barbarossa in 1162. This church remained standing for many years into the fifteenth century, while the lofty walls of the new east end and south transept rose round it; only when those parts had been well advanced was it finally demolished and with it the octagonal baptistery.

The actual date when the work was begun is quite unknown but it must have been well under way when, in 1387, Simone da Orsenigo was appointed "engineer and general master" on account of the work he had already done. The original designer remains anonymous and how far his initial plan was carried out is conjectural. The importance of trans-Alpine Gothic influence on the ultimate design (79) does not imply that in the first place the new cathedral was other than a product of the North Italian Gothic school, as it is represented, for example, at Como (15), Verona, Venice and Bologna. However, so imposing were the dimensions that a succession of French and German masters were

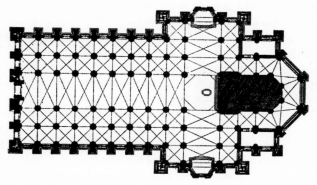

77 Milan, begun by 1387

invited to assist in solving the difficult structural problems involved. Not one of these stayed long enough, nor were the committees of Italian masters prepared to permit them, to give the work the unqualified stamp of the "High Gothic" style. It is the most considerable example of Italian transformation of trans-Alpine architectural elements and decorative motives in terms of the traditional Lombard sense of mass and geometrical design; while the flying buttress was adopted, the verticality of other Gothic structural members was negated at every possible point by a broadening of wall-surfaces and breaking of the continuity of line. In plan (77) the ambulatory and the short double-aisled transepts were accepted, but side-chapels in the nave, a triforium and aisles of equal height in the German style were vehemently excluded; nor was there to be a steeply pitched roof. The significant Italian insistence on a geometrically based design so early as 1391 is without parallel in North Europe. It was determined that the elevation should be built up on equilateral triangles so that each aisle should have half the width of the nave; the height of the springing of each aisle vault should be equal to twice, and two-and-a-half times, the aisle width respectively; the nave vault should start at a height twice the width of the nave, and so on, until the apex of the nave vault stand as high as the width of nave and aisles combined. This geometrical principle was logically pursued to govern the height of the cupola vault. The formula was established with the aid of a geometrician, Gabriele Stornaloco of Piacenza. Such mathematical calculations were no part of the practice of the German masters, like Heinrich von Eisingen, the architect of Ulm cathedral and of the left tower of Strasbourg cathedral, and the Frenchman, Jean Mignot. Yet it was the same Jean Mignot who bitterly remarked "art without science is nothing"; the Italian masters retorted that "science is one thing and art another". These alien masters were quite unable to countenance the Lombard techniques. They criticized all and everything, and even proposed to start again from the foundations; their greatest *bête-noire* was the unstepped buttress. So, in spite of the advice asked of and given by the "Gothic" masters, Milan cathedral was in fact erected almost entirely by Italian craftsmen.

The work began at the east end and by 1398 at latest the plan and details of the elevation, including the form of the walls, piers and capitals, had been established. In 1403 the first of the forest of pinnacles was put up, the "Guglia Carelli", and the only remaining problems were how to erect the main vault and what form the cupola and spire of the crossing should take. The vaulting, designed in 1410, was begun in the apse six years later and in the nave at the middle of the same

78 FERRARA: the great façade and the loggias of the south side, begun in 1113 and continued in the thirteenth century in the French Gothic style; the campanile begun 1405, continued by Alberti (1451)

79   MILAN: a view from the south-east. Begun little before 1387, the first pinnacle was added in 1403; the façade was undertaken in the seventeenth century and, with the north side, only completed in the nineteenth century

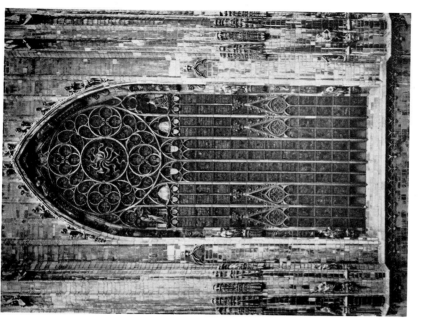

80 MILAN: the spire and high pinnacles seen from the roof; the lantern, designed by Amadeo and Dolcebono in 1490, was only given its spire in 1750

81 MILAN: one of the east windows of about 1390 – the largest in Europe

82   MILAN: the nave and choir of the fifteenth century

century, but was still not completed so late as 1576. The cupola was given most serious attention from 1390 when the stability of the main piers of the crossing was discussed. In 1481, Il Moro invited Johann Naxenperger of Graz to give his opinion, but the work he did had to be partly dismantled; in 1487 Leonardo da Vinci, Pietro da Gorgonzola and Bramante were called upon to provide models, but their respective proposals were not adopted. In 1490, Giovanni Amadeo and Giovanni Dolcebono entered for a competition. These two were disciples of Bramante who had already propounded the principles that should govern the design: conformity with the rest of the building, solidity, lightness and beauty. Bramante advocated that Amadeo's design be preferred even to his own; and it was accordingly followed for the cupola and the octagonal lantern above; the open-work spire, 350 feet high, was only begun in 1750. Although the façade was designed in 1653 it, with much else, remained incomplete, so that an engraving of 1735 shows the whole north side and main front devoid of pinnacles and even a permanent roof. Napoleon, in 1805, ordered the overdue completion of the work – at half the estimated cost of the old design. Bronze doors have been added in recent years and other details are still to be finished.

The fabric of this remarkable building is of brick, with facings and window mullions of pinkish marble from Candoglia where quarries, owned in perpetuity by the Cathedral Chapter, are still worked for all restoration purposes. The overwhelming complexity and detail of the ornamentation of the exterior defies close description, yet it conforms to the regular structural pattern with which it is integrated. The serried ranks of pinnacled and canopied buttresses on the massive plinth round the main walls, the labyrinth of pinnacled and fretted flying buttresses above the high aisles, and the slender perforated spire shooting up from the lantern give brilliant movement to the colossal body of the building. The majestic fourteenth-century polygonal apse at the east end is the finest and most attractive part. The three open faces of the apse, between the lofty unstepped buttresses at each angle, are occupied by spacious windows, almost flamboyant in the swirls of tracery that fill them (*81*). These windows were originally designed by Nicolas de Bonaventure (an Italian?) from Paris (1389–90), but modified by Filippo degli Organi who also made important contributions to the internal decoration; there are sculptured figures in the tracery as well as in niches in the concave jambs. The wall surfaces and the broad-faced buttresses are panelled with a screen of slender mouldings and canopied niches running up to a pierced frieze of cusped gables, pointed and ogee arches which lines the parapets and flying buttresses. All the other windows of the church are tall and relatively narrow with similar, though less rich, tracery. The great height of all the structural members, accentuated by the relative narrowness of the bays between the buttresses along the aisles, is counteracted by the scale and apparent weight of the series of canopies and niches with their statues. This method was employed to blunt the lines of pinnacles and turrets up which statues and gargoyles are marshalled in increasing numbers to the topmost finial. Saints serenely poised, giant ruffians on watchful guard, anxious men and women clinging to the precipitous walls and surrounded by grotesque corbels and gargoyles, make up this stony populace. There are sculptures in every style from the fourteenth to the nineteenth centuries, many by skilful masters, Italian, German and French; Milan became one of the most active centres for international art.

Above the marble paved high roofs of the nave and transepts, surrounded by the forest of pinnacles, stands the lantern, an outstanding triumph of engineering. The high windows of the octagonal lantern admit light to the interior of the church through the smaller windows of the inner cupola which was designed by Amadeo. The upper part continues in all its details the decorative friezes and pinnacles with flying buttress supporting the daring central needle on which the figure of the Virgin was placed in 1774. The octagonal spiral staircases emerging from the roofs and admitting to the lantern were also conceived by Amadeo with their imaginatively pierced inclined friezes (*80*).

Work on the façade (*79*), designed by Carlo Buzzi in 1653, was conducted along with the completion of the westernmost bays of the nave, and was well advanced in the first quarter of the eighteenth century. It is generally condemned because its Baroque pedimented windows are out of keeping with the Gothic fretwork and traceried windows. That is unjust to the architect, for none of these had been added so far west in the seventeenth or even eighteenth centuries. There have been many schemes for this façade, including contributions by English, French and German academic architects who have sought to apply the studied Gothic forms of their respective countries, with singular unconcern for the environment in which they would reproduce a York Minster, a Notre Dame or Strasbourg cathedral. The completion of the façade, by repeating the motifs of the flanks and forming a steep-sided gable of fretted arches and pinnacles, was quite out of keeping with the principles governing the application of Gothic elements in the earlier work; in fact this may be considered the part of the whole design most close to trans-Alpine Gothic. The buttresses alone have been treated consistently; the window-filled spaces between them are unrelated to their pattern; the treatment over the side-aisles is particularly unimaginative. The Baroque scheme, on the contrary, if completed, would have had the strength of unity and boldness. The massive pediments and consoles and the deeply carved tympana and jambs of the five portals, with the sculptured reliefs on the panels of the plinth and caryatids, are on a scale entirely consonant with the size of the building. The richly ornamented and sculptured bronze doors are the work of Ludovico Pogliaghi (1913), with the Life and Passion of Christ narrated on the great central doors and the Coronation of the Virgin above.

The vast interior, lofty and austere (82), is a mystery to North European taste. It seems to belong to the great Gothic building tradition and yet does not conform to it. The essence of this difference is the optical effect resulting from the Lombard idiom of plain surfaces of the walls and piers and the lowering weight of the diminished upper parts, the small nave arches and clerestory and the relatively low vault. The uniformity of the design was determined when the ambulatory and choir, the principal structural components for the east end, had been built. The tall piers, with eight slender attached shafts, rise up to the springing of the vaults in aisles and nave, but the unique tabernacled capitals set below the level of the inner-aisle vault dominate and weigh down their vertical lines. This perplexing feature designed by Giovannino de'Grassi was approved in 1398. The standing figures in the canopied niches range in style from that date, in the choir, to the eighteenth century, at the west end. The nave is otherwise devoid of all sculpture, but the tone of the pinkish marble walls gives warmth to the severe simplicity of its lofty and noble vistas. The broad-aisled transepts, each with a tall polygonal apsidal chapel at the end, traverse the body of the nave west of the choir. The east end is richer in sculpture and furnishings than the nave; in the ambulatory and sacristies, all completed by the end of the first quarter of the fifteenth century, are finely carved doorways and niches. This sculptured decoration preoccupied the committees almost as much as the structure. Numerous German and French sculptors were employed, and each introduced their own Gothic styles, different from that of the Italian Campionese masters. However, they were all assimilated to create an appropriate pictorial effect. Among these contributors were Johann Fernach, responsible for the tabernacle work over the door of the south sacristy,

Peter of France and Johann Marchestem. The principal Italian sculptors were Giacomo di Campione, who found a new vitality in his association with the foreigners, and Giovannino de'Grassi, whose skill as a miniature-painter is oddly apparent in his designs and sculptures for the great capitals of the piers (82). The glazing of the enormous east windows was begun by Filippino da Modena from 1419 to 1430, but much of this was reset in the mid-nineteenth century, and continued in the nave into the sixteenth century; it is the greatest expanse of coloured glass in Italy.

The high vaults of the aisles and nave were worked out in detail as early as 1410, but only slow progress was made in erecting them. The compartments of the great quadripartite ribbed vaults are filled with curiously florid tracery. The same style was adopted by Amadeo for the cupola which springs from the regular octagon formed by the pendentive squinches between the arches of the crossing. Between the ribs of the cupola vault are tracery-filled pointed half-windows corresponding with the lower part of those in the lantern. This was the design recommended by Bramante; his disciple Amadeo was not just a Vitruvian theorist but a master engineer, capable of conforming to a set style and of raising a strong enduring structure on foundations that had been roundly condemned as inadequate by many other masters.

The choir-stalls in rich marquetry with the splendid organs on either side, the two bronze pulpits with sounding boards encircling the main crossing piers, and the baldacchino of the High Altar were added under the direction of Pellegrini from 1572 to 1596 and largely completed by 1620. In the north transept is the seven-branched Trivulzio candelabrum, a late twelfth-century bronze work by Nicolas of Verdun, given to the cathedral in 1560 and possibly obtained from Durham cathedral at the Dissolution of the English monasteries in 1540. The entire marble pavement is richly inlaid.

In 1606 was begun the crypt chapel of S. Carlo Borromeo who, as Cardinal Archbishop, had consecrated the cathedral in 1577. The octagonal chapel beneath the raised presbytery floor is reached by a corridor from the eastward side and adjoins a confessio arranged beneath the main crossing; this chapel has no architectural merit.

The prolonged labour completing so grandiose a building took nearly five hundred years. The impressive result is a tribute to the persistent adherence of a succession of architects to the design of the mediaeval masters.

83   RIMINI: the interior showing the chapel of Isotta

84   RIMINI: the exterior by Alberti, 1450

85   PAVIA: the crossing and presbytery seen from the west, begun in
1488 and not completed until the 1930's. Basic design by Bramante

RIMINI

PERHAPS the most celebrated single monument of the fifteenth-century Renaissance, the Tempio Malatestiano at Rimini, also known as S. Francesco, is an outstanding expression of the humanism that gripped the lesser figures of the age. Its founder, Sigismondo Pandolfo Malatesta, tyrant of Rimini, won glory as a Florentine condottiere against King Alfonso of Naples and, later, with the Venetian armies against the Turks. To fulfil his desire to celebrate himself, his family and, above all, his union with Isotta degli Atti, for long his mistress and later his wife, he commissioned Leon Battista Alberti, the leading architect of his time, to design a temple worthy of the descendant of Scipio Africanus.

This mausoleum was not a completely new building, but was the late thirteenth-century conventual church of the Franciscans, in which Sigismondo had had two private chapels erected in 1447 and 1448 by Matteo de'Pasti. In 1450 Alberti produced a design for the exterior which was executed by de'Pasti, who continued as architect charged with the conversion of the interior. The two parts are therefore independent and radically different in conception. In his important book *De Re Aedificatoria*, presented to Pope Nicholas V in 1452, Alberti said he wished "there to be so much beauty in a temple (church) that none would imagine more elsewhere". Though incomplete, the exterior of the Tempio gives substance to his words; the harmonious interpretation of classic motifs for a new purpose carries the new style in architecture a great step forward in its development (*cf*. Ferrara, campanile).

The work was promoted with great zeal for a few years, but, in 1464, it came to a halt in the absence of Sigismondo. The Franciscans themselves had to add the roof and later to complete the east end as best they could. In the Second World War the Tempio was seriously damaged by bombs, though the sculptures survived unharmed, and in the subsequent restorations the eighteenth-century east end has been reconstructed, excluding only the unlamented later furniture; the adjacent cloister and convent were destroyed. The Tempio was only made the cathedral of Rimini, with the dedication of S. Colomba in 1809, at the instance of Napoleon.

While Alberti interpreted the work of Vitruvius he sought inspiration among existing classical buildings as well, and in the Roman gateway standing today in Rimini is the theme he employed for the central portion of the façade, whilst it is probable that the Arch of Constantine

in Rome with its triple arch was the source of the rhythmic pattern
(*84*). This is indeed the first instance of a direct use of the Roman
arch for such a purpose in the Renaissance. That was only a part of the
whole project, however, as is known from a contemporary medallion
on which it is engraved. The arches on either side of the porch were to
have been recesses containing sarcophagi; above the porch, the incomplete piers and pilasters were to have supported a round-headed
arch surrounding a smaller round-headed window enclosing a tympanum. The roof of the church was intended to be semi-circular in
cross-section and the curved roofs over the side-chapels would have
been concealed by a curved gable. The cupola, with which Alberti proposed to cover the whole width of the presbytery and church, was
based on principles deduced from his study of the Pantheon. In spite of
the non-completion of the façade, its lower storey and the impressive
recessed arcading of the side-wall screen standing on the plinth show
his mastery of classical form and his reaction against the increasing use
of trans-Alpine Gothic architecture in North Italy. The sober decoration and the form of an imperial triumphal arch are fitting for the
mausoleum of a humanist warrior as are the garlanded marble discs in
the spandrels of the arches, the frieze of coats of arms and the monogram SI of Sigismondo and Isotta on the plinth and on the jambs of the
porch. Round the walls in the niches are disposed the sarcophagi of
favourite courtiers, including the poet Basinio, and Valturio, the author
of the treatise *De re militari*; it was Rimini's little Pantheon.

Before Matteo de'Pasti was invited to Rimini in 1446, he had already
acquired a high reputation as a medallist in his native city of Verona.
He was thoroughly steeped in the elaborately picturesque Veronese and
Venetian Gothic style, in terms of which he interpreted his knowledge
of classical decorative motifs. His scheme for converting the interior
of the simple aisle-less Franciscan church was partially governed by the
chapels he erected before 1450, and by the proposals of Alberti for a
cupola.

Like the exterior, the nave was only partially completed. On each
side of the nave three large vaulted chapels were erected to which, in
1709, a fourth was added in imitation of them and the wide apse put
up (*83*).

The walls of the broad nave are broken by the tall, boldly pointed
arches of the chapels, which are symmetrically placed opposite one
another, setting a rhythm of recesses and wall spaces. The first chapel
on either side of the west entrance is succeeded by an enclosed sacristy
followed by two contiguous chapels, another wall space, and the single

eighteenth-century chapel beside the apse. There is no clerestory, so the nave is lit only by the west window and the pairs of single lights in each chapel.

An essential part of de'Pasti's scheme is the rich decoration of the piers and spandrels, the monumental tombs and altar pieces. To execute these he was assisted by the Florentine Agostino di Duccio, the Umbrian Matteo Nuti da Fano, and the Dalmatian Francesco Laurana. Together they created an exquisite, albeit almost entirely pagan, array of sculpture. The glorification of the Malatestas and their patronage of the arts are the subject of a constantly repeated text. Round each great arch and across the architrave of the façade runs the inscription SIGISMUNDUS PANDULFUS MALATESTA PAN. F. FECIT. ANNO GRATIAE MCCCCL. In the spandrels of the arches are wreathed coats of arms of the family and everywhere in balustrades, on shields and panels recurs the monogram SI. The sepulchre of Sigismund within the west door, the blue and gilded tomb and draped pavilion monument to his ancestors in the first chapel to the left, and the gilded monumental tomb of Isotta in the second chapel to the right (*83*), declare the pomp of the Renaissance court in a blend of classical and Gothic ornament. Framed between fluted pilasters the high-plinthed piers of the chapels are panelled with sculptured reliefs. Each chapel is dedicated to a saint, but is best known by the theme of its decoration or the memorial in it; on the side the chapel of St Sigismund, the theological and cardinal virtues in high relief; the Chapel of Isotta, di Duccio's low reliefs of angelic musicians; the Chapel of the Sacrament, the planets and signs of the Zodiac; on the north side, the Chapel of S. Gaudenzio, low reliefs of the personified Arts and Sciences, by di Duccio; the Chapel of "the Childish Games" played by winged *putti*; the Chapel of Ancestors, like that of St Sigismund, but with sibyls and prophets and the famous medallion bust of Sigismondo. The doorways of the former sacristies between the first and second chapels, like the altar niches in the main chapels, have classically inspired pediments, architraves and jambs; the one containing the fresco painted by Piero della Francesca has low reliefs of the Evangelists and Apostles and the other the Kings of Judah with Sigismund. The walls above them, like the wall-spaces towards the apse, are given texture by pilasters with shield-bearing figures against their plinths, standing on an elaborate festooned cornice which continues the line of the capitals of the piers.

The harmonious variety of coloured marbles, red, white and grey, the blue ground of the reliefs and the rich sculptural texture, give added brilliance to the imaginative delicacy of the figures and floral ornament. It is, however, the fusion of the classical and Gothic members that basically distinguishes de'Pasti's scheme from the profound thought behind Alberti's exterior; classical pilasters, cornices and altar niches are confidently placed beside the Veronese pavilions and windows, the Venetian balustrades, and the exotic elephants with the delicate vigour of the Tuscan artists.

PAVIA

In 1487 it was decided to build a new cathedral worthy of the ancient commune of Pavia. The citizens had long lamented the dilapidated condition of the pair of old churches which together served as the bishop's seat. A willing patron was found in their bishop, the Cardinal Ascanio Sforza, brother of Lodovico Il Moro, Duke of Milan, whose liberality and authority made the scheme possible. But, though the building was begun in that year, the progress made was slow and, in fact, the work continues even today.

The proposal by Cristoforo Rocchi, that a reproduction of S. Sophia in Constantinople be made, was rejected and a new plan by the same man was only tentatively accepted. Giovanni Amadeo was called in to modify the design and direct the work on the vast scheme. Amadeo was an architect of Milan cathedral and of the Certosa of Pavia at the time, and he had come under the influence of Bramante. Donato Bramante, one of the most significant architects of the Human-

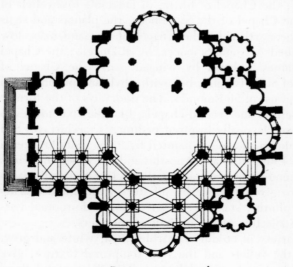

ist Renaissance (*see* p. 71) was himself, with Giovanni Dolcebono, directed to Pavia by Il Moro, to give his advice on the building. From that year, 1488, the work continued in accordance with his proposals; a brief visit made by Leonardo da Vinci is unlikely to have had any influence on it. A wooden model was made to

86 Pavia, 1488–1930's

guide the builders on the spot and Amadeo remained to supervise the construction. This model, now preserved in the Episcopal Palace, represents, in all probability, Bramante's intentions, though with some additions which resulted from a further review made by Amadeo, Dolcebono and Giovanni Fugazza. The building today (86) is a close likeness of the model, with two principal exceptions. The plan of the model is a Latin cross whereas Bramante probably intended what has now been made, an equal-armed or Greek cross; the elevation indicated by the model has since been heightened so altering the shape of the main arches and the clerestory. In 1760 a new model was made for the cupola which was ultimately erected at the end of the nineteenth century. The work has been completed with a close regard for that symmetry almost certainly intended by the original authors, in particular Bramante himself. The adoption of the Greek cross plan, as opposed to the Latin cross, is entirely consonant with the view of the leading architectural theorists of the Renaissance in that it afforded the perfection of architectural symmetry in every part. On being invited to prepare plans for the new St Peter's in Rome, Bramante produced a Greek cross design which was the germ of that mighty project. The character of Pavia cathedral has no little value as an indication of the texture and harmony that would have been given the Vatican basilica had he lived to carry out his most ambitious scheme.

The site of the cathedral of S. Siro was formerly occupied by the two small Romanesque churches of S. Stefano and S. Maria del Popolo. In the seventeenth century these were finally demolished, except for a part round the base of the contemporary campanile, to make way for the construction of the nave. The early changes made to the plan of the new work governed its final form. Only a limited part of the fabric is the certain work of Bramante himself, yet the whole effect of the interior (85) depends on the strictly economical concept of space and line that is the strength of his architectural style. The surfaces of the walls and piers are broken just enough to prevent monotony, and then only to strictly controlled architectural principles, by the foliate capitals, the projecting cornices, the subdued gallery and the circular clerestory windows; beyond these there is a bare minimum of superficial decoration. The interior is entirely faced with marble, slightly mottled and flaxen coloured.

From the beginning progress was slow. By 1492 the crypt had been completed to Bramante's design; its broad low arches and massive square piers supporting groined vaults, and the plain eye-shaped windows in the apses, are powerfully austere. Above it, the lower walls and windows of the main eastern apse, also by Bramante, are the pattern for the others completed in recent years. Externally, the five tall, narrow windows, with simple triangular pediments and lightly moulded jambs and sills, are separated by shallow pilasters standing on a massive plinth. Internally, the windows appear as deep round-headed niches completing the semicircle of the apse in seven bays and overtopped by a sharply contoured architrave which runs round each arm of the apse and each aisle. In the same year an order was made to build the polygonal octofoil sacristies. There were to have been four of these, one in each angle between the arms of the cross; but only two have yet been completed. These share the same pure style of the apses, with pilasters and niches giving way to round windows and a ribbed cupola vault. The main apse was completed in 1507, but just 100 years later, the exactly semicircular arch between it and the choir was raised. This change set the pattern for all the arches (85) and was the first significant alteration to the fifteenth-century design; it was in keeping with seventeenth-century taste but loosened the firm relation between the main storey and upper parts. The presbytery was vaulted and then work again ceased. From 1647 the piers of the octagon and parts of transepts and the nave were slowly erected and vaulted.

By 1760 it was possible to consider raising the cupola; it was to become the third largest in Italy, after those of St Peter's and Florence cathedral. A new model was made and the original design altered. From the new design only the drum was put up; its single heightened gallery took the place of a design comprising a gallery and splayed circular windows (cf. Florence). Only in 1884–85 was the cupola added with its lantern by the Milanese architect Carlo Maciachini, who conformed so far as possible to the fifteenth-century design.

Had it been decided to complete the ambitious nave of eight bays, as suggested in the wooden model, the cathedral would have been some 650 feet long, longer indeed than St Peter's, Rome, without its narthex. It was a happy decision to place the façade three bays from the octagon, leaving the nave equal in length to the other arms, even though, when this was first agreed in 1811, it was proposed to erect an infelicitous neo-classical façade and cupola. The façade, finally constructed in 1895, follows in its principal features the outline of the old model, with loggias matching those inside, above and below a central round window. As recently as 1930 the north and south apsidal arms were undertaken and have now been completed, 450 years after the first stone was laid. There is still the facing of the brick walls to be done externally, and possibly the western pair of sacristies to be built, but the idea of placing campanili on either side of the nave has long been rejected. Internally, at least, the great scheme to which Bramante and his followers gave form has been realized. It has been kept remarkably free of misplaced furniture and decoration. The altars in the main apses and those in the small apsidal chapels off the aisles have been limited to suitable proportions, while the seventeenth-century carved circular pulpit on the south-east pier of the crossing is an admirable example of the type also to be seen in Milan cathedral.

Liguria

GENOA

THE cathedral of S. Lorenzo at Genoa has a chequered architectural history. The first use of the site for the cathedral was in 985, in place of that of S. Siro. In keeping with the general movement of great church building, the present cathedral was begun in 1100 by the Consuls of the Republic, and the consecration by Pope Gelasius II took place in 1118. But, owing to the serious damage caused by fire in 1296, only part of this Romanesque work survives. The most important relic of that building, probably in fact the last part to be constructed, is the main façade. The nave was reconstructed in Gothic style in the first half of the fourteenth century. In the sixteenth century the interior at the east end was entirely redesigned and the cupola was raised over the crossing. As part of the general restoration undertaken in the nineteenth century, the piazza in front of the façade was lowered, greatly exaggerating the height of the west end.

The proximity of Genoa and Liguria to France facilitated the influence of trans-Alpine Gothic design on its architecture when, in the Middle Ages, the Republic maintained itself aloof from Lombardy and was not noted for its patronage of the arts. From the fifteenth century onwards, however, many noted artists from Lombardy, Tuscany and Rome left their mark in Genoa and, in the following century, Genoese artists of note made their appearance. A reserved people, the sea-faring Ligurians are more adventurous in commerce than art.

The west front of the cathedral seems to have been begun in the mid-thirteenth century, when French influence was at its height. The three great doorways with their deep recesses were direct Gothic importations. The multiple orders of the arches, moulded with dog-tooth chevron and spiral patterns, are supported by sheafs of colonnettes.

In the tympanum of the central porch is a bold relief of Christ in Glory between symbols of the Evangelists; on the architrave is represented St Lawrence on the gridiron of his martyrdom. On the jambs of the same portal are low reliefs relating the ancestry of Christ and the Mysteries of the Virgin. In spite of the part played by the French, the buttresses between the portals at the corners of the façade are unstepped in the Italian fashion; the central portion, with a fine wheel-window beneath the gable, is sandwiched between two massive towers up which rise the main buttresses. Only the south tower has been completed (1522); the north tower reaches as far as the nave roof, where it is terminated by a loggia designed by Giovanni di Gandria in 1427. The stages of the towers are marked by thin cornices, with three double lights, a single quadruple light and a single double light in ascending order from above the minor portals. The whole façade is banded horizontally after the Tuscan fashion with alternate courses of black and white stone above the portals, which are red and white with white stone sculpture. On the side of the north tower and in the walls of the south aisle are small twelfth-century portals, carved with men and beasts; over each is a loggia of later date.

Immediately within the entrance is an uncommon internal narthex or galilee; this seems also to have been constructed before the fire. It is vaulted in French style, with above a gallery which is lit by the wheel window. Where the narthex joins the side-aisles are the springings of the vaults intended by the French masters but not carried out. The nave (87) is in striking contrast to the richly decorated presbytery and transepts. The main arcade of classical columns on black marble Romanesque bases has moulded pointed arches on fine classical composite and twelfth-century Romanesque figured capitals. The brief space of black-and-white banded wall above the arcade is surmounted by a triforium of alternate piers and columns corresponding to the nine bays of the nave. The walls above, together with the round-headed arches and small clerestory, were completed without banding at a later date. The triforium is of the false variety in that it only forms a decorative screen between aisles and nave; the high aisles were vaulted at the same time as the nave, in 1550. During the fifteenth century two chapels were constructed on the north side of the aisle. The smaller of the two, the Cappella dei Fieschi, was given its fretted arch and cusped gable, with floral bas-reliefs in the spandrels, by Giovanni Gagini. Working in Genoa in the 1450's, Gagini imported the florid Gothic decorative technique widely found in Lombardy from the cathedral of Milan to St Mark's, Venice. At about the same time his brother Domenico, who

87 GENOA: the nave and "false" triforium from the east end of the south aisle, built during
the first half of the fourteenth century

88 GENOA: the north transept of about 1550 and the seventeenth-century organ

89 TURIN: the cathedral by Meo del Caprina, 1497; the campanile of 1469 with the lantern added by F. Juvara in 1720; the larger cupola is the Chapel of the Holy Shroud

90 TURIN: Chapel of the Holy Shroud by G. Guarini, 1668

had also had some experience in Tuscany, began the façade of the adjacent chapel of St John the Baptist which has panels in relief and a frieze of cusps and statues in the most ornamental Milanese manner.

The transformation of the presbytery and transepts was completed by 1550. The main entablature supported by giant fluted pilasters is surmounted by rectangular attic windows and a lofty barrel vault. Between the pilasters in the apse are single pointed windows set in square frames; between the attic lights are statues of St John the Evangelist, St Mark and St Luke. The richly frescoed vault, typical of Genoese work, depicts the judgement and martyrdom of the patron saint. The effect of this decoration is accentuated by the narrowness of the presbytery. The side-apses, refaced in the second half of the sixteenth century in similar style, are adorned with grandiose wall paintings by the Genoese Cambiaso. The octagonal cupola, designed by disciples of Galeazzo Alessi of Perugia, with its tall drum and narrow windows, rises high above the stilted crossing-arches. This gem of early Genoese Baroque is most effective in the transepts, where the richly decorated walls and the superb organ cases by Gian Antonio Ansaldo form a most harmonious ensemble (*88*).

Piedmont

TURIN

THE present cathedral of Turin, dedicated to St John the Baptist, was built on the site of three other churches which, reconstructed during the eleventh century, had existed from as early as the fifth century just within the gates of the Roman city. The close relations between the cathedral and the Palace of the Dukes of Savoy, subsequently Kings of Piedmont and Sardinia, the first kings of united Italy, have given it a particular place in history. In the seventeenth century the Chapel of the S. Sindone, the Shroud of Christ, was erected and became the mausoleum of the eighteenth-century kings (they were not buried in the Superga, Juvara's centrally planned masterpiece on a hill overlooking the city).

The cathedral church was built by Amadeo da Settignano, known as Meo del Caprina, and finished in the year 1497. Meo del Caprina was a Florentine artist whose reputation lies rather in his transmission of the forms of Renaissance architecture to Piedmont than in his originality. His work reflects the influence of Brunelleschi, Alberti and others, as has become more readily appreciable since the removal of heavy Baroque ornament in recent years. The plan of the church follows closely that of Brunelleschi's S. Lorenzo in Florence. The single aisles with shallow side-chapels are each a little narrower than the nave. Over the crossing of the nave and transepts, which overlap the outer line of the aisles, is an octagonal cupola. The east end was square, but has since been altered to provide a link with the Chapel of the Shroud. Externally the simple stone-faced upper and lower walls have an unpretentious entablature at the line of the roof-eaves, supported by flat pilasters and Tuscan capitals. Just as Alberti had utilized the theme of the classical triumphal arch for his façade at Rimini so Meo del Caprina sought to do so here (89). The outline of the façade is neatly composed, with coupled pilasters at the angles of the aisles and nave supporting the entablatures, giving proportion to the units of the structural pattern united by the gentle volutes between the nave and aisles. The simple pair of upper windows and the elegant pedimented portals combine the simplicity of northern Renaissance design with the architect's own sculptural decoration. The pilastered jambs and the spandrels of the doorways are attractively carved with trophies, putti and festoons. The church is dwarfed by its imposing campanile and the adjacent palace buildings. The campanile was built in 1469, but collapsed and had to be rebuilt in 1720 by Filippo Juvara, who added the stone-faced belfry with its groups of pilasters and columns at each corner supporting the full entablature and attic storey.

The austere but harmonious nave and single-aisles of seven bays have a stately arcade of semicircular arches between composite piers with attached half-shafts and Tuscan capitals. The half-shaft on the face of each pier is extended upward to support the depressed unribbed main vault. The vault springs from a plinth of Tuscan capitals between the clerestory windows, whose plain splayed rounded heads are framed by the smooth pendentives of the vault. The wide vaulted side-aisles are given colour and depth by the row of recessed chapels, the majority of which contain fifteenth-century altars, pedimented and richly decorated with festoons and twisted painted columns; one at least, the Cappella dei SS. Crispino e Crispiniano of the city gild of shoemakers, was transferred from the earlier church, thus perpetuating its traditions. The simple crossing, with slightly stilted semicircular arches on pilastered piers, is reduced to a small octagon by squinches on which stand the corbelled gallery and lofty windowed drum of the cupola. The transepts are filled with the late seventeenth-century organ to the south and the Royal Pew or gallery to the north. The presbytery is one of the most curious imaginable; behind the massive high altar, with its gilt-bronze corner pieces and array of candlesticks, is a screen of heavy wooden panelling and glass doors reaching up to the vault. Behind this screen may be discerned the Chapel of the Shroud. The aisles of the presbytery are occupied by the massive portals of this chapel, erected by Guarino Guarini in 1668 between the cathedral and the palace. The giant columns and fine staircases, all in black marble, make a sombre entry to the polygonal vaulted hall. The interior (90) is as forbidding as the exterior is bizarre (89). The main order of fluted pilasters supporting the entablature divides the walls into eight bays in which are arched recesses with broken entablatures on minor columns and pilasters. This classic formula is overwhelmed by the heavy frieze of corniced panels and broken pediments with tasteless festoons and scallop shells, and by the great circular windows surrounded by tortured panels and whirls. The vault rises up by tier on tier of flat arches diminishing towards the lantern, and appears from outside like an extravagant dove-cot above the well-designed windows. The Holy Shroud was transferred to the chapel in 1694 and encased in the shrine; it is only rarely exhibited. The monuments to four of the Dukes of Savoy and Kings of Piedmont and Sardinia were set up by King Carlo Alberto (1831–49). These monuments occupy niches round the walls of the mausoleum and add to the confusion of carved ornament.

Salernitano

THE province of Salerno and the hilly sea-girt fastnesses of the
Amalfitano, to the south of Naples, have rarely known the
blessings of peace or of plenty from the soil, but the inhabitants
have in the past won considerable wealth from trade and commerce on
the seas. Throughout their history they have succumbed to attacks
from the sea, but rarely from inland. In spite of all disadvantages the
small towns along the coast, celebrated for its natural beauty, contain
fine, even exotic, monuments. There is a brilliance in the variety of
their fortunes and the mingling of diverse cultures, Greek, Roman,
Saracen and Norman, represented by the Greek temples of Paestum,
the Republic of Amalfi, and the mediaeval medical school of Salerno.

SALERNO

IN 1077 the Norman adventurer Robert Guiscard conquered Salerno
and made it his capital. He personally provided the money for its new
cathedral, dedicated to S. Maria degli Angeli by Pope Gregory VII in
1084. One of the earliest of the great churches erected by the Normans
in their Italian territories, it suffered damage from earthquake in 1688,
and early in the eighteenth century was internally refaced by archbishops Poerio and Perlas. Nearly all the twelfth-century furnishing is
preserved, and the benevolent restorations of recent years have carefully revealed many of the church's most striking mediaeval features,
without prejudice to the work of the eighteenth century (92).

Leading to the church is a rectangular atrium (91), the eleventh-
century entrance of which (called the *Porta dei Leoni*, from the lions,
Strength and Charity, on either side at the top of a flight of steps) has
a tympanum over the architrave and carved jambs, like the main doorway of the church. The columns of the atrium arcade were brought
from Paestum, while the stilted arches and the arcade of the upper
cloister show the mark of Saracen architecture, with white, black and
yellow coloured walls, inlaid with geometrical patterns and roundels.
The central stoup, formerly in the middle of the nave, replaces a great
basin from Paestum (now in the National Museum, Naples). The
robust square campanile of the twelfth century, on the south-east

91   SALERNO: the façade seen from the atrium, *c.* 1080

92   SALERNO: the eleventh-century nave remodelled at the beginning of
the eighteenth century

93 AMALFI: the façade, rebuilt after 1861, and the twelfth-century campanile

94 RAVELLO: the ambo on the south side of the nave, 1272

95   AMALFI: the nave remodelled 1701–31

96 MOLFETTA: a view from the north-west showing the three roofed cupolas, two complete and one unfinished campanile of the late twelfth century

corner of the atrium, has a plain double light in each side of the three storeys above the basement, and is surmounted by an eighteenth-century cylindrical belfry (*cf.* Amalfi). The basilica has a broad nave with single aisles, a simple clerestory and timber roof, a transept across the east end (like Old St Peter's and Messina), with three apses, and simple fenestration. It is, in fact, the type for the majority of churches built in, around and south of Rome, during the eleventh and twelfth centuries. The three doorways of the church, especially the centre one, are not unlike those of similar date at Pisa. The bronze main doors have on them silver-damascened figures of Christ, St Matthew and other saints, along with the donors who had them made at Constantinople in 1099.

The interior of the nave (*91*) represents a sober Baroque manner not uncommon in the Kingdom of the Two Sicilies during the eighteenth century. The rhythm of the six bays of the main arcade and the elegant vault, springing from the bold cornice of the architrave, contribute to an unusually satisfying solution to the problem of the conversion of an ancient building to a "modern" style. The piers enclose the classical columns of Guiscard's church and, with the stilted arches, have been uncovered at the east end of the aisles. The long transept, raised five steps above the nave, has had its open timber-work roof restored, interlacing arches round the top of the walls have been exposed, and the single window of the main apse opened. The mosaics in these apses and on the upper walls of the transepts are in a much damaged state; those in the main apse have been admirably designed and executed anew by modern restorers of the Ravenna mosaics.

The twelfth-century furniture of the church is important not only for its completeness, but also because its mosaic decoration is the product of a local school. This school is strictly a part of that which flourished in Norman Palermo, and is to be distinguished from that of Rome. The skill available for preparing a greater variety of shapes than seems to have been possible in Rome, made possible far more complex and delicate patterns, including flowers, birds and animals, with a greater colour range. These were combined with imaginatively carved cornices, bosses, capitals and figures (*see* also Ravello and Monreale). The arrangement of the furniture is indicative of the general practice, and all of it is richly adorned. A wall, formerly with a pointed entrance arch (now in the sacristy), forms the enclosure or iconostasis of the paved choir and sanctuary. The choir is separated from the sanctuary by the transept and in the apse is the throne used by Gregory VII during his exile from Rome (he is buried in the right-hand apse). In front of the iconostasis are two great pulpits or ambos with lecterns attached, sumptuously decorated and supported by columns; against the right-hand ambo is a slender paschal candlestick. In other churches, individual pieces like these survive, but few so fine or forming such a complete series.

Beneath the transept is a crypt with three aisles and apses, faced with coloured marbles, by Domenico Fontana and his son, late in the sixteenth century. Here are interred the remains of St Matthew the Evangelist, brought to Salerno in 954 by the Lombard prince Gisulph I.

AMALFI

THE ancient Republic of Amalfi achieved great wealth and fame by its vigorous maritime trade. Its depots were located in every important port round the Mediterranean and the Black Sea, and the "Amalfi Tables" were the commercial law of the eleventh century. Living on a coast, inaccessible from the interior and devoid of fertile lands, the Amalfitani directed all their energies seawards, and were renowned for their independent spirit. The Republic had grown up by the late ninth century and lasted until its sack by the rival Pisans in 1135, but throughout much of a chequered history nominal allegiance was owed to a succession of alien powers, Byzantines, Normans and, later, various Italian princes.

An earlier cathedral was enlarged in the tenth century but completely rebuilt in 1203 and this basilica, formerly dedicated to the Assumption and now to St Andrew, was several times restored before the interior was converted in Baroque style, at the beginning of the eighteenth century. After the collapse of the façade in 1861, it was rebuilt on the scanty evidence of a few thirteenth-century fragments, though none can deny that the late nineteenth-century architects placed alongside the exotic campanile a truly enchanting composition, well suited to its picturesque setting (93). The cathedral, closely surrounded by the houses of the town, hemmed in by the steep cliffs of the valley behind, and the sea in front, is raised high up on a steep flight of sixty steps over streets tunnelled beneath. The design of the double-aisled and vaulted narthex or portico is a blend of Moorish and Gothic styles, with black and white banding, like a mediaeval Tuscan Church, and with decorative mosaics round the doorways and in the main gable. The fine bronze main doors were made in Constantinople before 1066 by Simeon of Syria, who was commissioned, according to an inscription, by the donor Pantaleon, head of the important Amalfitan colony there. On each door are twelve panels, the central group of four containing silver-damascened figures of Christ, the Virgin, St Andrew and St Peter in typically formal Byzantine style; in each of the other panels is bolted an elaborate cross. The jambs of the door way are carved in low relief, with a projecting architrave above and a half-round arch.

The elaborate decoration of the interior (1701–31) (95), of the main bays and rounded main apse, the square side-apses and short transept, completely hides the thirteenth-century fabric, which is only partially visible externally from the cloister. Originally there were probably double-aisles, now reduced to single-aisles and a row of side-chapels. The rich marble facings of the piers concealing the old columns, the applied stucco reliefs and the wooden ceiling, gilded and moulded with panels painted by Andrea Dell'Asta, are a highly successful creation in the ornate Neapolitan Baroque style (cf. Salerno). The architectural frame of the High Altar and the delicate glass chandeliers are happy accompaniments to the harmonious decorative scheme. In the sanctuary are two thirteenth-century ambos and two candelabra, inlaid with mosaic like those at Salerno. The crypt, divided into two aisles by piers, was renovated in 1719, with marble-veneered walls and piers and with frescoed stucco vaults, to the designs of Domenico Fontana. Beneath the altar are the relics of St Andrew brought here in 1208, from either Constantinople or Patras in Greece.

From the narthex can be reached the curious Cloister of Paradise, on the north side of the cathedral, designed as a cemetery for worthy citizens between 1266 and 1268. There is no more compelling evidence of Saracen influence than its simple white walls with triply-interlaced arcading and plain double columns; the walks are barrel-vaulted cross-wise, with open lights in the walls above the arcading. In glittering contrast is the twelfth-century campanile, sturdily squat but surmounted by turrets, on which the interlaced arcading and arches are picked out in bright colours sharpened by glazing (93).

RAVELLO

ON a ridge among the valleys behind Amalfi is Ravello; it, too, has a cathedral, but it has suffered heavily from neglect. The cathedral of S. Pantaleone was founded in 1086 in the simple basilican style of the region. Its general outlines are preserved with a robust detached campanile at the east end. The eighteenth-century refacing of the interior and exterior has no architectural distinction, but the interesting mediaeval furniture is well preserved. In front of the church, on the raised plinth, are four columns, part of a demolished narthex. The main doors, as at Amalfi and Salerno, are of bronze, but here they were made in 1179 by the outstanding craftsman Barisano da Trani (*cf.* Trani). They are divided into fifty-four main panels separated by raised and embossed strips, and in the panels are the low reliefs of saints (*104*), scenes of the Passion of Our Lord and men fighting.

In the nave stand two outstanding examples of the skill of the mosaic workers and stone carvers of the local school in the twelfth and thirteenth centuries. On the north side is a small ambo with a double staircase, made about 1130; it is a rare example of the type used in and around Rome. An eagle-lectern projects from the central platform and the marble side panels are inlaid with delightful, moralizing pictures in mosaic of Jonah being swallowed and disgorged by a green dragon-like whale. The decorative peacocks and flower capitals are imaginatively made of various marble shapes. The restored larger pulpit (*94*) on the south side was, according to an inscription, made by Niccolò di Bartolommeo da Foggia in 1272, at the expense of Niccolò Rufolo, husband of Sigilgaita della Marra, the remains of whose family's palace are near the cathedral overlooking the sea. The high box of the pulpit, beneath which is a small oratory, is reached by a walled staircase. The richly carved cornices and capitals are abundant with flowers and crisp foliage; within the roundels of the formal mosaic pattern on the panels are the Paschal Lamb, the Virgin and Child and birds, while the twisted columns contain unusual star-spangled designs. The pretty lion feet are in the South Italian tradition from which, in all probability, Nicola Pisano had by this date drawn inspiration for his pulpits at Pisa and Siena. As well as the noble eagle-lectern there is, over the staircase entrance, a finely expressive diademed female head, whether of Sigilgaita or symbolical of the church it is not possible to say. There are also in the sanctuary an episcopal chair, in early style, and antique columns for candlesticks.

97 BARI: the nave and main apse built after 1156

98 BARI: the window of the main apse with rich carving of the Apulian school, after 1156

99   BARI: the south transept, nave, cupola and northern campanile seen
from the south-west

Apulia

THE plains of Apulia and the "heel" of South-East Italy are a
backward region today, notwithstanding beneficial developments
undertaken in this century. Over-population, the uncertainty of
crops, and a disastrous history of prolonged feudal tenure, blight much
fertile countryside. It has not always been so, for during the early
centuries of our era Apulia was noted for its grain and wool production,
and during the Middle Ages too its situation was highly favourable to
trade. The population is largely concentrated in numerous agricultural
towns. The Byzantine Catapans, representing the authority of the
Eastern Emperors, maintained a hold on this their last province in Italy
until the eleventh century, when they were finally ousted by the rebel
inhabitants. Factions among these called on Norman mercenary forces
for aid, and by 1070 the newly established communal institutions had
come under the control of Robert Guiscard, who assumed the title of
Duke of Apulia and Calabria. This unification, however much it may
have been disturbed by feudal dissidence, encouraged trade and
increased the wealth of the towns. Brindisi, an ancient Roman port,
and Bari, acquired particular importance as entrepôts for the luxury
trade with the Orient and as bases for the Crusades, though after the
greatest period, during Frederick II's reign, they suffered heavily in the
face of increasing Venetian power.

Little survives today of the monuments of the Byzantine period
beyond fragments incorporated in later buildings. The Normans, on the
other hand, have left an enduring record of their activity and wealth in
the numerous cathedrals and other churches they founded in the towns.
The independent development of Apulian architecture and sculpture
(98) has been called precocious by those best acquainted with more
northern Romanesque, but its brilliance is to be referred to a wider
circle of influences and owes much to the excellent quality of the local
freestone. Nor is this a mere provincial expression of Lombard art,
however much the style may owe to Lombard practice; its final products are quite distinctive. The great stone-built churches of Apulia
demonstrate a unique and effective assimilation of mediaeval Roman
planning, with accessory Byzantine, Saracen and Lombard features to

which the Normans contributed their ambitious craving for the massive and monumental. The Apulian style is simpler than that promoted by the Norman Royal Court at Palermo, but little less imposing; the hall-mark of the Norman is as readily recognized here as in England, Normandy or the Holy Land.

The prototype of the Apulian Romanesque style is the Palatine basilica of S. Nicola at Bari. From there a vigorous architecture developed, as in the cathedrals of Trani (*105*), Bari (*97*), and Troia (*103*), and persisted into the fourteenth century. A subsidiary group of Apulian churches is represented by the late twelfth-century Old Cathedral of S. Corrado at Molfetta (*96*). This type is characterized by the line of three hemi-spherical cupolas on octagonal drums over the nave, supported by the high round-headed arches surrounding each of the corresponding three bays; a combination of Byzantine and Roman-esque elements. Its bizarre appearance would have been the more striking if the two sturdy western towers had been completed with the slender eastern pair.

The neglect by the Angevins of their new possession, the Kingdom of Sicily (which included some mainland provinces), is reflected in the very limited diffusion of the alien Gothic style, current in France in the late thirteenth and fourteenth centuries, which the Angevins planted in their capital, Naples, and in Sicily. The appearance of Gothic forms in this part of the country is as uncommon and surprising as that of Pisan Romanesque design at Troia and in its vicinity. The few Gothic buildings, like Lucera and the east end of Barletta cathedral rebuilt with a chevet, are direct importations of that style.

The increasing poverty of the south, associated with the decline in political and economic fortune under the Spanish House of Aragon, has left a great gap in the history of its art. By the end of the eighteenth century, Apulia was one of the poorest parts of Italy. During the seventeenth and eighteenth centuries many churches were turgidly modernized in the Baroque manner. In one centre only the spirit of the Baroque is truly outstanding; at Lecce, where a local stone of a warm golden colour made vigorous carving possible and permanent, a great part of the town, including the cathedral, was enhanced by this purely local style which flourished from the mid-sixteenth century to the late eighteenth century. It is marked by the essentially Spanish inspiration of its exuberant decoration. But the structure of the buildings is in the standard style evolved in Rome and the essays in decoration show a marked indifference to correlation with the architecture. As a minor example, the seventeenth-century north façade of Lecce cathedral (*18*) exhibits its theatrical and almost wholly alien, though not ungracious, nature; bizarre in effect, it is the fruit of a rare fantasy.

Many of the Romanesque cathedrals of Apulia have been rebuilt or ornamented excessively, so losing their real architectural value; some of these have been restored to their original state in recent years.

BARI

THE greatest Byzantine centre in the west after 875, the important port of Bari was the residence of the Byzantine governor, the Catapan, and has continued to be the principal city of the province. There are two great churches in Bari; one is the cathedral and the other the palatinate and pilgrimage church of S. Nicola. When the city, including the cathedral, was virtually destroyed in 1156, only the Benedictine church of S. Nicola, built in 1087 within the "Court of the Catapan", survived. As the prototype for the greater Norman churches in Apulia it has a special interest, and some reference to it must be made if only to emphasize the importance of certain parts of the cathedral.

The present cathedral, dedicated to S. Sabino, was rebuilt after the destruction of 1156 and, largely completed sometime early in the thirteenth century, was consecrated in 1292. Although in its salient features the cathedral is similar to S. Nicola, its design was modified in the light of certain developments made in Lombardy in the first half of the twelfth century. This influence appears both internally and externally. The most characteristic and striking features are the strong simplicity of the stone wall masses, the long transept, standing as high as the tall narrow nave, and the deep arched recesses along the sides of the aisles. The apses of the east end are screened by a wall constructed so that, in plan (*100*), the cathedral appears to consist of two main rectangular blocks forming a T. Symmetry governs the arrangement of each part. The gabled west front with its rose-window and sparse small and round-headed windows, the flat buttresses and the carved friezes outlining the high narrow nave emphasized by the high shoulders of the steeply pitched aisle-roofs, has a simple dignity typical of the churches of the period in the region. The three portals, now altered by eighteenth-century Baroque additions, were originally quite plain, with a simple retaining arch above the architrave (*cf. 70*), though the main door probably once had a gabled porch, as at S. Nicola. The arcaded cornices of the aisles are corbelled with

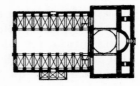

100 Bari, begun c. 1156

221

a variety of animal heads, which recur in the seven fine gargoyles round the hood of the rose-window. The tracery of the rose-window has been entirely lost, but is curiously recorded in the pavement of the nave and was similar to those in the transepts (99). The cornices across the façade continue round the side-walls of the nave and aisle and the drum of the cupola. Their ornament of stiff entwined foliage and the necklace-like motifs round some of the window jambs, show the flat conventional form of Saracen decoration. The tall deep arcading along the aisle walls surmounted by an arcaded gallery and multiple cornice (cf. 105) has little similarity to the shallow arcading of Lombardy. It seems, rather, a direct adaptation of the imposing arches of a Roman gateway or aqueduct, and, introduced early in the twelfth century in S. Nicola, is frequently met in Apulian churches; the gallery, too, was often made particularly attractive.

Although an imposing array of towers, one at each corner of the church, was intended at S. Nicola, as was later completed at Palermo (119), the cathedral has a central cupola and two towers over the eastern corners of the transept, flanking the central apse. Only one of the towers stands today, the other, which collapsed during an earthquake, reaches only to roof level; both seem to rise out of the body of the transept enclosed by the eastern screen wall (100). The tall slender campanile is pierced on all sides by double and quadruple lights; the quadruple set is curiously tall in a manner not uncommon in Byzantine Greece. The gabled belfry replaces an earlier one, removed as being unsafe. The octagonal cupola is quite unlike any in Lombardy; it has a shallow saucer-shaped vault of almost Saracen type, without an outer roof. Its sides are decorated with a carved frieze and arcaded cornice with pilaster shafts at the corner. The three walls of the transept are symmetrically panelled by tiers of blind-arcading and bold round-headed double windows without any intermediary buttresses or pilasters (cf. Modena). In the gables of the transepts are hooded wheel-windows with ornate spokes and richly carved rims; that at the south end (99) is a sixteenth-century copy of that to the north. In the middle of the east wall is the single window of the central apse (98) whose fine carved ornament is typical of that on other parts of the building and a notable product of the local school. It includes oriental animals, like the elephants, sphinx and peacocks, and little human and animal figures entwined in foliage on the jambs. Although the patterns exhibit a flat Saracenic formalism, the masterly carving of the expressive heads is evidence of the special nature of Apulian art.

The interior (97) has in recent years been swept clean of all its superficial Baroque decoration to reveal the fine simplicity of its Romanesque architecture. The nave arcade of nine bays is supported by odd classical columns with large stone capitals, partially restored with stucco and carved with stiff Romanesque acanthus leaves and bearing some resemblance to Byzantine capitals of earlier centuries. The timber roof was rarely displaced in this part of Italy, so there is no provision for vaults by means of piers in the main arcade, nor in the transept. Great prominence is given to the triforium, which has large retaining arches round the triple arches of the loggia, whereas the clerestory lights are very small. The triforium (*cf. 71*) is false in that the aisle is roofed above the level of the triforium and has two rows of small round-headed lights in the outer walls. The transepts are lit by the wheel-windows and other lights in the end-walls, and have blind windows on the east face, for the sake of symmetry. Over the three high arches of the crossing and the main apse, with pendentives at the angles, is the octagonal drum, pierced with a small window in each side, supporting the saucer-shaped vault. The apses in the east transept wall are tall and very shallow, but the presbytery beneath the high cupola is unusually spacious.

The furniture of the presbytery has also been restored. The baldac-chino over the High Altar, inspired by early examples in Latium round Rome, was made by Alfano da Termoli in about 1230. In the apse is a semicircle of presbyteral benches with carved steps on either side of the episcopal throne which has vigorous lion arm-rests. The presbytery is surrounded by a grille and a parapet wall of Byzantine-style carved panels. The stone pulpit on the south side of the nave is incomplete, but it has been reassembled in an exemplary fashion. It is rectangular, with panelled sides carved with beasts and foliate cornices, and has an internal staircase; projecting from the front is a semicircular bay on a single column with an eagle lectern. The pavement of the transept is roughly tesselated and that of the nave is, in part, of the fourteenth century with a centre-piece showing the design of the west wheel-window. The floor of the transept and presbytery is raised six steps above the nave over the crypt, which is entered down a flight of steps in either aisle. The crypt, in contrast to the main church, is still orna-mented with seventeenth-century frescos on the vaults and coloured marble sheathing on the piers and walls. Lying exactly beneath the transept and apses, its vaulting is supported by twenty-four columns in three rows, the capitals of which, surviving largely undamaged, exhibit a variety of styles of sixth- to twelfth-century date.

The twelve-sided building on the north side of the church, the "Trullo", was built on the site of a baptistery possibly of the sixth century; it is recorded that it once contained a round marble font. Presumably reconstructed in 1156, it was derelict for some centuries, until in 1618 an attempt was made to rebuild it. This work was not concluded until 1740 since when it has served as a sacristy.

TROIA

IN what is known as the Capitanata, some miles from Foggia towards the foothills of the Apennines, stands the tiny hill-city Troia. It was founded by the Byzantines in 1017 as a fortress. Today, like most other South Italian towns it is only a centre for local agriculture. But it has a cathedral of exceptional interest; a Romanesque masterpiece. Founded in 1093, it is largely a work of the twelfth century, remarkable for its resemblance to contemporary Pisan churches. There is little doubt that a Pisan master first erected the church, probably using as his model Pisa cathedral (q.v.) before it was altered in the twelfth century, whereas later additions are typical of Apulian work of the thirteenth century. Directly or indirectly, the Pisan style had a notable influence on architecture and sculpture in this neighbourhood.

A freestone building of modest size, Troia cathedral is a typical Pisan basilica. Its nave ends in a half-round apse, the side-aisles have square ends and, initially, there was no transept (*101*). The round-headed nave arcades have classical shafts and bases with a miscellaneous collection of fine classical Ionic, composite and Byzantine style capitals. There is no triforium but a simple clerestory and wooden roof. The groin-vaults of the aisles, whose wall-pilaster supports impinge on the window-arrangement, were probably added only when the transept was built in the thirteenth century. The presbytery of one bay ends in a low apse with a high triumphal arch, pointed like that at Pisa; its cross-vault and the circular window over the apse seem contemporary with the arches of the transepts. The dimness of the interior is accentuated by the tarnished gaudiness of the seventeenth-century painted and gilded walls. Beside a main pier of the crossing is a rectangular stone pulpit of 1169, standing on four columns with capitals. The cornices round the side panels are richly carved with scrolled vines,

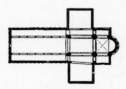

bunches of grapes and other foliage. On one side is an eagle-lectern, and on the end panels scenes of wild life are carved in high relief. The High Altar and the balustrade around the presbytery are ornately carved in polychrome marble and, with the organs on either side, show the florid

101 Troia, begun 1093 taste of the seventeenth century.

The most impressive and interesting part of the building is the exterior (*103*) which, with the exception of the later wheel-window and the transepts, is treated in the Pisan fashion. Round the aisle walls and lower part of the façade runs the typical blind round-headed arcading with carved capitals and pilaster-strips on a high pediment. In the arcading are circles, lozenges and other shapes cut into the wall, and patterns in Saracen style are carved in the spandrels. The main apse is ringed by two tiers of free-standing columns; its single-window is set between two columns on a pair of lions. Framed by higher arches in the arcade, the doorways are heavily constructed with thick jambs and flatly carved capitals and architrave beneath a hooded tympanum arch. On the architrave of the west portal are Christ enthroned between the Virgin and St John the Baptist and other local saints, with symbols of the Evangelists; on the tympanum of the north doorway is a relief of Christ between two angels. The prominent cornice round the eaves of the aisles and across the façade is remarkable for its series of grotesquely carved animals and birds serving as corbels. The clerestory in the upper nave walls has quite simple windows, but the upper part of the west front was altered in the thirteenth century by the addition of the amazing wheel-window. The development of such lavish sculptural ornamentation by the Apulian school may well have had significant influence on northern art. If Nicola Pisano was indeed Apulian by birth he must have drawn a large part of his inspiration from the vigorous work of this province as represented here at Troia and elsewhere. The full relief and lively expression of the animal and human figures (*cf.* *98*), even where grotesque, are the measure of the superiority of local sculptors. With naturalistic motifs were combined the formal design of intricate pierced panels in the sectors of the wheel, derived from Saracen art.

The bronze doors of the west and south portals are also important in that they must have been known by Barisano da Trani, whose work is found in a number of centres in South Italy (*106*). The main pair of doors, dated 1119, have fourteen panels each containing embossed lions' heads with rings in their mouths, ornate Byzantine crosses or silver-damascened figures, including Christ in Judgement, local saints, the donors Count Berardus and William the bishop, and Oderisius the artist. Parts of the work were recut in 1573, but the massive doors, which run on their own wheels, reflect a new sense of variety and unity of form. The other doors, by the same Oderisius of Benevento, were made in 1126, with twenty-four panels containing figures of saints and bishops, once damascened in silver, and with similar embossed lions' heads.

TRANI

TRANI possesses one of the finest of the stone-built Apulian cathedrals (*105*). Great height and attractive honey-coloured walls give it particular distinction, enhanced by its site on the sea-wall of the port. The present church, dedicated to S. Nicola the Pilgrim, was begun in 1084, though not completed until the thirteenth century. Its predecessor, possibly built in the second half of the seventh century, now forms a sixteen-feet-high crypt beneath the nave – to this is due the unusual loftiness of the exterior which is emphasized by the narrowness of the tall transept.*

In plan the church is a T-cross, inscribed within a rectangle, with projecting eastern apses (*102*). The roof line of the transept is unbroken and the only tower, not begun until the mid-thirteenth century, is at the south-west corner. The main portal is reached up a double-staircase and preceded by a platform, on which is provision for a covered narthex. Across the foot of the façade is a colonnaded blind-arcade with soffits and capitals, richly carved with Byzantine-style foliage (*106*). On each capital remains the root of an arch by which the narthex would have been vaulted. Of the three doorways, the side two are very simple, but the main portal is an important example of local sculpture; the jambs and half-round arch are faced with interlaced foliage and tendrils, stylized in the Saracen manner with, on the inner face, a series of vigorously contorted figures; at the base of the jambs are lions mauling their prey. The bronze-sheathed doors made by Barisano da Trani (1175–79), are the prototype of his later work at Ravello and Monreale (*104*) where several motifs were repeated. There are thirty-three panels in eight rows, surrounded by broad frames decorated with foliage and containing in medallions figures of centaurs, Hercules and the Lion, sirens and bowmen, griffins, men hunting and animals fighting, while the panels include figures of saints, more men fighting, the Deposition from the Cross and Barisano himself at the feet of S. Nicola. The progress made by Barisano over his Byzantine and Apulian predecessors (*cf.* p. 225), whose designs are formal and static, is evident. The freedom and movement of the figures and the design of some of the groups like the Deposition show advances not attained either by the Byzantines or northern masters like Bonanno of Pisa (*q.v.*)

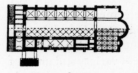

102 Trani, begun 1084

* Trani cathedral is at the moment undergoing extensive restoration, and its tower is being reconstructed after long showing signs of collapse.

103 TROIA: the façade; the lower
half is in the twelfth-century
Pisan style, the upper half is of
the thirteenth century

104 A bronze panel from doors by
Barisano da Trani, as found at
Trani, Ravello and Monreale
(1175–c. 1180)

105 TRANI: a view from the north-east
showing the high transepts and
apses, begun in 1084

106 TRANI: the west portal and the
arcading of the narthex with the
bronze-sheathed doors by Barisano
da Trani (1175–79)

The high gabled façade between the inclined shoulders of the aisle roofs is not ornamented except by an harmonious group of windows; high above each doorway is a single round-headed light, with a simple circular window higher up and a small light in the gable. The jambs of each are carved like the main portal and round the central one and the wheel-window project free-standing elephants and lions. The sides of the aisles, as at Bari, are flanked by tall, deep-recessed arches with a line of projecting lion gargoyles. No gallery like that at Bari was added (cf. 99), so the round-headed windows of the aisles open below and those of the triforium above the arcade; the windows of the clerestory are slightly pointed. On the end-walls of the transepts (105) there is plain blind-arcading with richly carved twin-lights and a wheel-window above; round the eaves (cf. 103) is a prominent corbelled and sculptured cornice.

The campanile, attached to the south corner of the façade, rises from a massive base pierced by a high pointed archway. The tower has five storeys and an octagonal spired belfry; the ground lights in each side at every stage are graduated upwards, from the lowest plain double-light to the uppermost of five arches. The top three storeys and the projecting cornice were completed during the first half of the fourteenth century and the belfry finally added by 1365.

Though the interior is largely bereft of its normal fittings, the rhythm of the main arcade, with its coupled pairs of tall classical columns, the judicious proportions of the triple arches of the triforium gallery, joined across the west front by an arcaded loggia, and the careful spacing of the small clerestory windows, stamp this a masterpiece of Romanesque style. The aisles are vaulted with cross-arches supported by the main coupled columns and by half-shafts attached to the walls. The triumphal arch springs from tall composite angle-piers at a level above the triforium, and gives an unimpeded view of the crossing and the tall apse from the nave. Both the nave and the transept have restored open-work timber roofs. Of the internal sculpture little remains beyond the simple foliate capitals in the triforium arcade. The floor of the transept is only slightly raised over the eastern crypt, which is entered by a staircase in the north aisle. The part of the crypt beneath the transepts and apses has four aisles of twenty-eight Parian marble columns and a great variety of capitals which support cross-vaults. This part of the crypt cuts off the apsidal end of the ancient church, which forms a separate vaulted crypt beneath the nave.

Sicily

THE history of the island of Sicily begins long before our era. The temples of the Greek gods stand austere monuments of the civilization overthrown by the Romans. The advent of Christianity to the island was as early as to Rome and something of its long history there is to be found in Syracuse, one of the largest centres in the ancient world, a colony in Magna Graecia. The long domination of the island by the Byzantine Emperors has left its mark, in spite of the subsequent conquest by the Saracens. Byzantine influence was continued under the tolerant rule of the Saracens and reinforced by the encouragement of the Norman rulers.

Palermo was the royal capital of the Norman Kingdom, and there one can still sense a distinctive and exotic atmosphere in the dusty streets of the towns, and in the surrounding countryside of the fertile Conca d'Oro (110). The scattered pavilions and lodges, the great palace with the Cappella Palatina, and the numerous churches of the Norman period impress us by their diversity. The royal cathedrals of Messina, Cefalù, Palermo, the coronation church, and Monreale, the most favoured of all, stand witness to a material and artistic eminence that lasted from the eleventh to the thirteenth centuries.

SYRACUSE

MANY a great Christian shrine is known to stand on the site of a pagan temple. In Rome several classical buildings have been dedicated to the use of the Church, but the cathedral of Syracuse was at one time the famous Greek Temple of Athena, erected on the island of Ortygia in about 480 B.C. No other church building has so long a history. The oration of Cicero against Verres, the rapacious governor of Sicily, records the magnificence of the temple and we may still marvel at the noble proportions of its great fluted columns and the spaciousness of the transformed *cella*. The temple was a Doric peripteral hexastyle of thirty-six columns, 28 feet high with a diameter of 6 feet 6 inches, fourteen on each side and six across each end, before the columned porticos, the *pronaos* and *opistodomos*. It stood on a massive stylobate, or podium, three steps high and measuring 184 feet by 72 feet, of truly

Cyclopean construction. The colonnades surrounded the inner hall, the *cella*, which formerly enshrined the statue of the goddess and is now the nave of the cathedral.

At Syracuse was established one of the earliest Christian communities in Europe. In the seventh century, when the city was among the most important Byzantine centres in the West, the Byzantine bishop Zosimo converted the temple into a basilica by blocking up the spaces between the columns, opening eight arches in each wall of the *cella* (*108*) and adding three eastern apses. The walls of the nave were heightened by the Normans, but any later mediaeval alterations were completely effaced in the seventeenth and eighteenth centuries, when, after two particularly disastrous earthquakes, the east end was extended, the side-chapels added, and the whole transformed by eighteenth-century stucco ornament. In 1927 the nave and aisles were restored, so far as possible, to their primitive state, revealing the columns and walls and diminishing the flagrant contrasts created by the gaudy coloured decoration.

Curiosity is immediately aroused on first seeing the cathedral (*107*). The long crenellated flank of the north aisle is not merely a rough stone wall, for exposed along it are twelve of the fluted monolithic shafts and chamfered circular capitals of the Greek temple, standing on the massive podium. In a semicircular piazza of Baroque palaces stands the façade designed by Andrea Palma and built from 1728 to 1754 to replace the Norman one destroyed in an earthquake a few years previously. A distinctive work of the Sicilian Baroque style, it characteristically bears little relation to the body of the church. The boldly projecting cornices and broken pediments on the tall free-standing columns, with sharply carved volutes and fronds, and precariously perched cherubs sensitively arranged, contribute to an imposing scenographic composition. Within the portal is a vestibule in the same style, though incomplete, which prepares the way to the nave.

The cathedral, first dedicated to the Nativity of Mary, is now known as S. Maria delle Colonne. Its nave is chilling and unrelentingly austere. The piers of the seventh-century arcade, coarsely cut from the ancient stone-walls, and the equally severe Norman clerestory are unrelieved by any form of decoration other than that of the restored sixteenth-century open-work timber roof. But in turning to face the west end the significance of those walls is revealed by two mighty Doric shafts and capitals which support the architrave of the *naos* of the temple. Then through the arches on either side appear the fascinating vistas of the ranks of massive columns emerging from the aisle walls beneath the barrel vaults; in the south aisle there are nine, and in the north aisle ten shafts. In these stands the 2,400-year history of this place of worship. Again from the unadorned nave the richly furnished presbytery and sanctuary draw the eye towards the High Altar. After the catastrophic earthquakes of 1542 and 1693, in which thousands of people were killed, the cathedral was seriously damaged, columns bulged outwards and the apses collapsed. In their place, the square-ended sanctuary was built beyond the limits of the colonnades during the first half of the eighteenth century. In the restorations the stucco vault of the presbytery was replaced by the coffered wooden ceiling.

Opening off the south aisle are the baptistery and the chapels of S. Lucia, of the Sacrament and, on the site of the apse, that of the Crucifixion. The most important of these, the Chapel of the Sacrament, was erected in the first half of the seventeenth century, and is attributed to one Giovanni Vermexio. The frescoed panels of the vault, and the imaginative treatment of the pilasters and cornices of the walls indicate the quality of the local Baroque style. The superb iron gates of this chapel (*108*) were made in 1809–11 by a local craftsman, Domenico Ruggeri.

It must always be a matter for concern when drastic restorations are carried out in a building where the art of many centuries has accumulated, but it seems vindicated in this case, for Syracuse cathedral is undoubtedly unique and its ancient character fully deserves to be laid bare.

MESSINA

MESSINA has suffered much in its history, above all from the appalling devastation of earthquakes; the most calamitous occurred in 1908 when, with ninety per cent of the city, the Norman cathedral was almost completely destroyed. The upper walls and roof collapsed, ruining most of the nave and south transept. The whole building was faithfully restored then, and again later after being severely damaged during the invasion of Sicily in 1943. The restorations in this century have revealed the principal features of the mediaeval church and its Renaissance fittings, not all of which have been irreparably damaged.

The Norman cathedral was built by Roger I of Sicily in 1092, completed by King Roger II and consecrated to Mary in 1197 in the presence of the Emperor Henry VI. The simple form of this building has been revealed and restored, and in spite of the coldness of the bare walls and the sharpness of the reworked materials, its original character is evident. The tall nave and transept, T-shaped in plan, are typical of

107 The façade (1728–54) and the north wall revealing columns of the Greek temple

108 The south aisle from the west, showing Doric columns and seventh-century arches

109 CEFALÙ: a view from the south-east. Largely built 1131–48

110 MONREALE: view from the north-west. Abbey church begun 1174

111 CEFALÙ: Pantocrator, the mosaics in the presbytery, 1148

the mediaeval Roman style adopted also in the contemporary cathedral at Salerno. The Moorish influence here is, however, more evident; it puts beyond all doubt that the use of the stilted pointed arch (cf. 12) in Sicily in the twelfth century was not due to Gothic developments in North Europe. The pointed arcades of the nave are supported by twenty-six monolithic granite columns with square abaci and massive capitals carved with stiff-leaved foliage, reworked after the originals. Above the arcades is a broad high wall space (cf. Monreale), with a clerestory of single pointed lights placed high up beneath the open-work timber roof, now painted with patterns and figures of the Holy Family and saints in Byzantine style. In the walls of the single-aisles are windows in similar style. The triumphal arch opening into the transept and the arch of the broad deep main apse, are both supported by two tiers of columns and capitals. The transept, which projects slightly beyond the line of the aisle walls, is as high as the nave, and on either side of the central main apse are smaller apses. The main apse, semi-circular inside but polygonal externally, is encircled at the springing of its vault with a cornice of classical fragments. In the half-dome is a colossal mosaic figure of the Redeemer giving His Blessing in the Greek manner, and seated between the kings Peter and Frederick of Aragon (about 1322), the archangels Michael and Gabriel, the Virgin and John the Baptist, and the archbishop Guidotto, who commissioned the work. Round the face of the apse arch are roundels in mosaic containing half-figures of saints and the Annunciation, with half-figures of the Apoca-lyptic Elders in the archivolt; though damaged, these mosaics have been no more restored than was necessary and are, for this area, a rare survival from the fourteenth century.

The exterior has also been restored to its mediaeval state, ignoring certain Baroque additions to the façade. The elevation and plan of the nave and transept are an instructive link in the chain of influences affecting architecture of the Norman period; they are the key to the Roman source of the high transepts and shallow apses of the Apulian school. The towerless façade, with its three Norman style windows in the upper wall of the nave, was given its three Gothic portals in the fourteenth and fifteenth centuries. Though damaged in some details the greater part of the central portal, reminiscent of those of S. Maria del Fiore at Florence, is still well preserved. Its design is attributed to Antonio Baboccio, but the charming sculptures are the work of the Tuscan Pietro de Bonitate (1468). The jambs are carved with kings and prophets, and the architrave and the tympanum beneath its steep gable are richly and delicately carved with the Coronation of the Virgin surrounded by angels. The projecting gable is supported by projecting piers which are carved with sheafs of colonnettes and capitals in two tiers veiled by vine-stems and bunches of grapes, among which clamber innumerable agile boys, naked and tiny. The smaller doorways are typical of the Gothic style as it was imported into the Kingdom by the Angevins from France in the fourteenth century. The lower part of the façade is striped with bands of mosaic inlay and narrow panels of figures in low relief, in the style of those on the central portal.

In about 1547, Montorsoli, a pupil of Michelangelo's, came to Messina to erect the great fountain in front of the main façade. He was also responsible for an unusual group of subsidiary altars in the aisles of the church. Six altars are arranged on each side in an impressive screen of arches which are framed by fluted pilasters supporting an entablature. The segmental pediment of the reredos of each altar is broken by a panel in relief and in the niche stands the vigorous statue of an Apostle.

As part of the restoration, a new campanile nearly 200 feet high was built to the design of Francesco Valenti. In it has been set the largest mechanical astronomical clock in the world, built by Theodore Ungerer of Strasburg and inaugurated in 1933.

CEFALÙ

THE cathedral of Cefalù is one of the most notable of the Norman kings' foundations even though its decoration was never more than partially completed. It dignifies a poor shrunken town, but enjoys a superb natural setting. It stands on ground which slopes gently down to the sea nearby on the north side; its south side is overhung by a high cliff of golden limestone. Built between 1131 and 1148 by Roger II, who wished to be buried there, it is contemporary with the beautiful Cappella Palatina of the Royal Palace in Palermo. In its plan, which consists of a nave and single-aisles with a high transept, projecting apsidal presbytery and side-chapels (109), it owes more to Lombard or French Romanesque architecture than do the other great churches in this group. The walls between the presbytery and the side-chapels are unbroken, so that there is not the close relation with Byzantine practice as at Monreale. Nevertheless, the full blend of cultures in the Norman court is marked by the Byzantine mosaics with their inscriptions in Latin and Greek, the Moorish stilted arches and windows, and the Romanesque plan and vaulting.

The massive exterior, typical of the Norman school, is dominated by the squat towers and high walls. Externally, the east end has an unusual form. The main apse, which rises to the full height of the presbytery, is faced with eight slender coupled shafts on pilaster-plinths which support a row of arcaded cornices. The side-apses are only half as high, with similar pairs of shafts supporting blind interlaced arcades and smaller arcaded cornices just beneath the eaves. The transept from which the apses and presbytery project by the length of two bays is partly vaulted at the same height as the presbytery, but it is considerably higher than the nave. The east face of the transept and the presbytery are strongly buttressed to their full height, and have a blind interlaced arcade around the top of the walls. The plain tall pointed windows are hooded by a cornice; in the main apse there is one single-light window lighting the interior, but the three annular windows do not appear inside.

A strong and characteristic feature of the Siculo-Norman churches is the contrast in volume between the east end and the nave. The short low-built nave is compressed between the transept and the pair of eastern towers, which flank the projecting open narthex. The two tiers of arcading across the upper façade and the single window, dated 1240, are richly moulded with the favourite Norman chevron ornament. The interlaced-arch pattern already noticed on the east walls, occurs frequently and, although it is known on tenth-century Saracen buildings, it also appeared about 1100 at Durham cathedral, and, with other details, may well have come in the train of the new rulers. The pointed arches on either side of the middle rounded arch of the lofty vaulted narthex, supported by shafts and richly carved Romanesque capitals, have an entablature inserted in a later restoration; the single doorway is only lightly carved, and has a polygonal hood.

The impressive interior presents difficult problems of interpretation. The low openwork timber roof of the undecorated nave impinges on the mouldings of a great blind arch on the west face of the transept. While it is possible that the nave was reduced in height, it would seem more probable that a decision was taken to complete it more economically than the vaulted presbytery which is, undoubtedly, on account of its mosaics part of the initial building project. The low wall-space between the stilted pointed arches and clerestory windows does not conform with the usual practice (see Messina and Monreale) probably for this reason. The seven bays of the nave have fine columns and miscellaneous richly carved Roman capitals, and the aisles are cross-vaulted. The capitals of the great columns supporting the lofty Moorish transept arch are, with those in the narthex, remarkable examples of bold Romanesque figure-sculpture combined with stiff acanthus leaves, which, with others having formal Saracen motifs, suggest an Apulian source. The windows of the transept are set high in the wall, but at the clerestory level there is an arcaded loggia with small columns and carved capitals beneath the high quadripartite vault.

The most spectacular part of the cathedral is the brilliantly decorated presbytery (*111*). The tall narrow apse and one bay of the quadripartite vaults, with the walls beneath, are adorned with Byzantine mosaic pictures of the highest quality. The superb definition of the features of the Redeemer, the Pantocrator, and the calm benevolence with which He blesses the faithful, make this one of Europe's most beautiful and expressive works of art; the mantle is a pastel blue, the undergarment gold streaked with blue, and the background is gold; the Redeemer's hand is raised and the fingers held in the Greek manner. In the vault above are Cherubim and the six-winged Seraphim; on the wall of the apse below are the Virgin, her hands raised in prayer, between the archangels, and the Apostles, who stand in two rows with hieratic dignity. On the side-walls are Greek and Latin Fathers splendid in the robes of their respective Churches, saints in vestments or armour, and the prophets announcing the Word of God. All the wall surfaces, cornices, windows and arches are sheathed in mosaic, richly coloured with variegated patterns to make a decoration of great splendour in the sunlight that pours through the windows on either side. The individual figures are all named and their scrolls and books inscribed in Latin or Greek; an inscription gives the date of these mosaics as 1148. At the entrance to the presbytery is a contemporary parapet wall, and mosaic-decorated panels mark the places for the royal and episcopal thrones. The decoration of the presbytery was continued in different fashion in 1588 by the bishop Francesco Gonzaga, in the reign of Phillip II of Spain. The marbled stucco on the walls and vault and the racked marble statues bear full witness to the influence of Spain on late Sicilian art. In any place but this they would earn considerable praise for vivacity and imagination, but they are vulgar when set next to the refined dignity of the twelfth century.

The cloister on the north side of the nave is not large, but the simplicity of its coupled shafts with their carved capitals is striking, since it is contemporary with that at Monreale (*113*) built in the reign of William II (1166–89).

MONREALE

MONREALE is a small town on the side of the valley leading into the fertile Conca d'Oro surrounding Palermo (*110*). Here, on the edge of the royal park, William II, in 1174, founded a Benedictine monastery and the metropolitan church of S. Maria la Nuova. It was rapidly completed and is the most magnificent of the Norman churches in Sicily to come down to us. It is in an excellent state of preservation owing to reasonable restoration and the fact that additions made have, in the main, conformed in decorative treatment with the original where they impinge on it. It is unique for its harmonious proportions and the prodigious luxury of the vast series of pictorial mosaics, much advanced even by 1182, ever since when "they have been celebrated as without parallel from antiquity to the present day".

The plan of the church (112) is a successful combination of the nave with the *trichora*, the tri-apsidal east end of Byzantine Greek churches; it is not correct to call the broad block of the presbytery and its aisles a transept, to which it has only a superficial resemblance (110). The broad nave and narrow aisles, with their lofty pointed arcades and superb set of granite columns and capitals (many with heads of Ceres and Proserpina and almost all from a single classical building), and massive abaci, have an incomparable spaciousness and stately rhythm (12). The walls of the presbytery are each pierced by two principal arches, the larger spans the choir, which was possibly intended to have a cupola, and the smaller joins the sanctuary and the side-aisles which, in the Byzantine tradition, served as sacristies. The springing of each of the arches and of the apse vault is delineated by a simply moulded cornice. Above these arches are clerestory windows beneath the separate roofs of each bay. The tall apse, in which stands the main altar, is framed by a broad vaulted bay. The timber roofs of the church were destroyed by fire in 1811. In the restoration the open-work roof of the nave was richly painted with imitation Moorish patterns; that over the choir was given the honeycomb form of the twelfth-century roof of the Cappella Palatina; the smaller bay over the sanctuary was given a simply coffered pitched-ceiling.

The simplicity of line in every part of the church gives a sensuous form to the broad wall-spaces, which are the canvas for the glass mosaic decoration. This area of some 7,500 square yards is employed to the full, and carefully divided up into regular zones of greater importance, like the apse, the walls of the nave, the presbytery and their aisles, and of lesser importance, as the soffits of the arches and windows.

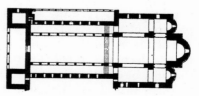

112 Monreale, begun 1174

Along the walls runs a dado of grey- and white-veined marble veneer with borders of mosaic patterns and a frieze of mosaic lilies.

The magnificence of the mosaics reflects the aspirations of the Norman kings in Sicily and the strength of Byzantine influence in the island. Though these, like the older mosaics at Cefalù and in the Cappella Palatina in Palermo, are probably the work of local craftsmen, they indicate a considerable decline from the power of expression possessed by the earlier generation. However fine the execution is here, it depended too much on the earlier models; their masterly design was imitated and adapted to the broader space available. There was a consequent loss of dignity and vigour which is particularly apparent in the treatment of the Pantocrator, who dominates the whole scheme from the main apse (*118*); the features are coarser and the arms of the Redeemer, slightly raised in Benediction, are obscured by the deep curves of the apse vault and only clumsily communicate their universal embrace. On the walls of the apse below are the Virgin and Child enthroned between the archangels and the Apostles ranged on either side and round the side-walls with saints below; all are accompanied by appropriate legends in Greek and Latin.

In the vault between the Seraphim is the *Hetimasia*, the symbol of the Invisible Deity. The presbytery-aisles are devoted to the Christian Feasts, signifying the Terrestrial Church, and the cycle of the Miracles of Our Lord and His Passion. Between these, on the upper walls of the sanctuary and presbytery, is the story of the Annunciation; the side-apses show the Apostles Peter and Paul with their lives and martyrdoms. The walls of the nave, divided into two principal zones, depict the Old Testament from the Creation to Jacob's vision of the Angel, and the Life of Christ, with, in the aisles, His preaching. All these large-scale pictures are set against a bright gold background, while the friezes round the arches, cornices and window jambs are strengthened by their depth of colour in abstract patterns and icons. The marble pavement of the nave and aisles is patterned with interlacing bands of red and white. The presbytery and its aisles are paved throughout with mosaic guilloches and arabesque patterns with squares and roundels of porphyry and serpentine and, in unexpected corners, charming inlaid pictures of rabbits and other animals.

The choir, partly restored after the fire, contains the high dais of mosaic-decorated panels for the thrones of the king and archbishop; the back of each is veneered with veined marble and above is a mosaic picture; that above the royal throne, to the north shows William II receiving the crown from the hands of Christ in emulation of the

Emperors, and in the other, above the episcopal seat, he offers the cathedral to the Virgin. In the south aisle stand two sarcophagi; one of William I in porphyry (*cf. 10*), and the other of William II, remade in white marble with gold arabesque patterns in 1575. Another king partly buried here is St Louis of France, who, after dying of the plague at Tunis in 1270, left his heart and entrails to be preserved in a little wall-shrine in the north apse.

The side-chapels, added at a later date, do not impinge on the mediaeval building. Notable among them is the Chapel of the Crucifix, off the north apse, by Frate Giovanni da Monreale (1687–92); its exuberant carved and inlaid ornament is not untypical of the Baroque style prevalent in Palermo (*115*).

The exterior is curiously distinctive for the cubical mass of the east end and the ponderous incomplete towers of the west front (*110*). The highly ornamented triple apses (*114*) make a bizarre effect, with their three tiers of blind interlaced arcading, simple arcading and cornices, all inlaid with black lava and sandy-coloured limestone shapes which form abstract patterns, chiefly of Saracen origin. The west front is similarly arcaded above the tall portico, re-erected between the pair of towers in the eighteenth century; the long arcaded portico of the north side was designed by Gian Domenico and Fazio Gagini (1547–69). Both the principal doorways into the church have precious bronze doors. The composite jambs of the single west doorway are richly carved with floral motifs and figures and inlaid with imitation columns in mosaic, and have capitals carved with griffons, lions and hunting scenes all akin to work of the Apulian school. The bronze doors (*117*) are the work of Bonanno of Pisa, and dated 1186; the forty-two panels contain scenes from the Old and New Testaments like those he executed for Pisa cathedral a few years earlier. The doorway under the north portico is framed by a mosaic frieze; the panelled doors, with scenes of the Passion and saints, are by Barisano da Trani (*see also* p. 226), working at about the same date. There is a striking contrast in style; whereas Bonanno had absorbed possibly Rhenish influence for his modelling, the more sophisticated work of Barisano holds more closely to his Byzantine models (*104*).

Some of the buildings of King William's monastery, including the refectory and dormitory and the superb cloister, still stand on the south side of the cathedral. Round the four sides of the exotic cloister 216 columns in coupled pairs, and in fours at the corners, support the curious arches inlaid with black lava and limestone shapes. The slender shafts are decorated with an infinite variety of imaginative designs, fluted or zig-zagged with pretty coloured glass mosaic infillings and carved with patterns and floral motifs. Each pair of shafts has a double capital, on which the sculptured subjects range from the expulsion of Adam and Eve from Eden (116), to knights fighting and monkeys playing tricks. This important collection of sculpture has raised many doubts as to its origin, for it is certainly not Saracen, Byzantine, or Roman by derivation, nor does it seem to be of the Apulian school. There is so little similar work in Sicily, as for example certain capitals at Cefalù, that a foreign source is likely, perhaps France. In the corner of the cloister is a small enclosure surrounding the twelfth-century fountain which consists of a tall pylon rising from a saucer-shaped bowl (113); this follows a widespread ancient tradition.

PALERMO

THE cathedral of the Assumption (S. Maria Assunta) at Palermo is the largest of all the royal Norman buildings in Sicily and was the coronation church of the kingdom. It stands on the site of a sixth-century basilica which was reconsecrated after having been made a mosque by the Saracens, who took the city in 831. This ancient church was not replaced until 1185, when the new work was begun and dedicated by the Anglo-Norman archbishop, Gualterius Offamilius – Walter of the Mill. The east end of the cathedral, at least, was soon completed but the long nave, though continued in similar style, was still being built in the fourteenth century. Considerable decorative alterations were made after that, but when, at the end of the eighteenth century, it was decided to modernize the cathedral, the interior was completely transformed – the cupola was added at the same time, though the external grandeur of this monumental edifice was not otherwise seriously affected (119).

The only likely remains of the original basilica are the lower walls of the curious crypt of the present church. This crypt, with vaulting of the Gothic period, projects beyond the great twelfth-century apse and consists of a line of seven small apses and two colonnaded aisles. Partly above and partly below the present ground level, this remnant had no effect on the design of the new structure.

The grandiose plan and elevation of the Norman work is difficult to distinguish because of the chapels and sacristies built around the lower walls in later periods. The design is similar in its general features to that of Monreale; the broad nave, nearly four times the width of the single aisles, was joined to the *trichora* of the east end, but with an intervening

113 MONREALE: the late twelfth-century
cloister with its fountain

114 MONREALE: the east end begun 1174

115   The Chapel of the Crucifix (1687–92)

116   A double capital in the late
twelfth-century cloister arcade

117   Two panels of
the   bronze-sheathed
doors by Bonanno of
Pisa (1186)

MONREALE

118　MONREALE: Pantocrator, the mosaics in the main apse (*c.* 1180)

119 PALERMO: view from the south-east; the east end, the transepts and nave begun 1185; the south porch added in 1426; the cupola erected by F. Fuga after 1781

transept. At each angle of the building is a tower; two flank the triple
apse, and two the later west front. The characteristic decoration of
the east end, the tall billet-moulded blind arches on the upper walls,
the interlaced arcading on the apses, the crenellation and the arcaded
cornices all round is in the same manner as that at Monreale, but here
the pattern is even more elaborate and more richly inlaid with abstract
patterns in black lava and the local buff stone. Though it is uncertain
how far work on the nave had advanced in the twelfth century, the
multiple-hooded windows and blind arches of the clerestory follow
entirely the style of that period. The majestic nave of ten bays was
unique in having four classical columns coupled together, in place follow
the usual one, with antique and Romanesque capitals supporting the
pointed arcade, and, for Sicily, in having a triforium gallery. The upper
parts of the four towers and the remarkable massive campanile, joined
to the west end by great arches, were continued with the elegant
triple portal of the west façade in the Gothic style of the Angevin
period, when the building was largely completed.

As well as being the coronation church, the cathedral was, like
Westminster Abbey, the principal royal mausoleum. The tombs of the
kings and members of the royal family buried here have been relegated
to two side-chapels in the south aisle. Four of these tombs contain the
remains, as ascertained in 1781, of King Roger II († 1154), the
Emperor Henry VI († 1197), his Empress Constance, daughter of
Roger († 1198) (10), and the Emperor Frederick II († 1250), and
are of the greatest magnificence. All of these tombs are made of red
porphyry, three of them richly carved and moulded, with canopies
supported by six columns; two of them have porphyry columns and
canopies and two are adorned with glass mosaics on the shafts and
canopy. Such sarcophagi were the prerogative of the Eastern Emperors
and some examples survive in Constantinople; it was a typical part
of the pluto-Byzantine policy of the Normans in Sicily that their
memorials, especially, should follow Imperial example. The working of
porphyry is at any time a process of utmost difficulty, for it is among the
hardest of rocks. The skill of the craftsmen of the Court School of
architecture and decoration was without equal in Italy; the experience
of the Byzantine Greeks and of the Saracens was at the service of this
remarkable kingdom. This same skill was also available for mosaic
work, and the variety of shapes it was possible to cut in the twelfth and
thirteenth centuries made for the delicacy of imaginative design found
on all kinds of furniture (cf. p. 213), often combined with exquisite
sculpture. The influence of the Siculo-Norman school of art was to be

of great importance to North Italy from the thirteenth century onwards.

The coronations of the kings of Sicily, whether Norman, Angevin or Aragonese, continued to take place in the cathedral up to the eighteenth century. Close to the west front is a small loggia from which the kings were presented to the people at their coronation, a rare survival of a very ancient practice.

In the first half of the fifteenth century, a brief revival occurred in the bizarre fusion of Gothic and Moorish motifs in native Sicilian art. The impressive south portico of the cathedral is a leading example and is contemporary with the fine doorway by Antonio Gambara (1426) beneath it.

In the fifteenth and sixteenth centuries there was some activity by artists of the North Italian Renaissance in redecorating the interior. Of this work only a fraction has survived; there is a fine holy water stoup by Francesco Laurana (1469), who had earlier worked at Rimini; in the Chapel of the Crucifixion are bas-reliefs of the Passion by Fazio and Vincenzo Gagini, and in the Chapel of the Assumption sculptures by Antonello Gagini. The prolific Gagini family, who in earlier generations worked in Lombardy and Genoa, made a considerable contribution of high quality to the sixteenth-century art of Sicily.

In 1761 the archbishop, Serafino Filangieri, expressed his fears for the stability of the fabric and begged the king in Naples to send Ferdinando Fuga, the best architect in the kingdom, to restore it. The proposal made was to strengthen parts of the cathedral, or to redesign the interior, only preserving the old exterior; the scheme for modernization was a foregone conclusion, and the work began in 1781. The interior was, indeed, entirely transformed (21); the nave was narrowed, the aisles widened and a line of side-chapels added; the antique shafts were cut down to a uniform height and placed in pairs to support the arches and the piers, over which runs the deep entablature beneath the clerestory and the barrel vault. Though it is said that Fuga had not in fact intended to alter the presbytery, it was made to conform with the rest, bare and cold in the grey and white of the stuccoed walls, capitals and gaunt trabeation. This was not enough; there had to be a cupola, and for this the nave was reduced in length by two bays, the piers of the crossing strengthened and the Norman roof-line broken (119). Although the cupola is in Fuga's most competent style, it could be more happily judged elsewhere.

GLOSSARY

Abacus. Flat slab on the top of a capital.

Acanthus. A leafy plant conventionally carved on Corinthian capitals and on imitative derivations.

Ambo. A pulpit, usually in pairs, for the reading of the Gospel and Epistle.

Ambulatory. An aisle encircling an apse.

Apse. The semicircular termination of a nave, aisle or side-chapel, usually vaulted.

Archivolt. The under-surface of an arched wall.

Baldacchino or *ciborium.* A canopy usually supported by four columns over an altar.

Baptistery. A church or chapel provided for the baptism of converts and children, also used for the instruction of converts.

Campanile. A bell-tower.

Campionese masters. Stone workers and carvers from the Italian Alps.

Catechumen. A convert under instruction.

Chevet. An arrangement of small chapels radiating from the ambulatory of an apse, common in France.

Ciborium. See Baldacchino.

Classical orders. The Greek *Doric,* *Ionic* and *Corinthian* orders were used by the Romans who added the *Tuscan* and *composite* (Ionic with Corinthian) orders. Each of these forms was adopted by the masters of the Renaissance. An Order comprises the column with base, capital and entablature but has often been modified or only partially applied.

Clerestory. The range of windows set high in the nave and choir walls of a church.

Cloister. A rectangular enclosure, comprising a covered and arcaded "walk" surrounding a central "garth", part of the conventual buildings of a monastery or large church.

Coffering. Sunken panels in wood or stucco ceilings and vaults.

Comacene masters, so-called. Master builders, probably from Lake Como in the Italian Alps, forerunners of the Campionese masters.

Cross-plan. Three church plans are most common, the T, the *Latin* (with a long nave and projecting east end), the *Greek* (with equal arms.)

GLOSSARY

Crypt. A chamber or chapel contrived under the east end of a church. Normally contains the shrine of the patron saint.

Cusp. A pointed or pyramidal feature.

Diaphragm arch. A great arch across the body of a church but not supporting high vaults.

Façade. The distinctively decorated external end-wall of the nave or transepts.

Gable. The triangular or curved head of an end-wall (see also *Pediment*).

Guilloche. A ribbon-like pattern.

Iconostasis. A screen in front of the sanctuary on which icons or pictures of saints are hung, after the practice of the Byzantine Church.

Loggia. A gallery open on one side and commonly arcaded.

Matroneum. An internal gallery round the nave of a church at a low level. How far such a gallery was ever reserved for women must remain uncertain since few examples survive. Cf. *Triforium*.

Narthex. A narrow portico across the façade of a church.

Ogee arch. A pointed arch made up of a convex and a concave curve.

Paschal Candlestick. A great free-standing candlestick only lit at Easter-tide.

Pediment. The triangular or curved head of a façade, window, door or niche.

Pendentive. The triangular concave wall-surface between arches supporting a cupola.

Pier. A pillar of masonry as distinct from a column.

Pilaster. A shallow wall-buttress.

Pontile. The bridge formed where a crypt is only partly below the level of the nave, and the presbytery raised above it.

Presbytery. The part of the church reserved for the clergy either in front of, or behind, the High Altar.

Pulvin. A block or secondary capital placed on a Byzantine style capital to relieve it of the weight of the wall above (alternative to an *abacus*).

Sacristy. A room, usually near the High Altar, for vestments and church plate.

Soffit. The under-side of an arch.

Spandrel. The triangular wall-surface on each side of an arch.

Squinch. A minor arch across the angle between two arches to support a cupola.

Symbols of the Evangelists. The angel of St Matthew; the winged lion of St Mark; the winged bull of St Luke; the eagle of St John.

Tabernacle work. A canopied niche often repeated as a decorative motif.

Transept. The arms of the cross in the usual church plan.

GLOSSARY

Triforium. The arcade or arcaded gallery running round the nave and choir of a church directly above the main arcade.

Trophy. The arms and armour of the hero commonly used as a decorative motif during the humanist Renaissance.

Tympanum. The semicircular (sometimes segmental) surface enclosed in the arched head of a doorway.

Vaulting. *Barrel*—has a semicircular cross-section and a plain surface; *Groined*— or *cross*—results from the intersection of two equal barrel-vaults. *Ribbed*—is constructed with ribs on the diagonal lines of the groined vault.

Appendix

THE CATHEDRAL CHURCHES OF ITALY

THE following list includes all those churches in Italy that have cathedral status today and a number of others that have once had, but no longer retain that status (those monasteries entitled *abbeys nullius* are not listed). None is included where the title is doubtful and others have probably escaped the author's attention. Altogether 363 church sites are cited. Where possible a brief statement is given of the history and status of the diocese, the dedication of the church, the chronology of important phases in the architectural development of the church and of such ancillary buildings as the baptistery and campanile; dimensions are given in only few cases for lack of published details.

It is not possible to indicate the survival of early structural features where rebuilding has taken place. That process has, however, often entailed the preservation of parts of the old fabric. With certain notable exceptions, rebuilding undertaken from the end of the fifteenth century to the present day has been complete; often this was necessitated by the severe damage caused by earthquakes, especially in the central and southern provinces. Further information on the dioceses and their organization is available in the *Annuario dei diocesi d'Italia*. Useful summaries of the works of art to be found in the churches are given in the *Guide-books of the Touring Club Italiano* in Italian, or in more compact form in *Muirhead's Blue Guides to Italy* (Ernest Benn, London) in English.

Cathedral cities to which reference is made in the first or second part of this book are indicated by **BOLD CAPITALS**; the date of the establishment of the diocese and the date of its elevation into an archbishopric where applicable are given in SMALL CAPITALS. Where the city is not a provincial capital, the province is added in parenthesis; the dedication of the church is in *italics*. References inside square brackets are to the map on pp. 14–15.

Abbreviations

METR. – metropolitan archbishopric. IMM. SUBJ. – immediately subject to the Holy
See. SED. SUBURB. – sedia suburbicaria, or suffragan of the Holy See. C. – century.
INT. – interior.

Acerenza. 4C. METR. 11C.
  Assumption & *S. Clelio*, begun ? 1080;
  rebuilt after 1281.
Acerno. 12C. (Salerno).
  S. Donato, 17C.–18C.
Acerra. 6C. (Naples).
  Assumption, rebuilding begun 1791–
  1843; rebuilt afresh 1874.
Acireale. 1844 (Catania).
  Annunciation, 1597–1618; remodelled
  18C.
Acquapendente. 1649 (Viterbo).
  Holy Sepulchre & *S. Ermete*, remodelled
  mid-18C.
Acquaviva delle Fonte. 1848 (Bari).
  S. Eustachio.
Acqui. 4C. (Alessandria).
  Assumption, 1067; later alterations.
Adria. 7C. (Rovigo).
  SS. Peter & *Paul* (new cathedral), early
  19C. by G. BACCARI.
    Campanile, 1686.
[E9] Agrigento. 1C.
  Assumption & *St James*, ? on site of
  Greek temple of *Jupiter Polieus*; 13C;
  remodelled 14C.
Alatri. 6C. (Frosinone).
  St Paul.
Alba. 4C. (Cuneo).
  St Lawrence, rebuilt 1486; restored
  1861; façade, 1861.
Albano. 4C. SED. SUBURB. (Rome).
  St John Baptist, now *S. Pancrazio*, 4C.
  restored.
A3] ALBENGA. 5C. (Savona).
  St Michael, 11C.; int. 16C.
    Baptistery, about 400; misguidedly
    restored 19C. *See* fig. 5.
Ales. 7C. (Cagliari).
  SS. Peter & *Paul*, rebuilt 2nd half 17C.

Alessandria. 1175.
  St Peter, 1170; rebuilt 1280 & 1810;
  restored 1874–79. *216 ft* long.
Alghero. 12C. (Sassari).
  Immaculate Conception, rebuilt 18C.–19C.
Alife. 5C. (Benevento).
  Assumption & *S. Sisto*, 11C.–12C.
Altamura. ? DATE, PALATINE BASILICA
  (Bari).
  Assumption, 1232; rebuilt after 1316;
  altered 1543.
AMALFI. 6C. ARCHB. 987, IMM. SUBJ. **[F6]**
  (Salerno).
  Assumption now *St Andrew, see* pp. 214–5.
Amelia. 5C. (Terni).
  S. Fermina, ?11C.; remodelled 1640.
    Campanile, 1050.
Ampurias. 12C. (Sassari).
  S. Antonia.
Anagni. 5C. (Frosinone).
  Annunciation, 1074–1179.
ANCONA. 3C. ARCHB. 1904, IMM. SUBJ. **[E4]**
  S. Ciriaco, 4C. or 6C.; rebuilt 11C.–
  13C.; restored 1883, 1920, also since
  heavy damage in World War II.
    Campanile, before 1314.
Andria. 5C. (Bari).
  S. Riccardo now *Assumption*, rebuilt 12C.
  & 1438–63; remodelled later;
  façade, 1844.
    Campanile, 1118–15C.
Anglona. 968 (Matera). City destroyed.
  S. Maria, 13C.
Aosta. 4C.
  St John Baptist, restored 12C.; re-
  modelled late 15C.–early 16C.; façade,
  1848.
AQUILEIA. MID-3C.–1751, PATRIARCH. **[E2]**
  Assumption, see pp. 123–7. *213 ft* long,
  transepts *95 ft* wide.
    Campanile, *240 ft* high.

APPENDIX

Aquino. 5C. IMM. SUBJ. (Frosinone).
S. Costanzo.

Arezzo. 3C.
S. Donato, about 1278 by MARGARI-
TONE D'AREZZO, finished 1510; façade,
1901–11.

Ariano. 11C. (Avellino).
Assumption, ?11C.; rebuilt after 1456,
about 1836 & after 1930.

Ascoli Piceno. 4C. IMM. SUBJ.
S. Emidio, 12C.; enlarged & remodelled
1482, restored late 19C.

Ascoli Satriano. 11C. (Foggia).
S. Potito, ?12C.–13C.; remodelled
15C.–16C.

[D4] ASSISI. 3C. IMM. SUBJ. (Perugia).
S. Rufino, 9C.; enlarged 11C.; rebuilt
1144 by GIOVANNI DA GUBBIO;
restored 1217; int. remodelled 1571
by G. ALESSI. *See fig. 8.*

Asti. 3C.
Assumption, 11C.; rebuilt 1324–about
1354; remodelled & extended 1764–9
by B. VITTONE.
Baptistery, crypt 7C.–8C.

Atri. 1152, IMM. SUBJ. (Teramo).
S. Reparata & Assumption, 9C.–10C.;
rebuilt 2nd half 13C. & early 14C.;
int. altered 15C. *186 ft long, 81 ft.*
wide.
Campanile, ? 13C. *179 ft high.*

Avellino. 2C.
Assumption, 10C.; repeatedly rebuilt up
to 1868.

Aversa. 11C. IMM. SUBJ. (Naples).
St Paul, 1062–1090; restored 1255;
largely rebuilt 1703–15, by C. BERATTI.

Avezzano. 9C. (Aquila).
St Bartholomew.

Bagnoregio. 6C. IMM. SUBJ. (Viterbo).
Ss. Donato, Nicola & Bonaventura.

[G6] BARI. 4C. METR. 6C.
S. Sabino, see pp. 221–4.

[G6] Barletta. 1860 (Bari).
S. Maria Maggiore, before 1150;
extended about 1307, enlarged 15C.

Belluno. 2C.
S. Martino now *Assumption,* rebuilt early

16C. to design of T. LOMBARDO;
restored after 1873.
Campanile, 1732–43 by F. JUVARA.
223 ft high.

Benevento. 1C. METR. 969.
Assumption & S. Fotino, 7C.; enlarged
9C.; rebuilt 2nd half 12C.; restored
after 1688 & 1702; largely destroyed
1943.

Bergamo. 4C.
S. Vincenzo now *S. Alessandro,* rebuilt
1459 with collaboration of A. FILA-
RETE; remodelled 1689 by C.
FONTANA; altered later; façade, 1886
by A. BONICELLI.
Baptistery, 1340 by GIOVANNI DA
CAMPIONE.

Bertinoro. 1360 (Forlì).
S. Maria degli Angeli, late 16C.

Biella. 1772 (Vercelli).
S. Stefano Nuovo, 14C.–1402; enlarged
& remodelled after 1772; portico,
1825.
Baptistery, 9C.–10C.

Bisaccia. 12C. (Avellino).
Nativity of Mary, rebuilt 1747 by
PIETRO DI PAGANO.

Bisceglie. 8C. (Bari).
St Peter, 1073–1295.

Bisignano. 12C. (Cosenza).
Annunciation, 11C.–12C.; altered since.

Bitetto. 1089–1818 (Bari).
St Michael, 1355; int. 1735.
Campanile, 1735.

Bitonto. 9C. (Bari).
S. Valentino now *Assumption,* 1175–
1200.

Bobbio. 11C. (Piacenza.)
Assumption (not the monastery), 13C.;
extended 15C.

Boiano. 11C.–1927 (Campobasso.)
St Bartholomew, 14C.; rebuilt since.

BOLOGNA. 3C. METR. 1582.   **[C3]**
St Peter, rebuilt after 1141; rebuilt
1605 to design of F. AMBROSINI;
façade, 1743–7 by A. TORREGGIANI.
See fig. 19.

Bosa. 5C. (Nuoro).
Immaculate Conception.

256

Bova. 7C. (Reggio-Calabria).
S. Teodoro, rebuilt 1783.
Bovino. 5C. (Foggia).
Assumption, 905; rebuilt 13C.; restored 1930's.
Brescia. 1C.
La Rotonda (old cathedral), 6C.–7C.; rebuilt 9C.–11C.; restored 1881–97; presbytery added 15C.
Assumption (new cathedral), 1604 by G. B. LANTANA (on site of old summer cathedral, *S. Piero de Dom*); cupola completed 1825, to design of L. CAGNOLA.
Bressanone. 6C. IMM. SUBJ. (Bolzano).
Assumption, rebuilt 13C.; rebuilt 1745–1754 to design of G. DELLAI; façade, 1790 by G. PIRCHSTALLER; int. decor. 1896.
    Baptistery, before ? 1080.
[H6] **Brindisi.** 4C. METR. 10C.
Visitation, 1140; rebuilt 1746.
    Campanile, 1780.
Brugnato. 12C. (La Spezia).
St Peter, 8C. abbey church; rebuilt after 1133.

Cagli. 4C. (Pesaro & Urbino).
Assumption, rebuilt 1790.
Cagliari. 4C. METR. 11C.
S. Cecilia, 13C.–14C.; restored 17C.
Caiazzo. 9C. (Benevento).
Assumption, rebuilt 2nd half 13C.; altered later.
Caltagirone. 1818 (Catania).
S. Giuliano, 1818.
Caltanissetta. 1844.
Immaculate Conception, 1570–1622.
Calvi. 5C. (Naples).
S. Casto, 9C.; restored about 1452.
Camerino. 3C. ARCHB. 1787, IMM. SUBJ. (Macerata).
Annunciation, rebuilt 1832 by A. VICCI & C. FOLCHI.
Campagna. 1525, IMM. SUBJ. (Macerata).
S. Maria della Pace.
Campobasso. 1927.
Holy Trinity now *Assumption*, 1829 by B. MUSENGA.

Canosa. 6C.–1818 (Bari).
S. Sabino, mid-11C.; restored 1689.
Caorle. 598–1818 (Veneto).
Capua. 2C. METR. 966.
St Stephen, 856; rebuilt 1120; additions 1719; largely destroyed 1943.
Carpi. 1779 (Modena).
Assumption, 1514 by B. PERUZZI (incomplete); façade, 1667; (cupola removed 1771).
Carrara. (Massa Carrara q.v.).
St Andrew, 12C.–13C.; façade, 12C., altered 14C.
    Campanile, begun about 1281.
Casale Monferrato. 1474 (Alessandria).
S. Evasio, 11C.–12C.; restored 1859–61 by A. MELLA.
Caserta Vecchia. 12C. (Naples).
St Michael, 1113–about 1128. *151 ft* long.
    Campanile, finished 1234. *105 ft* high.
Caserta Nuova (succeeds C. Vecchia).
St Michael, before 1844.
Cassano all'Ionio. 5C. (Cosenza).
Nativity of Mary.
Castellamare di Stabia. 4C. (Naples).
Assumption, 1587; altered 1875.
Castellaneta. 11C. (Taranto).
SS. Peter & Paul now *Assumption*, 12C.; rebuilt 15C. & 18C.; façade, 1771.
    Campanile, 15C.
CATANIA. 1C. ARCHB. 1844 IMM. SUBJ. [F9]
S. Agata, 1092; rebuilt 1169 & 1693; rebuilt 1736 by G. B. VACCARINI.
Catanzaro. 1121, ARCHB. 1844, IMM. SUBJ.
Assumption & *SS. Peter & Paul*, 12C.; rebuilt after 1783.
Cava. 1394, IMM. SUBJ. (Salerno).
S. Adiutore, 18C.–19C.
CEFALU. 1131 (Palermo). [E9]
S. Saviour, see pp. 238–40. *243 ft* long, transepts *95 ft* wide.
Ceneda. 6C.–1939 (Treviso).
S. Maria Maggiore, rebuilt 1755 by A. SCHIAVI DI TOLMEZZO.
Cerignola. 1818 (Foggia).
St Peter.

Cervia. 6C. (Ravenna).
Assumption.

Cesena. 1C. (Forlì).
St John Baptist, late 14C. by UNDESVALD; altered later; restored 1890.
Campanile, 1450–mid-18C.

Chiavari. 1892 (Genoa).
Madonna dell'Orto, enlarged 1613; remodelled since.

Chieti. 6C. METR. 1526.
St Thomas now S. Giustino, restored 840; restored 1877.
Campanile, 1335 by BARTOLOMEO DI GIACOMO; finished 1498 by ANTONIO DI LODI.

Chioggia. 7C. (Venice).
Assumption, before 11C.; rebuilt & reorientated 1633 by B. LONGHENA.
Campanile, 1347–50.

Chiusi. 5C. (Siena).
S. Secondiano, 5C.–6C.; restored 1887–94.

Cingoli. 5C. IMM. SUBJ. (Macerata).
Assumption, 17C.

Città di Castello. 7C. IMM. SUBJ. (Perugia).
S. Florido, 11C.; enlarged 1356; largely rebuilt 1466–1529; int. 18C.; façade, 1632 by F. LAZZARI.
Campanile, 13C.

Città della Pieve. 1600, IMM. SUBJ. (Perugia). *Ss. Gervasio & Protasio,* 12C.; remodelled 16C.–17C.

Cividale. 5C. (Udine).
Assumption, 1453; rebuilt after 1502 by T. LOMBARDO.
Baptistery, 8C.
Campanile, 1634.

[D5] CIVITA CASTELLANA. 990, IMM. SUBJ. (Viterbo).
Annunciation, façade 1210, see fig. 6; int. remodelled 1736–40.

Civitavecchia. 4C. IMM. SUBJ. (Rome).
St Francis of Assisi.

Colle Val d'Elsa. 1592 (Siena).
S. Marziale, rebuilt 1603 by F. BUGLIESI DA MONTEPULCIANO.

Comacchio. 6C. (Ferrara).
S. Cassiano, 17C.; façade, 1817.

COMO. 4C. [B2]
S. Maria Maggiore, rebuilt late 14C. by L. D. SPAZZI; continued 15C. by P. DA BREGGIA, & T. RODARI; apse, 1513; cupola, 1730–70 by F. JUVARA (rebuilt since 1935 to original form).
See fig. 15.

Concordia Sagitaria (Portogruaro). 6C. (Udine).
St Stephen, ?12C.
Baptistery, ?12C.; restored 1880.

Conversano. 5C. (Bari).
Assumption, 11C.–12C.; renovated 1359–73; restored after 1911.

Conza. 8C. METR. 11C. (Avellino).
S. Erberto.

Cortona. 1325, IMM. SUBJ. (Arezzo).
Assumption & S. Vincenzo, about 1100; int. enlarged 2nd half 15C. by G. DA SANGALLO; altered by A. GALILEI, early 18C.
Campanile, about 1556.

Cosenza. 7C. METR. 1050, IMM. SUBJ.
Assumption, about 1185; remodelled 1750; façade, 1831.

Crema. 1579 (Cremona).
S. Maria Maggiore, 14C.–15C., probably by G. & A. DI MARCO DA CAMPIONE.

CREMONA. 4C. [C3]
Assumption, 1109; rebuilt after 1124; continued & enlarged 13C.–14C.; main façade finished 14C., altered 1491 & 1501.
Baptistery, 1167 by ? T. ORLANDINO.
Campanile, 1250–67 or '84, cusp 1287–1300. *364 ft high.*

Crotone. 6C. IMM. SUBJ. (Catanzaro).
S. Dionigi.

Cuneo. 1817.
Nostra Signora del Bosco (Our Lady of the Wood) or *The Presentation of Mary,* ?12C.; rebuilt 1662; restored 1745; façade, 1865 by A. BONO.

Fabriano. 1728 (Ancona).
S. Venanzio, remodelled 14C.; largely rebuilt 1617 by M. ODDI; restored 1920.

Faenza. 3C. (Ravenna).
S. Maria Foris Portam (first cathedral), ?8c.; rebuilt later.
St Peter (present cathedral) now *S. Terenzio*, 1474 by G. DA MAIANO, finished by L. DI PIGNO PORTIGIANI IL GIOVANE, early 16c.; altered 1581.

Fano. 1C. IMM. SUBJ. (Pesaro & Urbino).
Assumption, rebuilt 1113–40 by MAESTRO RAINERIO; altered 13c.; remodelled later.

Feltre. 6C. (Belluno).
St Peter, ?9c.; altered 15c.; largely rebuilt 16c.
 Campanile, 1392, top 1690.

Ferentino. 4C. IMM. SUBJ. (Frosinone).
St Peter, about 1100.

Fermo. 3C. METR. 1589 (Ascoli Piceno).
Assumption, 5c.; ?10c.; rebuilt after 1176 by MAESTRO GIORGIO; int. 1789 by C. MORELLI.
 Campanile altered 1340 & 1731.

[D3] FERRARA. 4C. ARCHB. 1735, IMM. SUBJ.
S. Giorgio, see pp. 177–82.
 Campanile, *177 ft* high.

Fidenza. 1601, IMM. SUBJ. (Parma).
S. Donnino, 1207–late 13c.

[C4] FIESOLE. 1C. (Florence).
S. Romolo, 1028; enlarged 1256 & 14c.; restored 1883–87.
 Campanile, 1213. *139 ft* high.

[C4] FLORENCE (Firenze). 1C. METR. 1420.
S. Maria del Fiore, see pp. 158–66. *492 ft* long; nave & aisles, *124* ft wide; octagon diameter, *295 ft*; cupola, diameter of drum, *149 ft*, height (without lantern), *298 ft*.
 Baptistery, see pp. 166–67. Diameter *84 ft*.
 Campanile, see p. 159. *268 ft* high.

[F6] FOGGIA. 1855, IMM. SUBJ.
S. Maria Icona Vetere, about 1170; largely rebuilt after 1731.

Foligno. 1C. IMM. SUBJ. (Perugia).
S. Feliciano, 1133, by MAESTRO ATTO; enlarged 1201; altered 16c. & 18c.; int. early 16c., by C. DA CAPRAROLA

to design of A. DI SANGALLO IL VECCHIO; remodelled by G. PIERMARINI, ?1771, to modified design of L. VANVITELLI.

Fondi. until 1818 (Littoria).
St Peter, rebuilt 1158–80; altered 13c. & 14c.; restored 1935.
 Campanile, 1278.

Forlì. 2C.
Holy Cross now *St Thomas of Canterbury*, 12c.; largely rebuilt 15c.; restored 1841.

Fossano. 1592 (Cuneo).
Ss. Maria & Giovenale, 1789, by M. L. QUARINI.

Fossombrone. 5C. (Pesaro & Urbino).
S. Maurenzo, rebuilt 1772–84, by C. MORELLI.

Frascati. 3C. SED. SUBURB. (Rome).
St Peter.

Gaeta. 8C. ARCHB. 1848, IMM. SUBJ. (Littoria).
Assumption with Ss. Erasmo & Marciano, late 11c.; restored 1792.
 Campanile, 1148–74, by N. D' ANGELO; lantern about 1279.

Gallese. 8C. IMM. SUBJ. (Viterbo).
Assumption, 1796.

Gallipoli. 6C. (Lecce).
S. Agata, 1629 by G. B. GENUINO D' GALLIPOLI.

GENOA. 3C. METR. 1133. **[E3]**
Holy Apostles (first cathedral) now *S. Siro*, rebuilt 11c. & 16c.
St Lawrence (cathedral since 985), see pp. 201–5.

Gerace. 5C. (Reggio-Calabria).
Assumption, consecrated 1045; restored 14c. & after 1783.

Giovinazzo. 11C. IMM. SUBJ. (Bari).
Assumption, 12c.; int. 17c. & 18c.

Gorizia. 1751, METR.
Ss. Ilario & Taziano, 14c., later enlarged; rebuilt after World War I.

GRADO. 6c.–? (Gorizia). **[E2]**
S. Eufemia now *Ss. Ermagora & Fortunato*, see pp. 122–3. *151 ft* long.

Gravina. 9C. IMM. SUBJ. (Bari).
St John Baptist now *Assumption*, 1092; enlarged 1420; rebuilt after 1447.
    Campanile, 1698.

Grosseto. 1138.
Assumption & St Lawrence, rebuilt 1190–about 1250; remodelled 1294 by S. DI PACE RUSTICHINI; restored 19C.
    Campanile, 1402; restored 1611.

Gualdo-Taddino. 5C. (Perugia).
S. Benedetto, 13C.; int. altered later.

Guastalla. 1828 (Reggio-Emilia).
SS. Peter & Paul, 1343–71 by FRANCESCO DA VOLTERRA; façade, 1719; altered 1890.

Gubbio. 5C. IMM. SUBJ. (Perugia).
Ss. Mariano & Giacomo, 13C.

Iesi. 6C. IMM. SUBJ. (Ancona).
S. Settimo, 13C.–15C.; rebuilt 1732–41 by D. BARRIGIONI.
    Campanile, 18C. by F. MATELICANI.

Iglesias. 1763 (Cagliari).
S. Chiara, 1285–88; int. 16C.

Imola. 4C. (Bologna).
S. Cassiano, 1187–1271; rebuilt, consecrated 1782; façade, 1849.
    Campanile, 1473–85.

Irsina. 15C. IMM. SUBJ. (Matera).
Assumption, 13C.; rebuilt 1777.
    Campanile, 13C.

Ischia. 12C. (Naples).
Assumption, 14C.; abandoned after 1809.

Isernia. 5C. (Campobasso).
St Peter, rebuilt 1837.

[A2] **IVREA.** 7C. (Aosta).
Assumption, 4C.; rebuilt 11C.; restored 2nd half 18C.; façade, 1854; two belltowers and cupola, 11C.

Lacedonia. 11C. (Avellino).
Assumption.

Lanciano. 1515, METR. 1562 (Chieti).
S. Maria del Ponte, 1389–15C.; rebuilt 1785–88 by E. MICHITELLI.
    Campanile, 1610–14. *121 ft* high.

Lanusei (Ogliastra). 1824 (Nuoro).
S. Maria Maddalena.

L'Aquila. 1257, ARCHB. 1876, IMM. SUBJ.
Ss. Massimo & Giorgio, late 13C.; rebuilt after 1703; restored 1887 & after 1915; façade, 19C. *249 ft* long.

Larino. 5C. (Campobasso).
S. Pardo, finished 1319.
    Campanile, 1451.

La Spezia. 5C.
Assumption, 14C.–1550; destroyed 1943, rebuilding.

LECCE. 1057.   **[H7]**
Assumption, 1114; rebuilt 1659–70 by G. ZIMBALO. *See fig. 18.*

Lipari. 5C. (Messina).
St Bartholomew, rebuilt 1654.

Livorno. 1806.
St Francis of Assisi, 1581–95 by A. PIERONI; portico by ? INIGO JONES, 1605; restored 1856.
    Campanile, 1817 by L. PAMPALONI.

Lodi. 4C. (Milan).
Assumption, about 1158–63.

Loreto. 1586–1934 (Macerata).
Basilica containing the *Santa Casa*. Begun 1468 by ? M. DI MARCO CEDRINO; completed by G. DA MAIANO; additions by G. DA SANGALLO; work by D. BRAMANTE & A. SANSOVINO; restored late 19C.
    Campanile, 1750–4 by L. VANVITELLI. *248 ft* high.

LUCCA. 1C. ARCHB. 1726, IMM. SUBJ. **[C4]**
S. Martino, rebuilt 1060; remodelled 13C.; façade, about 1200 by GUIDO & GUIDETTO DA COMO; int. late 14C. & early 15C. *276 ft* long, *90 ft* wide. *See fig. 9.*

LUCERA. 4C. (Foggia).
Assumption, 1300–11. *See p. 64.*   **[F6]**

Lungro. 1919, IMM. SUBJ. (Cosenza).
S. Nicola di Mira.

Luni. 5C.–1016, transferred to La Spezia. Destroyed about 1000.

Macerata. 1320.
S. Giuliano, 1771–90 by C. MORELLI.
    Campanile, 1478; altered later.

Magliano-Sabino (Sabina). 5C. SED. SUBURB. (Rome).
S. *Liberatore*, restored 1735.

[G5] Manfredonia. 3C. METR. 1074 (Foggia).
St Lawrence.

[C2] MANTUA. 804.
St Peter, 1383; rebuilt after 1545 by GIULIO ROMANO, continued by G. B. COVO; façade, 1756.

Marsico Nuovo. 4C. (Potenza).
S. *Giorgio, Assumption* & S. *Gianuario.*

Massa Carrara. 1822.
St Francis now *St Peter*, 15C.; altered 17C.

Massa Marittima. 5C. (Grosseto).
S. *Cerbone*, about 1228 by ? ENRICO DA CAMPIONE; enlarged 1287–1304 by ? GIOVANNI PISANO.

Matelica. 5C. IMM. SUBJ. (Macerata).
Assumption.

Matera. 9C.
S. *Maria*, 1268–70; additions 17C. & 18C. *177 ft* long, *59 ft* wide.

Mazara del Vallo. 1093 (Trapani).
S. *Saviour*, 1075; remodelled 1690–4; façade finished 1906.

Melfi. 11C. IMM. SUBJ. (Potenza).
Assumption, 12C.; rebuilt 18C.
Campanile, 1153.

[F8] MESSINA. 5C. METR. 12C.
S. *Maria* now S. *Antonio*, see pp. 232–8. *318 ft* long, *111 ft* wide.
Campanile, *197 ft* high.

[B2] MILAN. 1C. METR. 4C.
S. *Maria Maggiore*, see pp. 182–92. *515 ft* long, *193 ft* wide; vault *148 ft* high; top of spire *350 ft* from pavement.

Mileto. 11C. IMM. SUBJ. (Catanzaro).
S. *Nicola*, rebuilt 1930.

[C3] MODENA. 3C. METR. 1855.
S. *Geminiano*, see pp. 168–73.

Modigliana. 1850 (Forlì).
St Stephen.

[G6] MOLFETTA. 12C. IMM. SUBJ. (Bari).
S. *Corrado* (old cathedral), 1150–late 13C. See fig. 96.
Assumption (cathedral since 1785), 17C.

Mondovì. 1388 (Cuneo).
S. *Donato*, 1743 by F. GALLO.

Monopoli. 11C. IMM. SUBJ. (Bari).
S. *Mercurio*, 1107; rebuilt 1742–70.

MONREALE. 1176, METR. 1183 **[E9]** (Palermo).
S. *Maria Nuova*, see pp. 240–4. *334 ft* long, *131 ft* wide; cloister, *170 ft* square.

Montalcino. 1462, IMM. SUBJ. (Siena).
S. *Saviour*, rebuilt 1818–32.

Montalto delle Marche. 1586 (Ascoli Piceno).
Assumption, 1586 by G. RAINALDI; altered 19C. by L. POLETTI; façade, 1896.

Monte Cassino. 1321–67 only.
Benedictine Abbey.

Montefeltro. 9C. (Pesaro & Urbino).
S. *Niccolò.*

Montefiascone. 15C. IMM. SUBJ. (Viterbo).
S. *Margherita*, 1519 by M. SAMMICHELI & C. FONTANA; façade, 1840–3 by P. GAZOLA.

Montepulciano. 1561, IMM. SUBJ. (Siena).
Assumption, rebuilt 1570, design of B. AMMANNATI, modified by I. SCALZA, finished 1680; restored 1888.

Monza. (Not a cathedral.) (Milan).
St John Baptist, Coronation church for Holy Roman Empire (founded by Lombard queen, Theodolinda), rebuilt 13C.; enlarged 1300–1400; façade, 1390–6 by MATTEO DA CAMPIONE, restored 1889–1908; int. 16C. & 18C., restored 1880–95.
Campanile, 1592–1606 by P. PELLEGRINI.

MURANO. 1659–1818 (Venice). **[D2]**
Ss. *Maria* & *Donato*, 7C.; restored & altered 12C.; restored 1866.

Muro Lucano. 11C. (Potenza).
S. *Nicola*, about ?1009; rebuilt 1696 & 1725–8; improved 1884–8.

NAPLES. 1C. METR. 10C. **[E6]**
S. *Restituta* (until 8C. S. *Saviour*); altered 14C.; restored 1688.
S. *Gennaro* (on site of 5C. *Basilica Stefania*), 1294–1323; partly rebuilt

APPENDIX

1484–1505; remodelled 1787 & 1837–44; façade, 1349, remade 1877–1905. *328 ft long.*
Baptistery, before 430.

Nardo. 1413, IMM. SUBJ. (Lecce).
Assumption (originally Basilian church, then, 1090, Benedictine), partly rebuilt 1230; enlarged 14c.; additions 18c.; restored 1892–1900.

Narni. 4C. IMM. SUBJ. (Terni).
Ss. Giovenale & Bartolomeo, consecrated 1145; int. 15c.

Nepi. 1C. IMM. SUBJ. (Viterbo).
Assumption, rebuilt 9c.; enlarged 1180; rebuilt 1831.

Nicastro. 11C. (Catanzaro).
SS. Peter & Paul.

Nicosia. 1816 (Enna).
S. Niccolò, before 14c.

Nicotera. 6C. (Catanzaro).
Assumption, 1785.

Nocera de'Pagani. 7C. (Salerno).
St. Mark.

Nocera Umbra. 5C. IMM. SUBJ. (Perugia).
Assumption, ?11c.; largely rebuilt 1450; int. remodelled later.

Nola. 2C. (Naples).
S. Felice, 1395–1402; rebuilt 1878–1909.

Noli. 1239 (Savona).
St Peter, consecrated 1239; remodelled 17c.

Norcia. 5C. IMM. SUBJ. (Perugia).
S. Maria Argentea or *della Plebe,* 1560; rebuilt after 1730; restored after 1859.

[F10] **NOTO.** 1844 (Syracuse).
S. Nicola, 18c. See fig. 20.

Novara. 4C.
Assumption, 11c.; rebuilt 1863–5 by A. ANTONELLI.

Nuoro. 12C.
S. Maria della Neve, 19c.

Nusco. 11C. (Avellino).
S. Amato.

Oppido Mamertina. 13C. (Reggio-Calabria).
S. Nicola di Mira, after 1783.

Orbetello. ? DATE (Grosseto).
?13c.–14c.; rebuilt 17c.

Oria. 1591 (Brindisi).
Assumption, rebuilt 1750.

Oristano. 11C. METR. (Cagliari).
Assumption, 13c.; rebuilt 1733; enlarged 19c.

Orte. 7C. IMM. SUBJ. (Viterbo).
Assumption, 1363–1422 by TADDEO DI BARTOLO.

Ortona. 5C. (Chieti).
St Thomas, remodelled 1127; int. remodelled 18c.?–19c.

ORVIETO. 6C. IMM. SUBJ. (Terni). [D5]
Assumption, see pp. 155–7. 293 ft long, 107 ft wide, 111 ft high; façade, *131 ft wide, 170 ft high.*

Osimo. 7C. IMM. SUBJ. (Ancona).
S. Leopardo now *St John Baptist,* 8c.; rebuilt 1200, altered later; façade, 16c.

Ostia. 3C. SED. SUBURB. (Rome).
S. Aurea.

Ostuni. 11C. (Brindisi).
Assumption, 1470–95.

Otranto. 7C. METR. 11C. (Lecce).
Nativity of Mary, 1080–8; restored after 1481, altered 18c., restored before 1940.

Ozieri. 13C. (Sassari).
Immaculate Conception, 16c.; rebuilt 19c.

PADUA. 1C. [D2]
Assumption, before 9c.; rebuilt 12c.; rebuilt 1552 to design of MICHELANGELO, much altered by A. DA VALLE & A. RIGHETTI, finished 1754.
Baptistery, 13c.

Palo del Colle. ? DATE (Bari).
S. Maria della Porta, 12c.; altered and restored 1581.

PALERMO. 1C. METR. 11C. [E9]
Assumption, see p. 244.

Palestrina. 4C. SED. SUBURB. (Rome).
S. Agapito, perhaps Roman Temple of Jupiter; additions 12c., restored and altered after 1437.
Campanile, 12c.

262

[E2] (PARENZO). 3C. (now in YUGO-SLAVIA).

Basilica Eufrasiana, see pp. 119–21.

[C3] PARMA. 4C. IMM. SUBJ.

Assumption, see pp. 173–6.
Baptistery, *see* pp. 176–7.
Campanile, *see* pp. *208 ft* high.

Patti. 12C. (Messina).
St Bartholomew.

[B2] PAVIA. 1C.

S. Siro now *St Stephen, see* pp. 198–201.

Penne. 5C. IMM. SUBJ. (Pescara).

S. Maria degli Angeli and *S. Massimo,* before 1000; rebuilt 11C. and 14C.; altered 1660, restored 1905.

Pergola. 1819 (Pesaro & Urbino).

St. Andrew & *S. Secondo,* 1258; rebuilt 19C.

Perugia. 2C. ARCHB. 1882, IMM. SUBJ.

St Lawrence now *Ss. Andrew* & *Lucia,* planned 1300, begun 1345, finished 1490. *223 ft* long.

Pesaro. 3C. (Pesaro & Urbino).

S. Terenzio, late 13C.–14C.; restored later.

Pescara. 1949.

S. Cetteo.

Pescia. 1726 (Pistoia).

Assumption.

[B3] PIACENZA. 4C. IMM. SUBJ.

Assumption, 1122; completed by R. SANTO DA SAMBUCETO: restored 1897–1901. *See* fig. *11.*

Piana dei Greci or **degli Albanesi** 1937, IMM. SUBJ. (Palermo). (for the Italo-Albanians of the Byzantine rite in Sicily).

S. Demetrio Megalomari.

Piazza Armerina. 1817 (Enna).

Assumption, 11C.–12C.; rebuilt 1627 by O. TORRIANI.

[D4] PIENZA. 1462 (Siena).

Assumption, 1459–62. *121 ft* long.

Pietrasanta. ? DATE (Lucca).

S. Martino, 1330; int. 16C., 17C. & 19C.

Pinerolo. 1746 (Turin).

S. Donato, ? 1044; enlarged & altered 1589, restored 18C. & 1874–94.
Campanile, 1425.

PISA. 4C. METR. 1092. **[C4]**

S. Maria Maggiore now *Ss. Leonardo* & *Ranieri, see* pp. 140–5. *311 ft* long, *112 ft* wide, *259 ft* across transepts; nave, *108 ft* high; cupola, *167 ft* high.
Baptistery, *see* pp. 145–7. Diameter *116 ft, 180 ft* high.
Campanile, *181 ft* high at highest point.

PISTOIA. 5C. **[C4]**

S. Zeno, altered 13C., remodelled 1599 & 17C.; façade 1311.
Baptistery, about 1337.
Campanile, 13C. *218 ft* high.

Pitigliano. 1844 (Grosseto).

S. Martino, restored 16C.; façade 18C.

Poggio Mirteto. ? 5C. SED. SUBURB. (Rome).

Assumption, 1641–1725.

Policastro Busentino. 11C. (Salerno).

Assumption, 1177.

Pontecorvo. 1725, IMM. SUBJ. (Frosinone).

St Bartholomew.

Pontremoli. 1797 (Massa Carrara).

Assumption, 1697 by A. CAPRA; façade, 1881.

Pordenone. ? DATE (Udine).

St Mark, rebuilt mid-15C.; façade, 1840.
Campanile, ?1219–1427, cusp 1616. *259 ft* high.

Porto Torres. ? DATE (Sassari).

S. Gavino, 11C.

Potenza. 5C.

S. Gerardo, 1197–1200; enlarged 1250; rebuilt 1783–99; restored 1930's.

Pozzuoli. 1C. (Naples).

S. Procolo, Roman Temple of Augustus (1C.); remodelled 16C.–17C.

Prato. 1653 (Florence).

St Stephen, 12C.; int. remodelled 1317–20; façade, early 15C. by NICCOLO D'AREZZO.

Priverno. 11C. (Littoria).

Annunciation, 12C. Cistercian church; int. remodelled 1782.

Ragusa. 1950.
St John Baptist.

Rapolla. 11c. IMM. SUBJ. (Potenza).
St Michael, 13c.

[F6] RAVELLO. 1086–1818 (Salerno).
S. Pantaleone, see pp. 215–6.

[D3] RAVENNA. 1c. METR. 5c.
Anastasis or *Resurrection, see* pp. 114–8.
New cathedral, *199 ft* long, *198 ft* across transepts.
Baptistery, *see* pp. 118–9. Diameter *36 ft*, with apses, *46 ft.*
Campanile, *115 ft* high.

Recanati. 1239, IMM. SUBJ. (Macerata).
S. Flaviano, late 14c.; int. about 1620.

Reggio-Calabria. 1c. METR. 11c.
Assumption, rebuilt after 1908.

Reggio-Emilia. 1c.
Assumption, 9c.; rebuilt 13c.

Rieti. 5c. IMM. SUBJ.
Assumption, 5c.; rebuilt 1109–1225; upper church rebuilt 14c.; int. remodelled 1639.

[D3] RIMINI. 3c. (Forlì).
(Tempio Malatestiano) S. Colomba, known as *S. Francesco, see* pp. 192–8.

Ripatransone. 1571 (Ascoli Piceno).
Ss. Gregorio & Margherita, 1597 by G. GUERRA; façade, 1842 by G. ROSSETTI.

[D5] ROME. THE PATRIARCHAL BASILICAS.
The Archbasilica of the Saviour, St John Lateran, see pp. 85–91. *426 ft* long.
Baptistery, *see* p. 91.
St Lawrence outside the Walls, 312–334; two basilicas joined together, early 13c.
S. Maria Maggiore, see pp. 108–12. *282 ft* long.
St Paul's outside the Walls, see pp. 102–8. *350 ft* long, *195 ft* wide; nave alone, *270 ft* long, *73 ft* wide, *95 ft* high.
St Peter's in the Vatican, old church, *see* pp. 91–4. *377 ft* long.
New church, *see* pp. 94–102. Overall length, *710 ft*; int. *600 ft*; nave, *84 ft* wide; transepts, *450 ft* across; main arcade, *83 ft* high; main vault, *150 ft* high; cupola, *137½ ft* diameter, springs from drum at a height of *257 ft*; cross

on cupola, *452 ft* above nave pavement.

Rossano. 7c. ARCHB. 1460, IMM. SUBJ. (Cosenza).
Holy Trinity.

Ruvo. 6c. (Bari).
Assumption.

Sacile. ? DATE (Udine).
? 9c.; rebuilt 15c.; restored 1836.
Campanile, 1568.

SALERNO. 6c. METR. 10c. **[F6]**
S. Maria degli Angeli now *SS. Matthew & Gregory, see* pp. 208–14.
Campanile, *183 ft* high.

Saluzzo. 1511 (Cuneo).
Assumption, 1491. *262 ft* long.
Campanile, 1771. *210 ft* high.

Sant'Agata de' Goti. 10c. (Benevento).
Assumption, 10c.; rebuilt early 12c.; int. remodelled 1723–34.

Sant'Angelo dei Lombardi. 12c. (Avellino).
S. Antonino, 11c.; rebuilt 16c.

Sant'Angelo in Vado. 1635 (Pesaro & Urbino).
St Michael.

San Leo. ? DATE (Pesaro & Urbino). 1173–13c.

San Marco. 12c. IMM. SUBJ. (Cosenza).
St Mark, 12c.; restored later.

San Miniato. 1622 (Pisa).
Assumption & S. Genesio, 9c.; remodelled 1703, restored 1860.

San Sepolcro. 1515 (Arezzo).
St John Evangelist.

Santa Severina. 7c. METR. 11c. (Catanzaro).
S. Anastasia, 1274–95; altered later; int. 20c.

San Severino Marche. 1586 (Macerata).
S. Severino (old cathedral), 944; rebuilt 1001; enlarged & altered later; façade, 14c.
Magdalene now *S. Agostino* (cathedral church since 1827), façade late 15c.; int. remodelled 1776 & 1827.

San Severo. 11C. (Foggia).
Assumption, enlarged 1583.

Sarno. 11C. IMM. SUBJ. (Salerno).
St Michael.

Sarsina. 4C. (Forlì).
Annunciation.

Sarzana. 1829 (La Spezia).
Assumption, 1204–1477; altered 17C.

Sassari. 5C. METR. 1073.
S. Nicola, 13C.; remodelled 1480–early 16C.; façade, 1650–1723.

Savona. 10C.
Assumption, rebuilt 1589–1604.
Baptistery, before 1000.

Scala. 987–1818 (Salerno).
St Lawrence, 10C.; restored 14C.; int. 1615.

Segni. 5C. IMM. SUBJ. (Rome).
S. Bruno now *Assumption,* finished 1185; rebuilt 1626–57; façade, 1817.

Senigallia. 6C. (Ancona).
St Peter, rebuilt 1790; façade, 19C.

Seravezza. ? DATE (Littoria).
Assumption, rebuilt 1235; altered 18C.

Sessa Aurunca. 5C. (Naples).
St Peter, rebuilt 1103; altered 1758.

Sezze. 8C. IMM. SUBJ. (Littoria).
S. Maria, 1347; remodelled 16C.–17C.

[C4] SIENA. 4C. METR. 1459.
St John Baptist, see pp. 147–55. *293 ft* long; nave & aisles, *80 ft* wide; crossing, *178½ ft* wide; new cathedral, *179 ft* long as it stands.

Siponto. ? DATE (Foggia).
S. Maria, consecr. 1117; partly remodelled 16C.–18C.

Sora. 3C. (Frosinone).
Assumption, on Roman substructure; consecr. early 12C.; rebuilt after 1229; remodelled 17C.

Sorrento. 5C. METR. 1068 (Naples).
SS. Philip & James, rebuilt 15C.; restored later; façade, 1913–24.

Sovana Pitigliano. 7C. (Grosseto).
SS. Peter & Paul, late 8C.; rebuilt mid-11C.; altered late 14C.

[D5] SPOLETO. 1C. ARCHB. 1820 (Perugia).
Assumption, rebuilt late 12C.; re-

modelled 17C.; façade, 1207 & 1491, see fig. 16.
Campanile, 11C.–12C.; belfry, 1461 and cusp, 1518.

Squillace. 4C. IMM. SUBJ. (Catanzaro).
Holy Trinity, rebuilt 1795; restored 1915.

Sulmona. 6C. IMM. SUBJ. (Aquila).
Our Lady now *S. Panfilo,* restored 1078–1119 & 13C.; remodelled 1463–1501; restored 20C.

Susa. 1772 (Turin).   **[A2]**
S. Giusto (once a Benedictine Abbey), 1st half 11C.
Campanile, 11C.; additions of 1481.

Sutri. 5C. IMM. SUBJ. (Viterbo).
Assumption, 13C.; remodelled 15C.–?16C.
Campanile, 1207.

SYRACUSE. 4C. METR. 1844.   **[F9]**
Nativity of Mary, known as *S. Maria del Piliero* or *delle Colonne,* see pp. 230–2.

Taranto. 6C. METR. 10C.
S. Cataldo, rebuilt 1071; altered 1569, 1657 & later; façade, 1713.
Campanile, 1413.

Tarquinia. 1435, IMM. SUBJ. (Viterbo).
S. Margherita, rebuilt about 1656; restored 1875–9; façade, 1933 by P. MAGNANI.

Teano. 6C. (Naples).
S. Terenziano now *S. Clemente,* 1116; rebuilt 1630 by A. VACCARO; façade, 1636–1873.

Teggiano (Diano-Teggiano). 1850 (Salerno).
S. Maria Maggiore, before 13C.

Telese. 5C. (Benevento).
Holy Trinity, consecr. 1740.

Tempio. 4C. (Sassari).
St Peter, 15C.–16C.; rebuilt 19C.

Teramo. 5C. IMM. SUBJ.
S. Maria Aprutiensis now *S. Getulia,* rebuilt 1158; enlarged 1317–35; remodelled 1739, restored to original 1935.
Campanile, late 12C.–1483.

Terlizzi. 11C. IMM. SUBJ. (Bari).
St Michael.

Termoli. 10C. (Campobasso).
S. *Maria* & S. *Basso*, ? 6c.; rebuilt
11C.–12C.; restored 18c. & 1932–5;
façade, about 1153 by ALFANO DA
TERMOLI.

Terni. 2C. IMM. SUBJ.
Assumption, 12c.; restored 1653.

Terracina. 1C. IMM. SUBJ. (Littoria).
S. *Cesario*, consecr. 1074, finished 13c.;
remodelled 17c.
Campanile, 14c.

Tivoli. 2C. IMM. SUBJ. (Rome).
St Lawrence.

Todi. 2C. IMM. SUBJ. (Perugia).
Annunciation, early 12c.; later addi-
tions.
Campanile, ? 13c.

Tolentino. 5C. (Macerata).
S. *Catervo* & *Assumption*, 8c.–9c.;
rebuilt 13c.; restored 1829.

[D2] **TORCELLO.** 7C.–1818 (Venice).
Assumption, see pp. 127–9. *118 ft* long,
70 ft wide.

Tortona. 2C. (Alessandria).
Assumption, 1574; façade, 1880.

[G6] **TRANI.** 6C. METR. 11C. (Bari).
Assumption & S. *Nicola Pellegrino, see* pp.
226–9. *193 ft* long, *90 ft* wide; façade,
123 ft high.
Campanile, *212 ft* high.

Trapani. 1844.
St Lawrence, 1635.

Treia. 1816 (Macerata).
Annunciation, rebuilt 18c. by A. VICI.
Campanile, 15c.

Trento. 2C. ARCHB. 1929, IMM. SUBJ.
S. *Vigilio*, 12c.–early 13c., finished
1515.

Treviso. 4C.
St Peter, 11c.; rebuilt 15c.–16c.;
enlarged 18c. by G. RICCATI.

Tricarico. 11C. (Matera).
St Peter, 11c.; remodelled 1638;
restored 1783.
Campanile, 13c.

[E2] **TRIESTE.** 6C.
Assumption & S. *Giusto*, about 1000;

14c. conjoined as *Immaculate Conception*
& S. *Giusto* with baptistery.
Campanile, enlarged 1337.

Trivento. 10C. IMM. SUBJ. (Campobasso).
Ss. *Nazario, Celso* & *Vittore*, 12c.;
altered later.

TROIA. 11C. IMM. SUBJ. (Foggia).   [F6]
Assumption, see pp. 224–5.

Tropea. 7C. (Catanzaro).
Assumption & *St Joseph*, 11c.; rebuilt
16c.; restored to original 1928.

TURIN. 5C. METR. 1515.   [A3]
St John Baptist, see pp. 205–7. *200 ft* long.
(originally three churches: S. *Salvatore*,
late 4c.; rebuilt 8c.–9c.; restored
11C.–12C.: St *John*, late 6c.–7c.; rebuilt
11C.: S. *Maria*, late 5c.)

Tursi. 1544 (Matera).
Assumption (*Chiesa della Rabatana*),
9c.–10c.; rebuilt 18c.

TUSCANIA. 3C. IMM. SUBJ. (Viterbo).   [D5]
1. S. *Maria Maggiore* (to 852), late 8c.;
   restored 12c.
2. *St Peter, see* pp. 138–40.
3. S. *Giacomo Maggiore* (from 16c.), rebuilt 18c.

Udine. METR. 1751, IMM. SUBJ.
S. *Odorico* now *Annunciation*, 1236; re-
modelled early 18c.
Campanile, 1441–50.

Ugento. 13C. (Lecce).
S. *Vincenzo.*

Urbania. 1635 (Pesaro & Urbino).
S. *Cristoforo.*

Urbino. 6C. METR. 1563 (Pesaro &
Urbino).
S. *Crescentino*, 1447 by L. LAURANA,
finished by B. PONTELLI or F. DI G.
MARTINI; rebuilt after 1789 by G.
VALADIER.

**Vallo della Lucania (Capaccio-
Vallo).** 12C. (Salerno).
S. *Pantaleone.*

Valva. 5C. IMM. SUBJ. (Aquila).
S. *Pelino* or *Basilica Valvense*, rebuilt
1075–1188; restored 1280; int. 1680–
1718.

Vasto. 5C. (Chieti).

S. Margherita, then *S. Agostino* now *St Joseph,* rebuilt 13C.; restored 1568; int. 1890.

Velletri. 5C. SED. SUBURB. (Rome).

S. Clemente, ? 4C.; largely rebuilt about 1300; rebuilt 1659–62. *167 ft* long.

Venafro. 11C. (Campobasso).

St John Evangelist.

[D2] VENICE. PATRIARCH 1451.

1. *S. Pietro di Castello* (until 1807), rebuilt 16C.–17C.

2. *St Mark, see* pp. 129–37. *250 ft* long overall; transept, *205 ft* across; façade, *170 ft* wide; atrium, *20 ft* wide; central cupola, *92 ft* high within, *141 ft* outside.

Venosa. 5C. (Potenza).

S. Felice, 1470–1502.

Ventimiglia. 7C. (Imperia).

Assumption, 11C.–12C.; restored 17C. Baptistery, ? 5C.; rebuilt 11C.

Vercelli. 3C. METR. 1817.

S. Eusebio, 6C.; rebuilt 1572 by P. PELLEGRINI, finished 1763–4.

Veroli. 8C. IMM. SUBJ. (Frosinone).

St Andrew.

VERONA. 3C. **[C2]**

1. ? *St Stephen,* rebuilt 10C. & ? 12C.

2. *S. Maria Matricolare (Assumption),* 8C.; rebuilt 1139–87 & 15C.; additions up to 1524.

    Baptistery, ?12C. (basilican plan).

VICENZA. 2C. **[D2]**

Annunciation, 6C.; rebuilt 12C. altered 13C., 15C. & 16C.; destroyed World War II, rebuilt since.

Vieste. 11C. (Foggia).

Assumption.

Vigevano. 1529 (Pavia).

S. Ambrogio, 10C.; rebuilt 14C.; rebuilt 1532–5 by A. DA LONATE, finished 1612; façade, 1680; cupola, 1708.

Viterbo. 6C. IMM. SUBJ.

St Lawrence, 12C.; façade, 1560–70. Campanile, 14C.

Vittorio Veneto. 1939 (Treviso).

S. Maria Nuova (Assumption), rebuilt 1755 by A. SCHIAVI DI TOLMEZZO.

Volterra. 5C. (Pisa).

Assumption, 10C.; int. altered 1514 & 1580.

Bibliography

THE greater part of the voluminous literature on Italian church art and architecture is written in Italian and much, too, in German and French. Although numerous monographs on individual artists and special aspects of Italian art are available in English, little has been published in England in recent years on Italian architecture that is not of a specialized nature. The following works are of general importance and contain useful bibliographies and valuable illustrations:

General Works

BUMPUS, T. F. *The Cathedrals and Churches of Italy*. London, 1926.
FLETCHER, B. F. *History of Architecture*. London (numerous editions).
VENTURI, A. *Storia dell'arte italiana*. Milan, 1901–39.

Early Christian Architecture

DALTON, O. M. *Byzantine Art and Archaeology*. London, 1911.
DIEHL, C. *Manuel d'art byzantin*. Paris, 1910.
TOESCA, P. *Storia dell'arte italiana: Il Medioevo* I. Turin, 1927.
TOYNBEE, J. M. C., & J. B. WARD-PERKINS. *The Shrine of St Peter and the Vatican Excavations*. London, 1956.

Mediaeval Romanesque and Gothic Architecture

CLAPHAM, A. W. *Romanesque Architecture in Western Europe*. Oxford, 1936.
RICCI, C. *Romanesque Architecture in Italy*. London, 1925.
RIVOIRA, G. T. *Lombardic Architecture*. Translated by G. McN. RUSHFORTH, re-edited with notes, II vols. London, 1933.
TOESCA, P. *Storia dell'arte italiana: Il Medioevo* II. Turin, 1927.
——. *Storia dell'arte italiana: Il Trecento*. Turin, 1951.

Renaissance Architecture

WITTKOWER, R. *Architectural Principles in the Age of Humanism*. 2nd edition, revised. London, 1952.

Baroque Architecture

RICCI, C. *Baroque Architecture and Sculpture in Italy*. Stuttgart, 1926.

INDEX

Bold figures indicate important references in the text. Italicised numerals refer to the *figure numbers* of illustrations. The references in square brackets relate to the grid on the map (pp. 14–15).

INDEX

INDEX

INDEX

INDEX

278

INDEX

279

INDEX